LAWS PREVENTING LAND ALIENATION
BY
SCHEDULED TRIBES AND CASTES

Books from COATS

- Forest Management in Tribal Areas: Forest Policy and People's Participation / *P.M. Mohapatra and P.C. Mohapatra*
- Development of a Primitive Tribe: A Study of Diḍayis/*Bhagyalaxmi Mohapatra*

About the Author

Sri Jagannath Shroff is a retired Officer, belonging to the Orissa Administrative Service Cadre with long and varied practical experience in the field of Land Administration of different parts of the State. He takes keen interest in presenting occasional papers expressing his views on land matters in the seminars and meetings as well as rendering consultancy services whenever sought for. He is utilizing his post retirement time in associating with the activities of some Religious, Research and Social Institutions, of good reputation.

Laws Preventing Land Alienation by Scheduled Tribes and Castes

Jagannath Shroff
Orissa Administrative Service (Retd.)
Koraput-764020

JOINTLY PUBLISHED
COUNCIL OF ANALYTICAL TRIBAL STUDIES (COATS), KORAPUT
and
CONCEPT PUBLISHING COMPANY PVT. LTD.
NEW DELHI-110059

ISBN-13 : 978-81-8069-926-9

First Published 2013

Published and Printed by

Concept Since 1974

Concept Publishing Company Pvt. Ltd.
A/15-16, Commercial Block, Mohan Garden
New Delhi-110059 (India)
T: 25351460, 25351794, *F*: 091-11-25357109
E: publishing@conceptpub.com, W: www.conceptpub.com
Editorial Office: H-13, Bali Nagar, New Delhi-110 015, India.

Cataloging in Publication Data--*Courtesy:* D.K. Agencies (P) Ltd. <docinfo@dkagencies.com>

Shroff, Jagannath.
Laws preventing land alienation by scheduled tribes and castes / Jagannath Shroff.
p. cm.
Includes index.
ISBN 9788180699269

1. Land tenure—Law and legislation—India—Orissa. 2. Restraints on alienation India—Orissa. 3. Orissa (India)—Scheduled tribes—Legal status, laws, etc. 4. Orissa (India)—Scheduled tribes—Economic conditions. I. Title.

DDC 346.541330432 23

Dedication

Offered at the lotus feet of the Lord
Sri Sri Jagannath
of Sabara Srikshetra, Koraput
seeking His devine blessings

Pyarimohan Mohapatra
Member of Parliament
Rajya Sabha

Member

Standing Committee on Industry
Committee on MPLADS (RS)
Committee on Rules (RS)
Consultative Committee for Ministry of Social Justice and Empowerment

January 4, 2009

Foreword

Land resource is central to the social, cultural and economic existence of the Tribal Societies. Transfer of land resource from Tribals to non-tribals through exploitative methods as well as compulsory acquisition is identified as the most potent political and administrative issue involving economic deprivation and leading to unrest and rebellion among the tribal population. Even though protection of land rights of tribal communities was enshrined in the Constitution of India in Schedule V and special laws enacted from time to time in the State of Orissa and instructions issued to safeguard tribal rights in land and to prevent exploitation, lack of adequate care in enforcement has led to large scale land alienation and consequent law and order problems. Provisions have been made in the Orissa Land Reforms Act and Regulation 2 of 1956 to prevent alienation of lands belonging to the Scheduled Tribes and Scheduled Castes as well.

The effort made by Shri Jagannath Shroff in compiling this Hand Book which contains all the Laws, Regulations, Rules and Instructions in the State of Orissa regarding restricting transfer of immovable properties of Scheduled Tribes and Castes is a timely and praiseworthy venture especially when such lands are under serious threat from industrialization.

I am sure that the present work of Shri Shroff will be useful not only to the Administrators but also to the legal needs of the professionals alike.

(PYARIMOHAN MOHAPATRA)

Bhubaneswar: *Plot No. A/111, Saheednagar, Bhubaneswar – 751007,*
Tel. (0674) 2545132 Fax (0674) 2543557
Delhi: *C-11/55, Satya Marg, Chanakyapuri,New Delhi – 119921,*
Telefax (011) 24122488
email: *pyarimohanap@sansad.nic.in / Pyarimohan@yahoo.co.uk*

Preface

Immovable property includes land, which is a permanent asset on which the agriculture community depends for livelihood. More often than not the Aborigines, mainly look upon land as the main source for their sustenance. They easily fall prey to the exploitation of the greedy land grabbers and the persisting poor socio-economic condition forces them to fall in the debt trap of the money lenders and alienate their lands for nominal price and become landless.

There was no restriction prohibiting transfer of lands by the aboriginal tribes in favour of the non-aboriginals who infiltrated into this region, till 1917 when the Agency Tracts interest and Land Transfer Act was enforced for the first time on 14th August, 1917. The list of Hill Tribes referred to in this enactment underwent change seven times between 25th January, 1918 and 14th January, 1943. A synopsis of the developments in this aspect is given in Appendix-IX of the Final Report of Major Settlement Operations in Koraput District which provided the guidelines for recording the rights of lands belonging to *Adivasis* during settlement. Thus a modest attempt has been made to protect the interest of the aboriginal tribes on land only in the areas which formed part of the ex-Madras Presidency.

Before the merger of the ex-State areas (that is to say, before the 1st January, 1948 in respect of all ex-States excluding Mayurbhanj and before the 1st January, 1949 in case of Mayurbhanj) occupancy tenants belonging to certain castes and tribes could transfer their lands only with the prior permission of the Durbar or some Revenue Authorities. Para. 12 (subsequently numbered as para. 10) of the Administration of Orissa States Order, 1948 which came into force in all the ex-States excluding Mayurbhanj on the 1st January, 1948, provided that an occupancy tenant would be entitled to freely transfer his holding, subject to the restriction that no transfer of holding from a member of an "aboriginal tribe" to a member of a non-aboriginal tribe shall be valid unless such transfer is made with the previous permission of the Administrator of the State concerned. This power of the Administrator was subsequently given to the Subdivisional Magistrate by an amendment of the order. The term aboriginal tribe was defined in the said order to mean any tribe that may from time to time be notified as such by the Provincial Government for the purpose of this order. When the ex-State of Mayurbhanj was integrated with the State of Orissa on the 1st January, 1949, a similar provision in para. 11 of the Mayurbhanj State Order 1949 was also issued. These provisions were repeated in section 7 (b) (i) of the Orissa Merged States (Laws) Act 1950. No notification was, however, issued by Government defining the term aboriginal tribe till the 22nd May, 1962 when notification No. 24507-Ten-15/62-R, dated the 22nd May, 1962 was issued explaining that aboriginal tribe shall mean any of the Scheduled Tribes specified in Scheduled Tribes list.

It is thus clear that with effect from the date of merger any occupancy tenant in any ex-State could transfer his holding or part thereof without the prior sanction of any officer or authority in the absence of any restrictions. The caste or tribe of the tenant was irrelevant for this purpose. In respect of other ex-State areas the restriction came into force with effect from the 22nd May, 1962 when notification No24507-Ten-15/62-R. dated the 22nd May, 1962 was issued defining the term of Aboriginal Tribe. The conclusions therefore are:

Prior to merger-Transfer of land by castes and tribes prior to the merger of Princely States will be regulated by the laws then in force in those States.

On and from the date of merger—(i) In the ex-State of Sundargarh there was no restriction of transfer of land by any occupancy tenant irrespective of his caste or tribe from the 1st January, 1948 to 3rd October, 1956 (both days inclusive).

(ii) Similarly in Mayurbhanj district there was no restriction on transfer of land by an occupancy tenant whether he is a Scheduled Tribe or not from the 1st January, 1949 to the 3rd October, 1956 (both days inclusive).

(iii) In other ex-States there was no such restriction from the 1st January, 1948 to the 21st May, 1962 (both days inclusive), when the notification defining aboriginal tribe was issued.

There were also certain laws in the agency areas regulating transfer of land by tribals to non-tribals. In the C.P. Tenancy Acts which are in force in Nawapara Subdivision of Kalahandi district and Bargarh and Sadar Subdivisions of Sambalpur district, there are certain restrictions on the transfer of land by tribals to others. Angul and Kandhamal Laws Regulation which apply to Angul and Kandhamal subdivisions respectively also put certain restrictions regarding transfer of land from tribal to non-tribals.

Regulation 2/56 promulgated under the Fifth Schedule of the Constitution which replaced the A.T.I and L.T Act 1917 came into force on 21st September, 1956, and prohibited transfer of lands of Scheduled Tribes only in the Scheduled Areas. With the coming into force of the Orissa Land Reforms Act 1960 on 1st October, 1965, analogous provisions have been made under Sections 22 to 23-A to prevent alienation of lands belonging to both Scheduled Castes and Tribes in other areas of the State. However Section 23-A is also applicable to the Scheduled Castes in the Scheduled Areas as well.

Bulk of the transfer of lands possessed by the *Adivasis* took place before the A.T.I and L.T Act came into force. The innocent people were neither educated nor conscious enough about their rights and the protection afforded to them even after passing of the Act. Taking advantage of the ignorance of the masses the Estate officials who maintained the land records of the zamindari played mischief and mutated the names of the non-tribal Tranferees in violation of the provisions of the Act. In most cases the Act was dodged by the *Adivasis* relinquishing their lands in favour of the Jeypore Estate and the shrewd non-*Adivasis* managed to get them leased from the Estate officials. All this happened when survey and settlement operations were not undertaken and before the abolition of the Estates in 1952. It was too late when the Act was amended in 1948 to make it applicable in case of relinquishments in favour of the landlord.

Under the A.T.I and L.T Act 1917 which was in force till the enactment of Regulation 2/56 as many as 98 tribes were declared as Hill Tribes whose lands were protected from alienation without permission. But with the promulgation of the Presidential Order termed as 'The Constitution (Scheduled Tribes) Order 1950' on 6th September, 1950. 66 tribal communities of the Hill Tribes list were excluded and some of them have subsequently been notified as Scheduled Castes or other Backward Classes and they remained outside the purview of Regulation 2/56 to get the benefit of restriction in the matter of land alienation. With the repeal of the Ganjam and

Vizagapatam Act 1839, the Koraput and Ganjam Agency Repealing and Extension of Laws Regulation 1951 came into force on the 1st January, 1953. During the period from 1.1.1953 and 20.09.1956 when Regulation 2/56 came into force there was no legal authority for according permission for transfer of Hill tribes' lands, and in this interval large extents of tribal lands were alienated. Similarly after enforcement of Regulation 2/56 all those who were excluded from the list of Original Hill Tribes and not declared as Scheduled Tribes, freely transferred their lands without any sort of restriction /control. Thus many of the non-tribals became the owners of lands belonging to tribals without any legal bar. The lacuna in the legislation was the contributing factor for this strange phenomenon.

It may be worth mentioning that the present legislations do not bring within their ambit all those Hill Tribes as were constituted / declared before coming into force of the Constitution of India, deserved equal protection of their interests like those declared subsequently as Scheduled Tribes and Castes under the Presidential orders of the Constitution or Acts of Parliament. Subsequently the Aborginal Tribes belonging to the merged States areas have been declared by Government to mean any of the Scheduled Tribes, specified in Part IX of the Schedule III of the Scheduled Castes and Scheduled Tribes Lists Modification Order 1956, in Notification No. 24507-Ten-15/62-R dated 22nd May, 1962 of the Revenue Department. On the same anology as well as in view of the definition of 'Traditional Forest Dwellers' provided in the Scheduled Tribes and other Traditional Forest Dwellers (Recognition of Forest Rights) Act 2006 and the Rules framed thereunder it seems expedient to declare the Hill Tribes, of the Ex-Agency Areas of Madras Presidency, included in the State of Orissa from 1st April, 1936, but not enlisted as Scheduled Tribes and Castes as belonging to Scheduled Tribes and Castes by issue of a similar notification as was done for Aboriginal Tribes by the State Government, so that the gross injustice done to them can be rectified and the restriction for free transfer of their lands to the non-tribals can be reimposed in the interest of natural justice and equality before law.

The Amendment of Section 3 of Regulation 2 of 1956 made in Regulation 1 of 1997 has a salutary effect as it completely prohibits transfer of land which is less than one standard acre in possession of an individual tribal, perhaps with a view to prevent him from being deemed as landless as defined in Clause (a1) of Section 3 of the

Orissa Prevention of Land Encroachment Act 1972 and Clause (b2) of Section 2 of the Orissa Government Land Settlement Act 1962. However, no such restriction of minimum ceiling has been prescribed in the corresponding provisions of Section 22 of the Orissa Land Reforms Act and there is need to make analogous provisions in both the laws. Had the present restriction been imposed in the original enactment from the very beginning, large extents of lands belonging to the tribes could have been prevented from alienation and they would not have been rendered landless to lead a miserable life being deprived of their main source of livelihood.

The insertion of new Sub-Section 3-B in Regulation 2 of 1956 with a view to bring about radical changes, has the adverse effect on the principle of peaceful co-existence giving rise to agitation and serious law and order situation. In the absence of specific definition of the words 'Fraud' and 'Tribal Lands', in the enactment, they are liberally interpreted to suit self interests leading to prolonged litigation and unlawful acts. To prevent any misgivings the real intention of the remedy provided under the law has to be made very clear, free from any controversy and direct conflict with any other prevailing law on land Rights. The cardinal principle of fundamental rights to seek redress for wrong decisions or injustice is denied and the law appears arbitrary. Judicial review is fundamental to the rule of law and courts of law are creatures of the constitution who act within their prescribed own limits. As reopening/rehearing of cases u/s 3-B in effect tantamount to review/ revision it is not proper on the part of the successor in office of the Sub Collector (S.D.O.) who granted the permission for alienation of land after satisfying himself to question the propriety and adjudicate the legality or otherwise of the order passed by the predecessor of the same rank and status. It, therefore, seems expedient that the powers u/s 3-B where the cases are covered by due permission granted in exercise of the powers conferred under the law, should be vested in the Higher Authority in rank and status to remove the existing anomaly, which has adverse impact.

This compilation incorporates the relevant Acts, Rules, statutory notifications and instructions to make it more cohesive and present developments covering the whole gamut of the legislation to make it coherent and comprehensive. It is hoped that it may help in providing adequate legal assistance and guidance to cater to the needs of professionals and officials as well as public alike.

It will be very much appreciated if ommissions and commissions if any, noticed in this compilation are promptly brought to notice for rectification.

Vivekananda Marg
DNK Road,
Koraput-764020

Jagannath Shroff
OAS (Retd.)

Acknowledgements

I humbly express my sincere gratitude to Sri P.M. Mohapatra, Member of Parliament, Rajya Sabha, Orissa who is kind enough to spare his valuable time for writing the thought-provoking Foreword to this publication. I remain deeply indebted to him for his kind gesture of goodwill and encouragement.

I am also grateful to the Chairman and Board of Governors of the Council of Analytical Tribal Studies, Koraput for the keen interest taken for the printing and publication of this compilation. Last but not the least, I extend my thanks to the staff members who are instrumental in typing and computerizing the Draft Handbook.

Jagannath Shroff
OAS, Retd.

Contents

Chapter I

(A) The Agency Tracts Interest and Land Transfer Act 1917 Madras Act of 1917 and Rules and Instructions thereunder

The 14th August, 1917

AN ACT to regulate the rate of interest and the transfer of land in the Ganjam, Vizagapatnam and Godavari agency tracts

Preamble.—Whereas it is expedient to limit the rate of interest and to check transfers of land in the agency tracts of the Ganjam, Vizagapatnam and Godavari districts; it is hereby enacted as follows:

1. Short title.—This Act may be called the Agency Tracts Interest and Land Transfer Act 1917.

2. Definitions.—In this Act unless there is anything repugnant in the subject or context—

(a) "Agency tracts" means the Scheduled districts as defined in Act XIV and XV of 1874 and included within the districts of Ganjam, Vizagapatnam and Godavari.

(b) "Agent" means "Agent to the Governor" in the districts of Ganjam and Vizagapatnam and "Government Agent" in the district of Godavari.

(c) "Hill-tribes" means anybody or class of persons resident in the Agency tracts not being a land-holder as defined in the Madras Estates Land Act 1908 that may from time to time be notified as such for the purpose of the Act by the (Provincial Government).

(d) "Immovable property" does not include standing timber, growing crops of grass.

(e) "Prescribed" means prescribed by rules made under this Act.

(f) "Transfer" means mortgage with or without possession, lease, sale, gift, exchange or any other dealing with property not being a testamentary disposition and includes a charge or any contract relating to immovable property.

3. Transfer of immovable property by a member of a hill-tribe—(1) Notwithstanding anything of anything of any rule of law or enactment to the contrary, any transfer of immovable property situated within the Agency tracts by a member of a hill-tribe shall be absolutely null and void unless made in favour of another member of a hill-tribe, or with the previous consent in writing of the Agent or of any other prescribed officer.

4. Where a transfer of property is made in contravention of Sub-section (1), in the Agent of any other prescribed officer may, either on application by anyone interested, or on his own motion, decree ejectment against any person in possession of the property claiming under the transfer and may restore it to the transferor or his heirs:

Provided that if the Agent or the prescribed officer is of opinion that the restoration of the property to the transferor of his heirs is impracticable, he may settle the property with another member of a hill-tribe on such terms as he may think fit.

(3) Subject to such conditions as may be prescribed, an appeal against a decree or order under Sub-section (2), if made by the Agent shall lie to the Revenue Commissioner and if made by any other officer shall lie to the Agent or to any other officer specially empowered by the Provincial Government in this behalf.

5. Suits against a member of a hill-tribe to be instituted in the Agency Courts notwithstanding the provision of any law to the contrary, every suit against a member of a hill-tribe instituted after the commencement of this Act shall be instituted only in the Courts of the Agency tracts.

6. Attachment of immovable property.—In execution of a money decree against a member of a hill-tribe, no immovable property owned by him within the Agency tracts shall be liable to be attached and sold except as and if prescribed.

7. Framing of rules.—(1) The provincial Government may from time to time to make rules to carry out the purpose of the Act.

(2) All rules made under this Section shall be published in the Official Gazette and on such publication, shall have the same effect as if enacted in this Act.

8. Saving.—(1) This Act shall not affect transfers made or debts of liabilities incurred before the coming into force of this Act.

(2) Nothing in this Act shall affect a land-holder's right to proceed against the ryot in accordance with the provisions of the

Madras Estate Land Act 1908 or the first charge declared by Section 5 of that Act.

(3) Notwithstanding anything contained in the Madras Estate Land Act 1908, no relinquishment of a holding or any part thereof by a ryot who is a member of a hill-tribe shall be valid unless after such relinquishment the land-holder either settles the holding or any part thereof, as the case may be, with another member of a hill-tribe; or else retains it in his possession or settles it with a person who is not a member of a hill-tribe after obtaining the written approval of the Agent or any other prescribed officer. Any relinquishment that is accepted in contravention of this Sub-section shall be deemed to be a transfer of property in contravention of Sub-section (1) of Section 4.

9. Penalty and burden of proof.—(1) If any person who is not a member of a hill-tribe is found in possession of immovable property in contravention of the provisions of this Act on or after the 1st day of March, 1948, such person shall, without prejudice to his liability ejectment under Sub-section (2) of Section 4, be also liable to penalty for an amount not exceeding rupees one hundred per acre of such his immovable property for each year or any part thereof during which his unlawful possession continues. Such penalty may be imposed the officer decreeing ejectment under Sub-section (2) of Section 4 and shall be recoverable as an arrear of land revenue.

(2) In any proceeding under this Act where the validity of the transfer of relinquishment of immovable property is called in question the burden of proving that such transfer or relinquishment was valid shall notwithstanding anything contained in the Indian Evidence Act lie on the transferee.

RULES UNDER THE AGENCY TRACTS INTEREST AND LAND TRANSFER ACT, 1917 (ACT 1 OF 1917)

(Home Department (judicial) Notification No. 79, Fort St. George, dated the 25th January, 1918. Home Department Order No. 187. Home (Judicial) dated the 22nd January 1918)

In exercising the powers under Section 7 of Act 1 of 1917 (Agency Tracts Interest and Land Transfer Act 1917) the Governor in Council is pleased to frame the following rules for regulating the transfer of lands in the Agency Tracts of Ganjam-Vizagapatnam and Godavari district:

(Rule relating to Act 1 of 1917, Agency Tracts interests and Land Transfer Act)

Rule 1.—For the purpose of this Act the following are declared as hill-tribes:

Ganjam	Khonds	Savaras	Panas, Haddies
Vizagapatanam			
Khondhs	Koyas	Dombs	Relli
Godabas	Paligarup	Dongiria Kondh	Palasi
Pangi Gadabas	Palli	Konda Dora	Mulia
Olar Gadabas	Bagata	Nukadora	Tikiria Kondh
Jodia Parajas	Kotia	Reddi Dora	Desia Kondh
Pengu Parajas	Mane Dora	Konda Kapu	Magatha Gouda
Bonda Parajas	Kapu Savara	Savara	Ojulus
Didua Parajas	Malaya Savara	Jadapulu	Yenity Kondh
Durva Parajas	Kodu	Maune	Ghasis
Gond			
Kutia Kondhs	Pydi	Malas	
Godavari			
Koyas	Konda Reddies		

Rule 2.—According to Section 4 (1), the transfer of immovable property to a non-hill-tribe, if it be a case of mortgage without possession can be sanctioned by the District Munsif who has power of trials, in writing, if necessary. The other aspects of transfer must be sanctioned in writing by the Assistant Agent.

Rule 2-A.—Notwithstanding anything contained in any rule for the time being in force all applications and petitions made under Section 4 shall be exempted from process fees payable therefor.

Rule 3.—According to Section 4(2) of the Act the ejectment order shall be made either by the Agent or Assistant Agent who has powers of trials.

Rule 4.—On the ejectment order issued by the Assistant Agent according to Section 4(2) an appeal lies to the Agent within two months from the date of orders of the Assistant Agent and within 3 months to Governor in Counsel from the order passed by the Agent. The appellate authority can, however, relax the period of appeal, if he is satisfied that for genuine and reasonable grounds the appeal could not be preferred in time. There can be no second appeal.

Rule 5.—Without the written orders of the Assistant Agent no immovable property can be sold according to Section 6. In such sales the property unless otherwise ordered for disposal by the Assistant Agent in writing must be sold only to hill-tribes. The sale should be done by public auction. Further after the property is attached the property cannot be sold within a month.

Rule 6.—The orders issued according to those rules by the officers subordinate to the Agent are subject to the general control of the Agent.

Instructions for the Guidance of Assistant Settlement Officers in Koraput District for deciding Cases relating to Recording of Illegal Transfer of Lands made by *Adivasi* to Non-*Adivasis*

The entire district of Koraput is predominantly populated by *Adivasis*. Transfer of land by *Adivasis* in favour of non-*Adivasis* is restricted to a certain extent in this district. The restrictions have been regulated in different laws and orders from time to time. The following instructions are issued for the guidance of the Assistant Settlement Officers working in Koraput district for deciding cases relating to recording of illegal transfer of lands made by *Adivasis* to non-*Adivasis*.

2. There was no restriction prohibiting transfer of lands by *Adivasis* in favour of non-*Adivasis* till the year 1917 when the Agency Tracts Interest and Land Transfer Act (briefly known as A.T.I.L.T. Act) was passed by the Government of Madras. So far as Orissa is concerned, this Act was applicable to the "Agency Tracts" (i.e., the Scheduled districts as defined in Acts XIV and XV of 1874) included, within the then districts of Ganjam and Vizagapatnam. The entire district of Koraput was then included within the "Agency Tract" of the district of Vizagapatnam. It came into force on 14th August, 1917. This Act provides in Section 4(1) that all transfer of lands situated within the Agency tracts by a member of hill-tribe to any person who is not a member of a hill-tribe shall be absolutely null and void unless the transfer is made with the previous consent in writing of the Agent or of any other prescribed officer. The prescribed officer for Koraput was the Assistant Agent (also called Special Assistant Agent in Koraput). It also provides in Section 6 that the land of a hill-tribe cannot be attached and sold in execution of a money decree against the member of a hill-tribe except to the extent prescribed under the rules framed under Section 7 of the Agency Tracts Interest and Land Transfer Act. The rules prescribe that in such sales the property, unless otherwise ordered for disposal by the Assistant Agent in writing, must be sold by public auction only to hill-tribes. Hill-tribe as defined in the Agency Tracts Interest and Land Transfer Act means any body or class of persons resident in the Agency tracts (not being a Land-holder under Madras Estates Land Act) that may from time to time be notified

as such for the purpose of the Act by the State Government. "Transfer" includes all cases of transfer such as mortgage, sale, gift, exchange and such other things not being a testamentary disposition. "Agent" means the Agent to the Governor. The Collectors of Ganjam and Vizagapatam were respectively appointed as Agents to the Governor in the Agency tracts of Ganjam and Vizagapatam. The original notification of the Government of Madras defining hill-tribes was issued in notification No. 79—Home (Judicial), dated the 25th January 1918. This notification was subsequently amended and so far as the district of Vizagapatam is concerned the list of hill-tribes has been amended several times by the Government of Madras in the following notifications—

(1) No. 516—Home (Judicial), dated the 23rd July, 1918;
(2) No. 59—Revenue, dated the 1st March, 1927;
(3) No. 207—Revenue, dated the 4th July, 1927;
(4) G.O. No. 1218—Revenue, dated the 18th June, 1931 and;
(5) No. 769—Revenue, dated the 4th June, 1932.

After creation of the province of Orissa on the 1st April, 1936, the district of Koraput was formed and it consisted of the major portion of the Agency tract of the district of Vizagapatam. The list of hill-tribes was amended by the Government of Orissa once in the year 1943 in Revenue Department notification No. 148-R, dated the 14th January, 1943.

3. It may be seen from the above that any transfer made before the 25th January, 1918 (i.e., the date on which the list of hill-tribes was first notified) by an *Adivasi* to a non-*Adivasi* is not to be considered as illegal. Only the transfer made after the 25th January, 1918, are to be treated as illegal. So the material point for consideration is the date of the transfer. The next point for consideration is whether the person who claims to be an *Adivasi* was included within the list of hill tribes on the date the transfer took place. Several tribes successively included in and excluded from the list of hill-tribes in different notifications. Appendix No. 1 shows the names of all the hill-tribes who have been included in or excluded from the list of hill-tribes in the notifications referred to above from time to time. While deciding cases of illegal transfers, the castes of the *Adivasis* have to be carefully checked up with this list to find out whether the said *Adivasi* was included in the list of hill-tribes on the date of transfer.

The most difficult point for determination is whether the case is one of transfer at all. Most of the people being illiterate and ignorant of their rights, have not kept any written record of their transfers. So most of the transfers are verbal. Even transfers of land exceeding Rs. 100 in value could be made previously either verbally or by unregistered documents. The Indian Registration Act (Act XVI of 1908) came into force in the district of Koraput in the year 1933 excepting Malkangiri, Pottangi, Bissemcuttack taluks where it came into force in the 1955 by Revenue Department notification Nos. 2041 to 2046—XIV-98/55-Regn. dated the 17th October, 1955. It has not yet come into force in Narayanapatna police station limits. So the question whether the case is one of transfer at all should be determined by some evidence other than looking for registered deeds. So far as the district of Koraput is concerned, the most useful documents are the tenants' ledger and other accounts which the Maharaja of Jeypore, the previous landholder, was filing annually before the Collector for cess valuation purpose. In those documents the names of the ryots who were paying rents in a particular year and the amount of their rent were recorded village by village. In Mustajari villages the names of the ryots as reported by the Mastajar was being recorded in those documents, although in actual practice he might be realizing more from the ryots of the village which he was appropriating himself. If in the old accounts of any particular year, the name of a particular *Adivasi* ryot occurs and if in any subsequent year the name of another person who is not an *Adivasi* is substituted for his *jama* or a portion of his *jama*, the obvious presumption is that the lands appertaining to that *jamabandi* have been transferred. Once this is established, then the burden of proof will lie on the transferee to prove that the transfer is legal, i.e., the transferee has obtained the permission of the agent or the Special Assistant Agent to the transfer (vide Sub-section 2 of Section 9 of the Agency Tracts Interest and Land Transfer Act as amended by Orissa Act II of 1948).

4. In many cases the transferees have managed to mutate their names in the estate records although the transfer was illegal. At the time of preliminary preparation of record-of-rights i.e., *khanapuri* and attestation *jamabandi* filed by the land-holder show that the transferees are the ryots and they are also in actual possession of the lands transferred. Unless somebody points out that this was an illegal transfer, it would not be possible for the A.S.Os. to record such transfers as illegal. If somebody puts up a claim, it will be decided on

merits. Mutation in the estate records does not entitle the transferee to be recorded as the ryot in the R.O.Rs. if the transfer has been made in contravention of the provisions of the Agency Tracts Interest and Land Transfer Act.

5. Although this was the position of law, the transfer could be made legal indirectly till the year 1948, i.e., till the 5th February 1948, when Orissa Act II of 1948 came into force amending certain provisions of the Agency Tracts interest and Land Transfer Act. Sub-section (2) of Section 8 of the Agency Tracts interest and Land Transfer Act provided that the provision regarding illegality of the transfer could not apply to relinquishment of a holding by a ryot under provisions of the Madras Estates Land Act. This otherwise meant that the *Adivasi* ryot could relinquish his holding to the land-holder and after relinquishment the land-holder was at liberty either to retain the land himself or to give it to some other person whether *Adivasi* or non-*Adivasi*. It is often said that the land belonged to an *Adivasi* and he left the land for some reason or other and so it was given to a non-*Adivasi* by the *mustadar* as land-holder's agent. In such cases it is to be examined whether the procedure of relinquishment as given in Section 149 of the Madras Estates Land Act has been followed. If the relinquishment was valid and the land was given to a non-*Adivasi* by the *mustadar*, the transfer cannot be considered as illegal if made before 5th February, 1948 when the Agency Tracts interest and Land Transfer (Orissa Amendment) Act 1948 (Act II of 1948) came into force. Under this amendment no relinquishment of a holding by an *Adivasi* ryot can be valid unless after such relinquishment the land-holder either settles the land of the holding with another member of a hill tribe or else retains them in his possession or settles them with a person who is not a member of a hill-tribe after obtaining the written approval of the Agent or any other prescribed officer. Any settlement of land which is made in contravention of this provision shall be deemed to be an illegal transfer under the Agency Tracts Interest and Land Transfer Act after the 5th February, 1948.

6. Then came the Constitution with effect from the 26th January 1950. Under Article 19 of the Constitution, a citizen has the fundamental right to acquire, hold or dispose of property subject to the condition that the State can make law imposing reasonable restrictions on the exercising of this fundamental right in the interest of the general public or for the protection of the interests of any

Scheduled Tribe. Under Article 342, the President has authority to specify, by notification, the tribes or tribal communities or parts of or groups within tribes or tribal communities which shall for the purpose of the Constitution be deemed to be Scheduled Tribes in particular States. The list of Scheduled Tribes once notified by the President can be amended only by Parliament by a statute. After coming into force of the Constitution, the President in "The Constitution (Scheduled Tribes) Order, 1950" in notification No. S.R.O. 510, dated the 6th September, 1950, specified 42 tribal communities to be Scheduled Tribes within the State of Orissa as per Appendix No. II. So with effect from the 6th September, 1950, the expression "Hill-tribe" should be deemed to have been substituted by the expression "Scheduled Tribes" and the list of hill-tribes which was in force on the date the Constitution came into force (this list included 65 tribal communities as per Appendix III) should be treated to have been modified by the President's "The Constitution (Scheduled Tribes) Order 1950", although there was no specific amendment to the Hill-tribe list of the Agency Tracts Interest and Land Transfer Act. On a comparison of both the lists, it will be seen that some communities included in the previous list of hill-tribes have been omitted from the Scheduled Tribe list of 1950 and some included in the 1950 list were not there in the last Hill-tribe list of 1943. It may be kept in mind that the 1950 list covers the entire State of Orissa including Koraput whereas the 1943 list was the list of Hill-tribes of Vizagapatnam district only including Koraput with Orissa Amendment of 1943 excluding Dombs from the list. The tribes which are commonly found in Koraput district are Kondhs, Porojas, Savaras, Gadabas, Koyas, Gondas, Jatapus, Kondadoras, Dhrubas, Bondaparajas, Didayis, Gondias, Bhumiyas, Ronas, Bhotodas, Kutiya Kondhs, Goudas, Doras, Ghasis, Rellis, etc., if some other tribes included in the list are also found they should be treated as hill-tribes or Scheduled Tribes as the case may be.

7. The Agency Tracts Interest and Land Transfer Act was repealed by the Orissa Scheduled Areas Transfer of Immovable Property (by Scheduled) Regulation 1956 (Regulation 2 of 1956). This regulation which came into force on the 21st September, 1956, repeated the Agency Tracts Interest and Land Transfer Act as amended in 1948 in all material particulars so far as illegality of the transfer is concerned except that the provision regarding in validity of the surrender or relinquishment of any holding by an *Adivasi* tenant would not apply to Government as

Land-holder. It may be mentioned in this connection that the Estate of Jeypore, i.e., the entire district of Koraput vested in State Government on the 29th December, 1952, and from that date the Collector as representative of Government stepped into the shoes of the land-holder. Even the Collector as representing the land-holder could not settle the surrendered or relinquished land of an *Adivasi* in favour of a non-*Adivasi* without the formal permission of the competent authority [as mentioned in Section 8(3) of the Agency Tracts Interest and Land Transfer Act] between the 29th December, 1952, when the Estate was abolished and the 21st September, 1956, when Regulation 2 of 1956 came into force. After the 21st September, 1956, the Collector has power to settle a surrendered or a relinquished land in favour of a non-*Adivasi* without the formal permission of the competent authority.

8. "Under Regulation 2 of 1956 the competent authority who will give permission for transfer of land by a member of the Scheduled Tribe to another who is not a member of the Scheduled Tribe is the Collector or any other officer appointed by the State Government by notification to perform the functions of a competent authority under that Regulation. The word "Agent" was omitted as the Act from which this expression came, namely, the Ganjam-Vizagapatnam Act 1839 was repealed by the Koraput and Ganjam Agency Repealing and Extension of Laws Regulation, 1951 (Regulation V of 1951) which came into force on the 1st January, 1953. Again Regulation 2 of 1956 is applicable to all the Scheduled Areas of the State as specified in the President's Scheduled Areas (Part 'A' States) Order 1950, issued under sub-paragraph 1 of paragraph 6 of the Fifth Schedule to the Constitution and not simply to the Agency tracts of the districts of Vizagapatnam and Ganjam to which the Agency Tracts Interest and Land Transfer Act was applicable.

9. Under the Agency Tracts Interest and Land Transfer Act which was in force till the 2nd September, 1956, the provisions of law regarding illegality of transfer was not applicable to lands sold in execution of a decree for arrears of rent under the Madras Estate Land Act. In other wards transfers made in execution of decree for arrears of rent under the Madras Estate Land Act before the vesting or under the Madras Revenue Recovery Act 1864 after vesting would not attract the provisions relating to illegality of transfer. To illustrate the point, a non-*Adivasi* who purchased land of an *Adivasi* in auction sale held in execution of a decree for arrears of rent under the Madras Estates Land Act before vesting

or under the Madras Revenue Recovery Act 1864 after vesting will not be liable for illegal transfer.

10. It has been pointed out in para. 8 that the Koraput and Ganjam Agency Repealing and Extension of Laws Regulation 1951 (Regulation V of 1951) came into force on the 1st January, 1953. The effect of this regulation is that it repealed the Ganjam-Vizagapatnam Act 1839 and so there was no "Agent" from that day who *could* give permission for transfer of land by *Adivasis* in favour of non-*Adavisis*. There was, therefore, no authority for giving this permission between the 1st January, 1953, and the 20th September, 1956. So if during this intervening period any permission for sale has been given by Collector or by Revenue Divisional Officers in their capacity respectively as "Agent" or "Special Assistant Agent" the permission should be treated as invalid and so the transfer effected by virtue of that permission should be treated as illegal.

11. The Constitution (Scheduled Tribes) Order 1950 has been amended by the Scheduled Castes and Scheduled Tribes Order (Amendment) Act 1956 (Act 63 of 1956), with effect from the 25th September, 1956. Appendix No. IV contains the list of Scheduled Tribes as per this 1956 Act. On a comparison of the two lists, i.e., 1950 and 1956 lists it will be seen that there are 62 tribal communities in Orissa in 1956 list whereas there were 42 tribal communities in the 1950 list. The 1950 list is valid till the 24th September, 1956 and it was replaced by 1956 list with effect from the 25th September, 1956, Appendix No. I also shows the tribal communities coming under 1950 and 1956 lists.

12. *Position regarding mortgage of lands.*—In Malkangiri taluk the claim generally put forth by some of the *Adivasis* is that their forefathers had mortgaged the lands in a question to the present cultivators or their predecessors-in-interest and the latter have managed fraudulently to get their lands mutated in the estate records. Mortgage also comes under "Transfer" as defined in the Agency Tracts Interest and Land Transfer Act or in Regulation 2 of 1956 and should be dealt with like any other case of transfer, such as sale, etc. If the mortgage is without permission of the competent authority, it is *ab initio* null and void and the entire transaction is illegal if made after 25th January, 1918. If it is with the permission of the competent authority, then the relevant provisions of the Orissa Money Lenders Act 1939, would apply. The Orissa Money Lenders Act 1939, was extended to the district of Koraput from the 6th April, 1940. Under

Section 17 of the Orissa Money Lenders Act, a possessory mortgage stands automatically discharged after the expiration of 15 years from the date of the mortgage which may be either before or after commencement of the Orissa Money Lenders Act and it is the duty of the mortgagee to deliver back possession of the property mortgaged to the mortgagor free from all encumbrances created by him. So the possession up to 15 years from the date of the mortgage should be considered as legal if made with necessary permission whereas the possession after the expiry of 15 years should be considered as illegal. So in the records it should be clearly written "auL jË[ö]Mmþ @cÊL [ÐeÞþM WÐeÊþ HaÕ ÒaAC_]Mmþ @cÊL [ÐeÞþM WÐeÊ"þ. It may be mentioned in this connection that for possessory mortgage, the mortgager has right to recover possession of the immovable property mortgaged within 60 years from the date when the rights to recover possession accrues, that is after expiry of 15 years from the date of the mortgage. So even though the possession may be considered as illegal after expiry of 15 years from the date of the mortgage, still the mortgagor can redeem the mortgaged property within 60 years under Article 148 of the Indian Limitation Act. The 12 years' rule of adverse possession does not apply to possessory mortgages, because "the possession by the mortgagee of the mortgaged property is not *prima facie* adverse to the mortgagor. Even the fact that the mortgagee is in possession after the mortgaged debt is paid off, does not make such possession adverse to the mortgager. His possession remains that of a mortgagee until some adverse title is set up by him. The mere assertion of the adverse title by a mortgagee in possession does not make his possession adverse to the mortgager or enable him (mortgagee) to abbreviate the period of 60 years which the law allows to a mortgager for redemption." vide Mitra's *Indian Limitation Act* (para. 614, page 742).

13. *Position regarding adverse possession.*—Sometimes transferees claim title through adverse possession. That is to say, they claim that they have been in possession of the land for twelve continuous years or more and have, therefore, perfected their title on the land by prescription. This question was considered in the Original Jurisdiction Case No. 3 of 1953 (P. Rama Murty and other *versus* Dhuba and other*) by a Division Bench of the Orissa High Court. The following is an extract from paragraph 14 of the judgement in that case.

* * * * *

In all these cases the transferees or their successors-in-interest have been in possession for more than twelve years. It cannot be said that they are persons 'claiming under the transfer as they have already acquired title on the land by prescription."

It, therefore, means that where the land of a person entitled to protection under the Agency Tracts Interest and Land Transfer Act or Regulation 2 of 1956 is in possession of another person for at least 12 continuous years then the person in possession has perfected his title over the land in question and he has to be recognised as the rightful owner.

14. This is the legal position regarding transfer of lands by *Adivasis* to non-*Adivasis*. The procedure of recording such illegal transfers in the record-of-rights is described in the *khanapuri* and attestation rules of Koraput Settlement. The Agency Tracts Interest and Land Transfer Act and the Rules thereunder and Regulation 2 of 1956 and the Rules thereunder are enclosed respectively as Appendices V, VA, VI and VIA for facility of reference.

---

* Reported at pages 617—622 of I.R. of Cuttack Series, 1952.

APPENDIX I

Sl. No.	*Name of castes notified as hill-tribes or Scheduled Tribes (with sub-castes)*	*Period or periods when they were treated as hill-tribes or Scheduled Tribes*
(1)	(2)	(3)
1.	Bagata	25-1-1918 to 28-2-1927
		4-7-1927 to up to date
2.	Bhottadas—	1-3-1927 to 5-9-1950
	Bodo Bhottada	25-9-1956 to up to date
	Muria Bhottada	
	Sano Bhottada	
3.	Bhumias—	1-3-1927 to 5-9-1950
	Bhuri Bhumia	
	Bodo Bhumia	25.9.1956 to up to date
4.	Barangijodia Bissoy—	18.6.1931 to 5.9.1950
	Binangi Bissoy	
	Daduva Bissoy	
	Frangi Bissoy	
	Hollar Bissoy	
	Jhoriya Bissoy	
	Kollai Bissoy	
	Kondi Bissoy	
	Paranga Bissoy	
	Pangajodia Bissoy	
	Sodojodia Bissoy	
	Takoda Bissoy	
5.	Bato Gaudas	18.6.1931 to 5.9.1950
6.	Bhiritiya Gaudas	18.6.1931 to 5.9.1950
7.	Baiga	6.9.1950 to up to date
8.	Bangara or Banjari	6.9.1950 to up to date
9.	Bathudi	6.9.1950 to up to date
10.	Bhuya or Bhuya	6.9.1950 to up to date
11.	Binjal	6.9.1950 to up to date
12.	Binjhia or Binjhoa	6.9.1950 to up to date
13.	Birhor	6.9.1950 to up to date

APPENDIX I—(*Contd.*)

(1)	(2)	(3)
14.	Bhumij	25.9.1956 to up to date
15.	Bhunjia	25.9.1956 to up to date
16.	Chenchu	6.9.1950 to up to date
17.	Domb—	25.1.1918 to 28.2.1927
	Adhinia Dombs	
	Chandal Dombs	
	Christian Dombs	4.7.1927 to 13.1.1943
	Mirgani Dombs	
	Oriya Dombs	
	Ponaka Dombs	
	Telega Dombs	
	Umania Dombs	
18.	Dhakkada	18.6.1931 to 5.9.1950
19.	Dudhokouria Gaudas	18.6.1931 to 5.9.1950
20.	Dal	6.9.1950 to up to date
21.	Desua Bhumij	25.9.1956 to up to date
22.	Dharua	25.9.1956 to up to date
23.	Didayi	25.9.1956 to up to date
24.	Ghasis—	25.1.1918 to 28.2.1927
	Bodo Ghasi	4.7.1927 to 5.9.1950
	Sano Ghasi	
25.	Gonds—	
	Madya Gond	25.1.1918 to 28.2.1927
	Rajo Gond	4.7.1927 to up to date
26.	Gadaba—	
	Bodo Gadaba	25.1.1918 to up to date
	Cerllam Gadaba	
	Franji Gadaba	
	Jodia Gadaba	
	Olaro Gadaba	
	Pangi Gadaba	
	Paranga Gadaba	
27.	Ghara	6.9.1950 to up to date
28.	Gorait or Korait	6.9.1950 to 25.9.1956
29.	Gandia	25.9.1956 to up to date

APPENDIX I—(*Contd.*)

(1)	(2)	(3)
30.	Ho	6.9.1950 to up to date
31.	Hato Gaudas	18.6.1931 to 5.9.1950
32.	Holva	18.6.1931 to 5.9.1950
		25.9.1956 to up to date
33.	Juang	6.9.1950 to up to date
34.	Jadapus	25.1.1918 to 28.2.1927
		4.7.1927 to 5.9.1950
35.	Jatapus	23.7.1918 to 28.2.1927
36.	Jatako Gaudas	4.7.1927 to up to date
37.	Juria Gaudas	18.6.1931 to 5.9.1950
		18.6.1931 to 5.9.1950
38.	Kosalya Gaudas—	
	Bisothoriya Gaudas	
	Chhiti Gaudas	1.3.1927 to 5.9.1950
	Dnagayat Gaudas	
	Dodukomariya Gaudas	
	Dudukamoro Gaudas	
	Ladiya Gaudas	
	Pullosoriya Gaudas	
39.	Khatis-Khati	1.3.1927 to 5.9.1959
	Kommar	
	Lohara	
40.	Kodu	25.1.1918 to 28.2.1927
41.	Konda Dora	4.7.1927 to 5.9.1950
42.	Konda Dora	25.1.1918 to 28.2.1927
		4.7.1927 to up to date
		25.1.1918 to up to date
43.	Kandhas—	
	Desaya Kondh	
	Dangaria Kondh—	
	Kotia Kondh	
	Tikiria Kondh	25.1.1918 to up to date
	Yenity Kondh	
	Isfanguli Kondh	
	Sitha Kondh	

APPENDIX I—(*Contd.*)

(1)	(2)	(3)
44.	Kotia—	
	Bartika	
	Bentho Oriya	25.1.1918 to 28.2.1927
	Dulia or Dhulia	4.7.1927 to 5.9.1950
	Holva Paik	25.9.1956 to up to date
	Putiya	
	Sanorana	
	Sidho Paika	
45.	Koyas	25.1.1918 to 28.2.1927
		4.7.1927 to up to date
46.	Kawar	6.9.1950 to up to date
47.	Kharia or Kharia	6.9.1950 to up to date
48.	Kharwar	6.9.1950 to up to date
49.	Kisan	6.9.1950 to up to date
50.	Kolan-kol-Loharas	6.9.1950 to up to date
51.	Kolha	6.9.1950 to up to date
52.	Koli including Malhar	6.9.1950 to up to date
53.	Kora	6.9.1950 to up to date
54.	Korua	6.9.1950 to up to date
55.	Kulia	6.9.1950 to 24.9.1956
56.	Kandha Gauda	25.9.1956 to up to date
57.	Kol	25.9.1956 to up to date
58.	Kulis	25.9.1956 to up to date
59.	Lodhai	25.9.1956 to up to date
60.	Malas or Agency	25.1.1918 to 28.2.1927
	Malas or Valmiles;	4.7.1927 to 5.9.1950
61.	Malis—	
	Korchia Maris	
	Paiko Mails	18.6.1931 to 5.9.1950
	Pedda Mates	
62.	Maune	25.1.1918 to 28.2.1927
		4.7.1927 to 5.9.1950
63.	Manna Dora	25.1.1918 to 28.2.1927
		4.7.1927 to 5.9.1950

APPENDIX I—(*Contd.*)

(1)	(2)	(3)
64.	Mukha Dora or	
	Nooka Dora	25.1.1918 to 28.2.1927
		4.7.1927 to 5.9.1950
65.	Muli or Mulia	25.1.1918 to 28.2.1927
		4.7.1927 to 5.9.1950
66.	Mum	18.6.1931 to 5.9.1950
67.	Mahali	6.9.1950 to up to date
68.	Mankidi	6.9.1950 to up to date
69.	Mandirdia	6.9.1950 to up to date
70.	Mirdhas	6.9.1950 to up to date
71.	Manda—	
	Munda Lohara	
	Munda Mohalia	6.9.1950 to up to date
72.	Mundari	6.9.1950 to up to date
73.	Madia	25.9.1956 to up to date
74.	Matya	25.9.1956 to up to date
75.	Magatha Ghudas—	
	Bennia Gaudas	25.1.1918 to 28.2.1927
	Bodo Magatha	18.6.1931 to 5.9.1950
	Dangayat Gaud	
	Ladya Gauda	
	Ponna Magatha	
	Sana Magatha	
76.	Magatha Gaudas	4.7.1927 to 7.6.1931
77.	Ojulas or Metta Kansalis	25.1.1918 to 28.2.1927
		4.7.1927 to 5.9.1950
78.	Omanaito	18.6.1931 to 5.9.1950
79.	Oraon	6.9.1950 to up to date
80.	Ormanatya	25.9.1956 to up to date
81.	Paigarapu	25.1.1918 to 28.2.1927
		4.7.1927 to 5.9.1950
82.	Palasi	25.1.1918 to 28.2.1927
		4.7.1927 to 5.9.1950
83.	Palli	25.1.1918 to 28.2.1927
		4.7.1927 to 5.9.1950

APPENDIX I—(*Contd.*)

(1)	(2)	(3)
84.	Pentias	1.3.1927 to 5.9.1950
85.	Pydi	25.1.1928 to 28.2.1927
		4.7.1927 to 5.9.1950
86.	Parenga	25.9.1956 to up to date
87.	Paraja—	
	Bodo Paraja	25.1.1918 to up to date
	Bonda Paraja	
	Daruva Paraja	
	Jodia Paraja	
	Mundili Paraja	
	Pengu Paraja	
	Salya Paraja	
88.	Reddi Doras	25.1.1918 to 28.2.1927
		4.7.1927 to 5.9.1950
89.	Relli or Sachandi	25.1.1918 to 28.2.1927
		4.7.1927 to 5.9.1950
90.	Rajuar	25.9.1956 to up to date
91.	Ronas	18.6.1931 to 5.9.1950
92.	Savaras—	
	Kapu Savaras	25.1.1918 to up to date
	Khuttu Savaras	
	Muliya Savaras	
93.	Seerithi Ghudas	18.6.1931 to 5.9.1950
94.	Santal	6.9.1950 to up to date
95.	Sfiabar or Lodha	25.9.1956 to up to date
96.	Saunti	25.9.1956 to up to date
97.	Therua	6.9.1950 to up to date

APPENDIX II

1. Bagata	15. Gorait or Korait	29. Korua
2. Baiga	16. Ho	30. Koya
3. Banjara or Banjari	17. Jatapus	31. Kulia
4. Bathudi	18. Juang	32. Mahali
5. Bhuya or Bhuyan	19. Kawar	33. Mankidi
6. Binjhal	20. Kaaria or Kharian	34. Mandirdia
7. Binjhia or Binjhoa	21. Kharwar	35. Miradhas
8. Birohor	22. Kond or Kandha or Nanguli Kandha or Sitha Kandha	36. Munda (Munda Lohara and Mudna Mohalia)
9. Bonda Paraja	23. Kishan	37. Mundari
10. Chenchu	24. Kolha-kol-Loharas	38. Oraon
11. Dal	25. Kolha	39. Paroja
12. Gadaba	26. Koli	40. Santal
13. Ghara	27. Konda Dora	41. Saora, Savar or Savura or Sohara
14. Gonds	28. Kora	42. Therua

APPENDIX III

1. Bagata
2. Bhottadas—
   Bodo Bhottada
   Muria Bhottada
   Sano Bhottada
3. Bhumias—
   Bhuri Bhumia
   Bodo Bhumia
4. Barangi—
   jodia Bissoy
5. Binangi Bissoy
6. Daduva Bissoy
7. Frangi Bissoy
8. Hollar Bissoy
9. Jhoriya Bissoy
10. Kollai Bissoy
11. Kondi Bissoy
12. Paranga Bissoy
13. Pangajodia Bissoy
14. Sodojodia Bissoy
15. Takoda Bissoy
16. Dhakoda
17. Gadaba—
    Bodo Gadaba
    Cerllam Gadaba
    Franji Gadaba
    Jodia Gadaba
    Olaro Gadaba
    Pangi Gadaba
    Pranga Gadaba
18. Ghasis—
    Bodo Ghasi
    Sano Ghasi
19. Gonds—
    Madya Gond
    Rajo Gond
20. Bato Gaudas
21. Bhiritiya Gaudas
22. Dudhokouria Gaudas
23. Hato Gaudas
24. Jatako Gaudas
25. Juria Gaudas
26. Kausalya Gudas—
    Bosothoria Gaudas
    Chiti Gaudas
    Dangayat Gaudas
    Dodukomoriya Gaudas
    Dudukamora Gaudas
    Ladiya Goudas
    Pullosoria Goudas
27. Magatha Gaudas—
    Bennia Gaudas
    Bodo Magatha Gaudas
    Dangayat Gaudas
    Ladya Gaudas
    Poona Magatha Gaudas
    Sana Magatha Gaudas
28. Seerithi Gaudas
29. Holva
30. Jadapus
31. Jatapus
32. Khatus—
    Kati Komaro
    Khati Labora
33. Kodu
34. Kommar

35. Konda Dora
36. Konda Kapus
37. Kandhas-
    Kasya Kondh
    Dangaria Kondh
    Kotia Kondh
    Tikira Kondh
    Yenity Kondh
38. Kotia—
    Baritika
    Bentho Oriya
    Dhulia or Dulia
    Holva Paiko
    Putia
    Sanrona
    Sidho Paiko
39. Koya
40. Mala or Agency Malas or Balmikites
41. Malis—
    Korchia Malis
    Paiko Malis
    Pedda Malis
42. Manue
43. Mannadora
44. Mukha Dora or Nooka Dora
45. Muli or Miulia
46. Muria
47. Ojulas or Metta Kansalis
48. Omanaito
49. Paigarapu
50. Palasi
51. Palli
52. Pentias
53. Bodo Parajas
54. Daruva Parajas
55. Didua Parajas
56. Jodia Parajas
57. Bonda Poroja
58. Mudili Parajas
59. Pengu Parajas
60. Saliya Parajas
61. Pydi
62. Reddi Doras
63. Relli or Sarchandi
64. Ronas
65. Savaras—
    Kapu Savara
    Khutu Savara
    Maliya Savara

APPENDIX IV

1. Bagata	20. Ganda
2. Baiga	21. Ghara
3. Banjara or Banjari	22. Gond, Gondo
4. Bathudi	23. Ho
5. Bhottada or Dhotada	24. Holva
6. Bhuiya or Bhuyan	25. Jatapa
7. Bhumia	26. Juang
8. Bhumij	27. Kandha-Gouda
9. Bhunjia	28. Kowar
10. Binjhal	29. Kharia or Kharian
11. Binjhia or Binjhoa	30. Kharwar
12. Birhor	31. Khond, Kond or Kandha including Nanguli Kandha or Sitha Kandha
13. Bondo Poraja	32. Kisan
14. Chenchu	33. Kol
15. Dal	34. Kolah-Kol-Loharas
16. Desua Bhumij	35. Kolha
17. Dharua	36. Koli including Malhar
18. Didaya	37. Kondadora
19. Gadaba	38. Kora

Chapter I (*Continued*)

(B) Extract from the Administration of Orissa State Order 1948 and Merged States Act, 1950

The provisions of this paragraph shall not apply to any claim against any Orissa State based on a cause of action which arose on or after the 1st January, 1948 and such claim shall be disposed of in accordance with the Laws applied or continued in force under paragraph 4.

Audit.—The Comptroller and Auditor General of Orissa shall perform such duties and exercise such powers in relation to the accounts of the Orissa States, as may be prescribed by rules made under this order by the Provisional Government.

Modifications of the Tenancy Laws.—(a) notwithstanding anything contained in the Tenancy Laws of the States as continued in force under sub-paragraph (b) of paragraph 4 an occupancy tenant shall be entitled:

(i) To freely transfer his holding subject to the restriction that no transfer of a holding from a member of an aboriginal tribe to a member of a non-aboriginal tribe shall be valid unless such transfer is made with the previous permission of the Sub-divisional Magistrate concerned.

(ii) To have full right over all kinds of trees standing on his holding.

(iii) To use the land comprised in the holding in any manner which does not materially impair the value of the land or render it unfit for the purposes of the tenancy.

(iv) (a) To presume that the rent for the time being payable by him is fair and equitable until the contrary is proved.

(b) Where a rent of an occupancy tenant is payable in cash, it shall not be liable to be enhanced except in accordance with the Tenancy Laws continued in force in the State concerned;

(c) An occupancy tenant shall not be liable to ejectment from his holding except in execution of a decree for ejectment passed on the ground that—

(i) he has used the land comprised in his holding in a manner which renders it unfit for the purpose of the tenancy; or

(ii) he has broken a condition consistent with the provisions of the Tenancy Laws in force in the State concerned and on breach of which he is under the terms of a contract between himself and his landlord, liable to be ejected.

(d) The interests of an occupancy tenant in his holding shall in his death pass by inheritance or survivorship in accordance with his personal law.

(e) A "Sukhbasi" shall be entitled to the right of an occupancy tenant over his homestead notwithstanding any law or custom to the contrary.

Explanation.—(1) An "Occupancy tenant" means a tenant or a raiyat having occupancy rights in his holding under the Tenancy Laws continued in force in the various States under sub-paragraph (b) of paragraph 4.

(2) An "Aboriginal tribe" means any tribe that may from time to time be notified as such by the Provincial Government for the purpose of this order.

(3) A "Sukhbasi" means any person holding only homestead whether or not recorded in the Settlement papers as "*ghar*", "*bari*" or "*gharbari*" or a person who is granted land by the *thekadar* or by a competent Revenue Officer for the purpose of using it as homestead.

10 A. Notwithstanding anything contained in the Tenancy Laws of the States as continued in force under subparagraph (b) of paragraph 4—

(a) When land is held as service tenure either under the Ruler or any member of his family the liability of the holder of such tenure to render service for the use and occupation thereof shall cease to and he shall on payment of full assessment to the Provincial Government acquire occupancy right therein.

(b) When a person holds *Khamer*, *Ni-jote* or any other private lands of a Ruler which have been recognised as such by the Provincial Government he shall not be liable to pay such fair and equitable rent as may be fixed by any competent authority appointed in this behalf by Commissioner and thereupon he shall acquire right of occupancy in respect of such lands;

Provided that such liability of the holder of any service tenure shall not cease and no occupancy right shall accrue to him therein if the application of the Ruler the Provincial Government direct that the holder shall continue to render such service.

EXTRACT OF SECTIONS 6 AND 7 OF THE ORISSA MERGED STATES (LAWS) ACT 1950

This Act ceases to have effect to the extent to which the law relates to matters with respect to which the (State Legislature has power to make laws).

6. (1) The repeal by section 5 of this Act of a corresponding law in force in the merged States immediately before the commencement of this Act shall not affect—

(a) the previous operation of any such law, or

(b) any penalty, forfeiture or punishment incurred in respect of any offence committed against any such law, or

(c) any investigation, legal proceeding or remedy in any such investigation, legal proceedings or remedy may be instituted, continued or enforced and any such penalty forfeiture of punishment may be imposed as if this act had not been passed.

(2) Subject to the provisions of sub-sections (1) and (3) anything done or any action taken, including any appointment or delegation made, notification, order, instruction or direction issued, rule, regulation, form, bye-law or scheme framed, certificate, patent, permit or licence granted or registration effected, under such corresponding law shall be deemed to have been done or taken under the corresponding provision of the Act or Regulation as now extended to, and in force in the merged States and shall continue in force accordingly unless and until superseded by anything done or any action taken under the said Act or Regulation.

(3) All rules, notifications, orders, bye-laws and regulations made or issued under any of the Acts or Regulations specified, in the Schedule whether before or after the date of this Act in exercise of the powers conferred by or under any such Act or Regulation shall, unless they have been applied immediately before the commencement of this Act apply to the merged States in the same manner as they applied to the (State) of Orissa before the merged, subject to such modifications not affecting the substance as may be necessary.

7. Notwithstanding anything contained in the tenancy laws of the merged States as continued in force by virtue of Article 4 of the States Merger (Governors' Provinces) Order, 1949—

(a) all suits and proceedings between landlord and tenants as such shall be instituted and tried in revenue courts.

EXTRACT OF SECTIONS 7 OF THE ORISSA MERGED STATES (LAWS) ACT 1950

Explanation.—In this clause, the expression "landlord" shall mean a person immediately under whom a tenant holds land, and the expression "tenant" shall mean a person who holds land under another person and is/or but for a special contract would be liable to pay rent for that land to that person.

(b) an occupancy tenant shall be entitled—
   (i) to freely transfer his holding[1] ....
   (ii) to have full right over all kinds of trees standing on his holding,
   (iii) to use the land comprised in the holding in any manner which does not materially impair the value of the land or render it unfit for the purposes of the tenancy,
   (iv) to the benefit of his presumption by any Court that the rent for the time being payable by him is fair and equitable until the contrary is proved;

1. The words "subject to the restriction that no transfer of a holding from a member of an aboriginal tribe shall be valid unless such transfer is made with the previous permission of the Sub-Divisional Magistrate concerned" repealed by the Orissa Scheduled Areas Transfer of Immovable Property (By Scheduled Tribes Regulation 1956) (Orissa Regulation 2 of 1956. Sec. 9 and Schedule).

Explanation.—(i) An "Occupancy tenant" means tenant or a raiyat having occupancy right in his holding under the tenancy laws continued in force in the merged States.

(ii) An "aboriginal tribe" means any tribe that may from time to time be notified as such by the (State)[1] Government;

(c) Where a rent of an occupancy tenant is payable in cash it shall not be liable to be enhanced except in accordance with the tenancy laws continued in force in the merged State concerned;

(d) an occupancy tenant shall not be liable to eviction from his holding except in execution of a decree for ejectment passed on the ground that—

  (i) he has used the land comprised in his holding in a manner which renders it unfit for the purposes of the tenancy, or

  (ii) he has broken a condition consistent with the provisions of the tenancy laws in force in the merged State concerned and on breach of which he is under the terms of contract between himself and his landlord, liable to the ejected;

(e) the interest of an occupancy tenant in his holding shall on his death pass by inheritance or survivorship in accordance with his personal law;

(f) a "Sukhbasi" shall be entitled to the rights of an occupancy tenanct over his homestead notwithstanding any law or custom to the contrary;

Explanation—A "Sukhbasi" means any person holding only homestead whether or not recorded in the settlement's paper as "Ghar", "Bari" or "Gharbari" or a person who is granted land by the Thekadar or by a competent revenue officer for the purpose of using it as homestead.

(g) when land is held as service-tenure, either under the Ruler or any member of his family the liability of the holder of such tenure to render service for the use and occupation thereof shall cease, and he shall, on payment of such rent as may be assessed by the (State) Government as fair an equitable, acquire occupancy right therein;

---

1. Substituted by the Adaptation of Laws Order 1950 for "provincial".

(h) when a person holds Khamar, Ni-jote or any other private lands of a Ruler, which has been recognised as such by the (State) Government, he shall not be liable to ejectment but shall be liable to pay such fair and equitable rent as may be fixed by any competent authority appointed in this behalf by the Revenue Commissioner, Northern Division, as the case may be and thereupon he shall acquire right of occupancy in respect of such lands

Chapter II

(A) The Scheduled Areas (Part A States) Order 1950

PART VII

C.O.9: In exercise of the powers conferred by sub-paragraph (i) of paragraph 6 of the Fifth Schedule to the Constitution of India, the President is pleased to make the following Order, namely—

1. (1) This Order may be called *The Scheduled Areas (Part A States) Order 1950*;
   (2) It shall come into force at once.
2. The areas specified below are hereby declared to be the Scheduled Areas within the States specified in Part A of the First Schedule to the Constitution—

Bihar

(1) Ranchi district.
(2) Singhbhum district, excluding Dhalbhum sub-division.
(3) Santal Parganas district, excluding Godda and Deoghar sub-divisions.
(4) Latehar sub-division of Palamau district.

CENTRAL RULES AND NOTIFICATIONS

Bombay

(1) Navapur Petha, Akrani Mahal, and the villages belonging to the Parivi of Kathi, the Parivi of Nal, the Parivi of Singpur, the Walvi of Gaohali, the Wassawa of Chikhili, and the Parivi of Navalpur, in West Khandesh district.

(2) The Satpura Hills reserved forest areas in East Khandesh district.
(3) Surgana Mahal, Kalvan taluka and Peint Petha, in Nasik district.
(4) Jawhar, Dahanu and Shahapur talukas and Mokhada and Umbergaon Pethas, in Thana district.
(5) Dangs district.
(6) Dharmpur, Vijara, Bansda and Songadh talukas and the villages in the Venkal Tappa and Nachal areas of the Mangrol Taluka in Surat district.
(7) Sagbara and Valia Mahals, and Dediapada, Nandol and Jhaghadia talukas in Broach district.
(8) Chhota Udepur taluka and the villages of Gad-Boriad Estate of Naswai taluka, in Baroda district.
(9) Limkheda, Deogadh—Baria and Sant talukas, and the villages in the old Sanejeli State include in Jhalod taluka, in Panch Mahals district.
(10) Khedbrahma, Bhiloda and Meghraj talukas, and Vijayangar Mahal, in Sabarkantha district.

Madhya Pradesh

(1) Melghat taluq of Amravati district.
(2) Baihar tahsil of Balaghat district.
(3) Antagarh-Narainpur and Dantewara tahsils, and Kutru and Bhopalpatnam zamindaris, of Bastar district.
(4) Bhainsdeshi tahsil of Betul district.
(5) Kenda, Matin, Lapha, Uprora, Chhuri and Korba zamindaris of Bilaspur district.
(6) Ahiri zamindari in the Sironcha tahsil and the Dhanora, Dudmala, Gewardna, Jharapapra, Khutgaon, Kotga, Muramgaon, Palagarh, Rangi, Sirsundi, Sonsari, Chandala, Gilgaon, Pai-Muranda and Potegaon zamindaris in the Gadhchiroli tahsil of Chanda district.
(7) Harrai, Gorakghat, Gorpani, Batkagarh, Bardgarh, Partapgarh (Pagara), Almod and Sonpur jagirs, and the portion of Panchmarhi jagir, in Chhindwara district.
(8) Ambagarh-Chauki, Aundhi, Koracha and Panabaras zamindaris of Durg district.
(9) Bazag, Samapur and Karnjia Revenue Inspectors' Circles of Mandla district.

(10) Khudia zamindari in Jashpur tahsil of Raigarh district.
(11) Balarampur revenue Inspectors' Circle in Pal tahsil and Samri and Changbhakar tahsil of Sarguja district.

Madras

(1) Laccadive Islands (including Minicoy) and Amindivi Island.
(2) East Godavari, West Godavari and Visakhapatnam Agencies.

Orissa

(1) Koraput, Mayurbhanj and Sundargarh districts.
(2) Ganjam Agency, including Khondmals, but excluding the Chokpad Khandam and Pandakhol Muttha of Surud Muliahs.

Punjab

Spiti and Lahaul in Kangra District

(3) Any reference in the preceding paragraph to a territorial division by whatever name indicated shall be construed as are reference to the territorial division of that name as existing at the commencement of this Order.

Chapter II (*Continued*)

(B) The Constitution (Scheduled Tribes) Order 1950

New Delhi, the 6th September, 1950

S.R.O. No. 510.—The following order, made by the President, is published for general information—

C.O. No. 22.—In exercise of the powers conferred by Clause(1) of Article 342 of the Constitution of India the President, after consultation with the Government and Rajpramukhs the States concerned is pleased to make the following order, namely—

(1) This order may be called the Constitution (Scheduled Tribes) Order 1950

(2) The tribes or tribal committees experts of or groups within tribes or tribal communities, specified {Part 1 to XII} of the Schedule to this order shall, in relation to the States to which those parts respectively relate, be deemed to be Scheduled Tribes so far as regards members thereof residents in the localities specified in relation to them respectively in those parts of that Schedule.

Notes.—Constitution (Scheduled Tribes) Order 1950—Para 2 and Part IX of the Scheduled-Bhotva Tribe comes under Scheduled Tribes. Plea should not have taken for the first time in the Second Appeal.

Paragraph 2 of the Scheduled Tribes Order 1950 provides to the extent material that the Tribes, or parts thereof, or groups within the Tribes specified in the Schedule to the Order shall also be deemed to be Scheduled Tribes. Whether Bhotras fall within any of the sub-groups of the Scheduled Tribes enumerated in Part IX of the Schedule to the 1950 Order is a question which could not have been permitted to be raised for the first time in the second appeal. The appeal, like the second appeal before the High Court must, therefore, be disposed of on the basis that respondent 3 is a member of the Scheduled Tribes, 47 (1979) C.L.T. P. 57 S.C.

3. Any reference in this order to a State or to a district or other territorial division thereof shall be construed as a reference to the State, district or other territorial division constituted on the 1st day or May, 1967.

SCHEDULE

PART XII—ORISSA

Throughout the State—

1. Bagats
2. Balga
3. Banjara, Bonjeri
4. Bethudi
5. Bhottada, Dhotad
6. Bhulya, Bhuyan
7. Bhumia
8. Bhumij
9. Bhunjie
10. Binjhal
11. Binjhie, Binjhoa
12. Birohor
13. Bondo Poraja
14. Chenuchu
15. Dal
16. Desua, Dhumij
17. Dharua
18. Didayi
19. Gadaba
20. Gandia
21. Ghara
22. Gond, Gondo
23. Ho
24. Holva
25. Jatapu
26. Juang
27. Kandha Gauda
28. Kawar
29. Kharia, Kharian
30. Kharwar
31. Khond, Kond, Kendha, Neguli Kandha, Sitha
32. Kisan
33. Kol
34. Kolah-Loharas, Kol
35. Kolha
36. Koli, Malia
37. Kondedora
38. Kora
39. Korua
40. Kotis
41. Koya
42. Kulia
43. Lodha
44. Madia
45. Mahali
46. Mankidi
47. Mandirdia Mandria, Mankidi
48. Matya

49.	Mirdas	56.	Pentia
50.	Munda, Munda-Lohara, Mundemahalis	57.	Rajuar
		58.	Santal
51.	Mundari	59.	Saora, Savar, Saura, Sahara
52.	Omanatya		
53.	Oraon	60.	Sabar, Lodha
54.	Parenge	61.	Sounti
55.	Paroja	62.	Tharua

1. Substituted by Scheduled Castes and Scheduled Tribes Lists (Modification) Order 1955. See, Orissa Gazette Extraordinary No. 539. Dt: 13-10-1956

2. Substituted by Central Act 108 of 1976 published in Orissa Gazette Extraordinary No. 980, dated 20th July, 1978.

Notes.—Scheduled Castes and Tribes—Constitution of India, 1950—Article 341 read with Constitution (Scheduled Tribes) Order, 1950 and Orissa Regulation 2 of 1956—Court not authorized to add or subtract entries in notification.

While examining as to whether a particular person belongs to Scheduled Tribe, a Court is not entitled to add or subtract the entry and whatever has been notified in relation to a particular State must be taken as final. It is the public notification issued by the President which is to be looked at to find out whether a particular tribe is a Scheduled Tribe or not—43 (1977) C.LT. Notes-128.

Chapter II (*Continued*)

(C) The Constitution (Scheduled Castes) Order 1950

PART III

No. 325. S.R.—The following order, made by the President, is published for general information—

0.0.19
NOTIFICATION

10th August, 1950

In exercise of the powers conferred by Clause (1) of Article 341 of the Constitution of India, the President, after consultation with the Government and Rajpramukhs of the State concerned, is pleased to make the following order, namely;

1. This order may be called the Constitution (Scheduled Castes) Order 1950.
2. Subject to the provision of this order, the castes, races of tribes or parts thereof, or groups within Castes or Tribes, specified in [Part 1 to XIX] of the Schedule to this order shall, in relation to the State to which those [Part 1 to XIX] respectively relates, be deemed to be Scheduled Castes so far as regards members thereof resident in the localities specified in relation to them in those parts of that Schedule.
3. Notwithstanding anything contained in Paragraph 2, no person who professes a religion different from Hinduism shall be deemed to be a member of a Scheduled Caste:

4. [Any reference in this order to a State or to a district or other territorial division thereof shall be construed as a reference to the State, district or other territorial division, constituted on the 1st day of May, 1976.]

(1) Substance by Scheduled Castes and Scheduled Tribes class (modification) Order 1956, See Orissa Gazette Extraordinary No. 539, dated 13th October, 1956.

2. Substituted by Central Act 108 of 1976, published in Orissa Gazette Extraordinary No. 960 dated 20th July, 1978.

SCHEDULE

PART XIII—ORISSA

Throughout the State—

1.	Adi-Andhra	24.	Dandasi
2.	Ament, Amat	25.	Dewar
3.	Audhelia	26.	Dhanwar
4.	Badaik	27.	Dom, Dombo, Duria, Dom
5.	Baghetl or Baghuti	28.	Dosadha
6.	Bajikar	29.	Ganda
7.	Bari	30.	Ghantaragade, Ghantra
8.	Bariki	31.	Ghasi, Ghasia
9.	Basor, Burud	32.	Ghogia
10.	Bauri	33.	Ghusuria
11.	Bauti	34.	Godegeli
12.	Bavuri	35.	Godari
13.	Bedia or Bejia	36.	Godra
14.	Beldar	37.	Gokha
15.	Bhata	38.	Gorait, Korait
16.	Bhoti	39.	Haddi, Haid, Hari
17.	Chachati	40.	Irika
18.	Chakali	41.	Jaggali
19.	Chamar, Mochi, Muchi	42.	Kandra or Kendara
20.	Satnami	43.	Karua
21.	Chandala	44.	Katia
22.	Cherua, Chhelia	45.	Kela
23.	Chandhia Maru		

46. Khadala
47. Kodalo, Khodelo
48. Kori
49. Kummari
50. Kurunga
51. Laban
52. Laheri
53. Madari
54. Madiga
55. Mahuria
56. Mala Jahala, Mala, Zala
57. Mang
58. Mangan
59. Mehra, Mahar
60. Mahtar, Bhangi
61. Mewar
62. Mundepotta
63. Musahar
64. Nagarchi
65. Namasudra
66. Paidi
67. Painda
68. Pamidi
69. Pan, Pano
70. Panchama
71. Panika
72. Panka
73. Pantanti
74. Par
75. Pasi
76. Patial, Patikar, Patratani, Patua
77. Rajna
78. Ralli
79. Sabakhia
80. Samasi
81. Sanei
82. Sapari
83. Sauntia, Santia
84. Sidhria
85. Sinduria
86. Siyal
87. Tamadia
88. Tamudia
89. Tanla
90. Tiar, Tior
91. Turi
92. Ujia
93. Valamiki, Valmikij

Chapter II (*Continued*)

(D) The Scheduled Castes and Scheduled Tribes Orders (Amendment) Act 1976

(Act No. 108 of 1976)

[Assented to on the 18th September, 1976]

AN ACT to provide for the inclusion in and the exclusion from the lists of Scheduled Castes and Scheduled Tribes, of certain castes and assembly constituencies in so far as such re-adjustment is necessitated by such inclusion or exclusion and for matters connected therewith.

BE it enacted by Parliament in the Twenty-seventh year of the Republic of India as follows:

1. Short Title and Commencement.—(1) This Act may be called the Scheduled Castes and Scheduled Tribes Orders (Amendment Act 1976).

2. Definitions.—In this Act unless the context otherwise requires—

(a) "Census authority" means the Registrar General and ex-officio Census Commissioner for India;

(b) "Commission" means the Election Commissioner appointed by the President under Article 324 of the Constitution;

(c) "Delimitation Act" means the Delimitation Act 1972, (16 of 1972);

(d) Last census" means the census held in India in 1971;

(e) "Scheduled Tribes Order" means the Constitution (Scheduled Castes) Order 1950, made by the President under Article 341 of the Constitution;

(f) "Scheduled Tribes Orders" means the Constitution (Scheduled Tribes) Order 1950 and the Constitution

(Andaman and Nicobar Islands) Scheduled Tribes Order 1950, made by the President under Article 342 of the Constitution; and

(g) "State" means a State included in the Scheduled Castes Order and the Scheduled Tribes Order and includes the Union Territory of the Andaman and Nicobar Islands.

3. Amendment of Scheduled Castes Orders.—The Scheduled Castes Order is hereby amended in the manner and to the extent specified in the first Scheduled.

1. See Orissa Gazette Extraordinary No. 980, Dt. 20-7-1978.
2. Came into force w.e.f. 27-7-1977 vide S.O. No 589 (E), Dt. 27-7-1977 See Gazette of India, Extraordinary, Part II, Section 3(ii) No. 335 Dt. 27-7-1977.

4. Amendment of Scheduled Castes Orders.—The Scheduled Castes Order is hereby amended in the manner and to the extent specified in the first Schedule.

5. Determination of Population of Scheduled Castes and Scheduled Tribes.—(1) As soon as may be after the commencement of this Act the population as at the last census of the Scheduled Castes or, as the case may be, of the Scheduled Tribes in each State shall be ascertained or estimated by the census authority.

(2) Whereby reason of the amendments made by Section 3 or Section 4—

(a) any locality in a State specified in relation to any caste or tribe in the said sections is varied so as to specify a large area in relation to such caste or tribe, the census authority shall take into account the population figures of the caste or tribe as ascertained in the last census and in any previous census wherein the population figures of the caste or tribe in respect of the increased area had been ascertained and determined the population of that caste or tribe as on the 1st day of April, 1971 by increasing or decreasing such figures by the proportion in which the general population of the State or, as the case may be, the division, district, taluk, tahsil, police station, development block or other territorial division in relation to which such caste or tribe has been specified by the said amendments has increased or decreased between the previous census as aforesaid and the last census; and

(b) Any caste or tribe which is deemed to be both a Scheduled Caste and Scheduled Tribe in relation to a State or part thereof is varied so as to specify such caste or tribe only as Scheduled Caste or Scheduled Tribe in relation to that State or part, the census authority shall take into account the population figures of such Scheduled Castes and Scheduled Tribes as ascertained in the last census:

Provided that it shall not be necessary for the census authority to determine the population of any Scheduled Caste or Tribe as on the 1st day of April, 1971, if the population of that caste or tribe was not ascertained at the last census and in any of the previous censuses and is, in the opinion of that authority, numerically small.

Explanation.—Where the population figures of any caste or tribe in respect of any increased area referred to in clause (a) had been ascertained in more than one previous census, the census authority shall take into account, for the purpose of that clause, the population figures of such caste or tribe as ascertained in the previous census which is nearest in point of time to the last census.

(3) The population figures ascertained or determined under Sub-section (2) shall be notified by the census authority in the Gazette of India.

(4) The population figures so notified shall be taken to be the relevant population figures as ascertained at the last census and shall supersede any figure previously published; and the figures so notified shall be final and shall not be called in question in any Court.

6. Readjustment of Constituencies by the Election Commission.—(1) After the population figures have been notified for any State under Section 5 it shall be the duty of the Commission to make such amendments as may be necessary in the Delimitation of Parliamentary and Assembly Constituencies, 1976 (Without altering the extent of any constituency as given in such Order) having regard to in the Delimitation Act and of this Act for the purpose of giving proper representation to the Scheduled Castes or, as the case may be, to the Scheduled Tribes of that State on the basis of the number of reserved seats as specified in that Order as hereunder amended by the Commission and the First Schedule and Second

Schedule to the Representation of the People Act 1950 shall be deemed to have been amended accordingly.

(2) In making any amendment under Sub-section (1), the Commission shall, as far as may be necessary, have regard to the provision of Clause (c) and (d) of Sub-section (1) of Section 9 of the Delimitation Act.

(3) The Commission shall—

(a) publish its proposals for the amendments in the Gazette of India and Official Gazette of the State concerned and also such other manner as it thinks fit;
(b) specify a date on or after which such proposals will be further considered by it;
(c) consider all objections and suggestions which may have been received by it before the date so specified; and
(d) thereafter make the necessary amendments in the order.

7. Procedure and Powers of the Commission.—In the discharge of its functions under this Act the Commission shall determine its own procedure and shall have all the powers of a Civil Court under the code of Civil Procedure 1908 while trying a suit in respect of the following matters, namely:

(a) Summoning and enforcing the attendance of witnesses;
(b) Requiring the production of any document; and
(c) Requisitioning any public record from any Court or office.

(2) The Commission shall have the power to require any person furnish any information on such point of matters as the opinion of those Commission, may be useful for, or relevant to, any matter under the consideration of the Commission.

(3) The Commission shall be deemed to be a Civil Court for the purpose of Sections 345 and 346 of the Code of Criminal Procedure, 1973.

Explanation.—For the purpose of enforcing the attendance of witnesses the local limits of the jurisdiction of the Commission shall be the limits of the territory of India.

8. Publication of Amendments and their Dates of Operation.—(1) The Commission shall cause the amendments made by it in the Delimitations for Parliamentary and Assembly

Constituencies Order 1976 to be published in Gazette of India and in the Official Gazettes of the States concerned.

(2) Upon publication in the Gazette of India, every such amendment shall have the force of law and shall not be called in question in any Court.

(3) As soon as may be after such publication in the Gazette of India, every such amendment shall be laid before the House of the People and the Legislative Assemblies of the State concerned.

(4) Subject to the provisions of Sub-sec. (5), the adjustment of representation of any territorial constituencies in the House of the People or in the Legislative Assembly of a State necessitated by any amendment made by the Commission in the Delimitation of Parliamentary and Assembly Constituencies Order 1976 and provided for in that Order as so amended shall apply in relation to after the publication in the Gazette of India under Sub-section (1) of such amendments and shall so apply in supersession of the provisions relating to representation contained in Representation of the People Act 1950.

(5) Nothing contained in the foregoing sub-sections shall affect the representation in the House of the People or in the Legislative Assembly of a State, existing on the date of publication in Gazette of India under Sub-section (1) of the amendments made by the Commission under this Act.

9. Certain Other Power of Election Commission.—(1) The Commission may, from time to time, by notification in Gazette of India and in the Official Gazette of the State concerned—

(a) Correct any printing mistake in the Delimitation of Parliamentary and Assembly Constituencies Order 1976 as amended under this Act or any error occurring therein from any inadvertent slip or omission; and

(b) Where the boundaries or the name of any district or any territorial division mentioned in the said Order are or is altered, make such amendments as appear to it to be necessary or expedient for bringing the Order up-to-date.

(2) Every notification under this section shall be laid, as soon as may after it is issued, before the House of the People and Legislative Assembly of the State concerned.

10. Validation of Acts done previous to the Commencement

of the Act.—All things done, and all steps taken, before the commencement of this Act by the census authority or the determination of population Scheduled Castes and Scheduled Tribes, or by the Commission for the purpose of re-adjustment of constituencies shall, in so far as they are in conformity with the provisions of this Act be deemed to have been done or taken under these provisions as if such provisions were in force at the time such things were done or such steps were taken.

THE FIRST SCHEDULE
(See Sec. 3)

In the Constitution (Scheduled Castes) Order 1950—

(a) In paragraph 2, for the figures "XVII", the figures "XIX" shall be substituted;

(b) for paragraph 4, substitute—

"4. Any reference in this Order to a State or to a district or other territorial division thereof shall be construed as a reference to the State, district or other territorial division as constituted on the 1st day of May, 1976",

PART XII

ORISSA

1. Adi Andhra
2. Amant, Amat
3. Audhelia
4. Badaik
5. Begheti, Beghuti
6. Bajikar
7. Bari
8. Bariki
9. Basor, Burud
10. Bauri
11. Bauti
12. Bavuri
13. Bedia, Bejia
14. Beldar
15. Bhata
16. Bhoi
17. Chachati
18. Chakali
19. Chamar, Mochi,
20. Chandala Muchi, Satnami
21. Chandhai Maru
22. Cherua, Chhelia
23. Dandasi
24. Dewar
25. Dhenwar
26. Dhoba, Dhobi
27. Dom Dombo, Duria Dom
28. Dosadha

29. Ganda
30. Ghantarghada, Ghatra
31. Ghesl, Ghasia
32. Ghogia
33. Ghusuria
34. Godagali
35. Godari
36. Godra
37. Gokha
38. Gorait, Korait
39. Haddi, Hadi, Hari
40. Irika
41. Jaggali
42. Kandra, Kandara
43. Karua
44. Katia
45. Kela
46. Khandala
47. Kodalo, Khodalo
48. Kori
49. Kummari
50. Kurunga
51. Laban
52. Laheri
53. Madari
54. Matiga
55. Mahuria
56. Mala, Jhala, Malo, Zala
57. Mang
58. Mangan
59. Mehra, Mahar
60. Mehtar, Bhangi
61. Mewar
62. Mundapotta
63. Musahar
64. Nagarchi
65. Namasudra
66. Paidi
67. Painda
68. Pamidi
69. Pan, Pano
70. Panchama
71. Panika
72. Panka
73. Pantani
74. Papa
75. Pasi
76. Patial, Patikar, Patratanti, Potua
77. Rajna
78. Relli
79. Sabakhia
80. Samasi
81. Sanei
82. Sapari
83. Sauntia, Santaia
84. Sidhria
85. Sinduria
86. Sivai
87. Tamadia
88. Tamudia
89. Tenle
90. Tiar, Tior
91. Turi
92. Ujia
93. Valamiki, Valmiki

PART XIII

ORISSA

1. Bagata	32. Kisal Naguli Kandha, Sitha Kandha
2. Balga	33. Kol
3. Banjara, Banjari	34. Lolah Loharas, Kol Loharas
4. Bathudi	35. Kolha
5. Bhottada, Dhotada	36. Koli, Malhar
6. Bhuiya, Bhuyan	37. Kondadora
7. Bhumia	38. Kora
8. Bhumij	39. Korua
9. Bhunjia	40. Kotia
10. Bainjhel	41. Koya
11. Binjhia, Binjhoa	42. Kulis
12. Birhor	43. Lodha
13. Bondo Paraja	44. Madia
14. Chenchu	45. Mahali
15. Dal	46. Mankidi
16. Desua Bhumij	47. Mankirdia
17. Dharua	48. Matya
18. Didayi	49. Mirdhas
19. Godaba	50. Mun Munda, Lohara, Munda Mahalis
20. Gandia	51. Mundari
21. Ghare	52. Omanatya
22. Gond, Gondo	53. Oraon
23. Ho	54. Parenga
24. Holva	55. Paroja
25. Jatapu	56. Pentia
26. Juang	57. Rajuar
27. Kandha Gaude	58. Santal
28. Kawar	59. Saora, Saver, Saura Sehare
29. Kharia, Kharian	60. Shabar, Lodha
30. Kharwar	61. Sounti
31. Khond, Kond, Kandha	62. Tharua

Chapter II (*Continued*)

(E) The Scheduled Areas (State of Bihar, Gujarat, Madhya Pradesh and Orissa) Order 1977

31st December, 1977

ORISSA

1. Mayurbhanj district
2. Sundergarh district
3. Koraput district.
4. Kuchinda Tahsil in Sambalpur district.
5. Keonjhar and Telkoi Tahsil of Keonjhar Sub-division and Champua and Barbil Tahsil of Champur Sub-division in Keonjhar district.
6. Khondmals Tahsil Khondmals Sub-division and Balliguda and G. Udayagiri Tahsils of Balliguda Sub-division on Boudh-Khondmals district.
7. R. Udayagiri Tahsils and Guma and Rayagada Blocks of Parlakhemundi tahsil of Parlakhemundi Sub-division on Boudh-Khondmals district.
8. Thuamul Rampur Block of Kalahandi Tahsil and Lanjigarh Block, falling in Lanjigarh and Kalahandi tahsils in Bhawanipatna Sub-division of Kalahandi district.
9. Nilgiri Community Development Block of Nilgiri Tahsil in Nilgiri Sub-division in Balasore district.
10. Any reference in the preceding paragraph to a territory all division by whatever name indicated shall be construed as a reference to the territorial division of that name as existing at the commencement of this Order.

Chapter II (*Continued*)

(F1) Updated List of Scheduled Castes (As per Second Amendment Act 61 of 2002)

1. Adi Andhra
2. Amant, Amat, Dandachhatra Majhi
3. Audhelia
4. Badaik
5. Bagheti, Baghuti
6. Bajikar
7. Bair
8. Bariki
9. Basor, Burd
10. Bauri, Buna, Bauri, Dasia Bauri
11. Bauti
12. Bavuri
13. Bedia, Bejia
14. Beldar
15. Bhata
16. Bhoi
17. Chachati
18. Chakali
19. Chamar, Mochi, Muchi, Satnami
20. Chandala
21. Chandhai Maru
22. Cherua, Chhelia
23. Dandasi
24. Dewar, Dhibara, Keuta, Kaibarta
25. Dhanwar
26. Dhoba, Dhobi
27. Dom, Dombo, Duria Dom
28. Dosadha
29. Ganda
30. Ghantarghada, Ghantra
31. Ghasi, Ghasi
32. Ghogia
33. Ghusuria
34. Godagali
35. Godari
36. Godra
37. Gokha
38. Gorait, Korait
39. Haddi, Hadi, Hari
40. Irka
41. Jaggali
42. Kandra, Kandara, Kadama
43. Karua
44. Katia
45. Kela, Sapua Kela, Nalua Kela
46. Khadala Sabakhia Kela, Matia Kela
47. Kodalo, Khodal

48. Kori
49. Kummari
50. Kurunga
51. Laban
52. Laheri
53. Madari
54. Madiga
55. Mahuria
56. Mala, Jhala, Malo, Zala, Malha, Jhola
57. Mang
58. Mangan
59. Mehra, Mahar
60. Mehtar, Bhangi
61. Mewar
62. Mundapotta
63. Muṣahar
64. Nagarchi
65. Namasudra
66. Paidi
67. Painda
68. Pamidi
69. Pan, Pano, Buna Pana, Desua Pan
70. Panchama
71. Panika
72. Panka
73. Pantani
74. Pap
75. Pasi
76. Patial, Patikar, Patratani, Patua
77. Rajna
78. Relli
79. Saakhia
80. Samasi
81. Sanei
82. Sapari
83. Sauntia, Santia
84. Sidhria
85. Sinduria
86. Siyal, Khajuria
87. Tamadia
88. Tamudia
89. Tanla
90. Tiar, Tio
91. Turi
92. Uija
93. Valamiki, Valmiki

Chapter II (*Continued*)

(F2) Updated List of Scheduled Tribes (as per Amendment Act 10 of 2003)

1. Bagata, Bhakta
2. Baiga
3. Banjara, Banjari
4. Bathudi, Bathuri
5. Bhottada, Dhotada, Bhotra, Bhatra, Bhattara, Bhotora
6. Bhiyan, Bhuyan
7. Bhumia
8. Bhumij, Teli Bhumij, Haladipokharia Bhumij, Haladi Pokharia Bhummija, Desi Bhumij, Desi Bhumij, Tamaria Bhumij
9. Bhunjia
10. Binjhal, Binjhwar
11. Binjhia, Binjhoa
12. Birhor
13. Bondo Poraja, Bonda Paroja, Banda Paroja
14. Chenchu
15. Dal
16. Desua Bhumij
17. Dharua, Dhuruba Dhurwa
18. Didayo, Didai Paroja, Didai
19. Gadaba, Bodo Gadaba, Gutob Gadaba, Kapu Gadaba, Ollara Gadaba Parenga Gadaba, Sano Gadaba
20. Gandia
21. Ghara
22. Gond, Gondo, Rajgond, Maria Gond, Dhur Gond
23. Ho
24. Holva
25. Jatapu
26. Juang

27. Kandha Gauda
28. Kawar, Kanwar
29. Kharia, Kharian, Berga Kharia, Dehelki Kharia, Erenga Kharia, Munda Kharia, Oraon Kharia, Khadia, Pahari Kharia
30. Kharwar
31. Khond, Kond, Kandha, Naguli Kandha, Sitha Kandha, Kondh, Kui, Buda Kondh, Bura Kandha, Desia Kandha, Dungaria Kondha, Kutia Kandha, Kandha Ganda, Muli Kondh, Malua Kondh, Pengo Kandha, Raja Kondh, Raj Khond
32. Kisan Nagesar, Nagesia
33. Kol
34. Kolah Kol Loharas
35. Kolha
36. Koli, Malhar
37. Kondadora
38. Kora, Khaira, Khayara
39. Korua
40. Kotia
41. Koya, Guba Koya, Koitur Koya, Kamar Koya, Musara Koya
42. Kulis
43. Lodha, Nodh, Nodha, Lodh
44. Madia,
45. Mahali
46. Mankidi
47. Mandirdia, Mandria, Mankidi
48. Matya, Matia
49. Matya, Matial
50. Munda, Munda Lohara, Munda Mahalis, Nagabanshi Munda, Oriya Munda
51. Mundari
52. Omanatya, Omanatyo, Amanatya
53. Oraon, Dhangar, Urau
54. Parenga
55. Paroja, Parja, Bodo Paroja Barong Jhodia Paroja, Chhelia Paroja, Jhodia, Paroja, Konda, Pajoja, Paraja, Ponga Paroja, Sodia Paroja, Sano Paroja, Solia Paroja
56. Pentia
57. Rajuar
58. Samta
59. Saora, Savara, Saura, Sahara Aris Saora, Based Saora, Ghumura

Saora, Jara Savar, Jadu Saora, Jati Saora, Juari Saora, Kindal Saora, Kumbi Kancher Saora, Kalapithia Saora, Lanjia Saora, Lamba Lanjia, Saora, Luara Saora, Luar Saora, Laria Savar, Uriya Saora, Raika Saora, Sudda Saora, Sarda Saora, Tankal Saora, Patro Saora, Vesu Saora

60. Shabar, Lodha
61. Sounti
62. Tharua, Tharua Bindhani

Received the assent of the President on 7th January 2008. Act published in Gazette of India, 8th January, 2003, Part II, Section I, Ext. P.i (No.10).

Chapter II (*Continued*)

(G) List of Hill Tribes of Koraput Region as Categorised Differently at Present

Sl. No.	*Name of Hill-Tribe and Sub-sects*	*Present Categorisation*	*Remarks*
(1)	(2)	(3)	(4)
1.	Bagata	Scheduled Tribe	
2.	Bhottadas— Bodo Bhottada Muria Bhottada Sano Bhottada	Scheduled Tribe	
3.	Bhumias—		
	Bhuri Bhumia	Scheduled Tribe	
	Bondo Bhumia	Scheduled Tribe	
4.	Barangi— Jodia Bissoy	Backward Class	
5.	Binangi Bissoy	Backward Class	
6.	Daduva Bissoy	Backward Class	
7.	Frangi Bissoy	Backward Class	
8.	Hollar Bissoy	Backward Class	
9.	Jhoriya Bissoy	Backward Class	
10.	Kollai Bissoy	Backward Class	
11.	Kondi Bissoy	Backward Class	
12.	Paranga Bissoy	Backward Class	
13.	Penga Jodia Bissoy	Backward Class	
14.	Sodojodia Bissoy	Backward Class	
15.	Takoda Bissoy	Backward Class	
16.	Dhakkada	Backward Class	

(1)	(2)	(3)	(4)
17	Domb	Scheduled Caste	Sl No. 17 was excluded from the list by way of amendment in 1943
18	Gadabas—	Scheduled Tribe	
	Boda Gadaba	Scheduled Tribe	
	Cevllam Gadaba	—	
	Franji Gadaba		
	Jodia Gadaba		
	Olara Gadaba	Scheduled Tribe	
	Pangi Gadaba		
	Parangi Gadaba	Scheduled Tribe	
19	Ghasis—	Scheduled Tribe	
	Bodo Ghasi	Scheduled Tribe	
	Sano Ghasi	Scheduled Tribe	
20	Gonds—	Scheduled Tribe	
	Madya Gond	Scheduled Tribe	
	Rajo Gond	Scheduled Tribe	
21	Bato Gaudas		
22	Bhiritiya Gaudas	Backward Class	
23	Dudhokouria Gaudas	Backward Class	
24	Hato Gaudas	Backward Class	
25	Jatako Gaudas	Backward Class	
26	Juria Gaudas	Backward Class	
27	Kausalya Gaudas—	Backward Class	
	Bosothoria Gaudas	Backward Class	
	Chiti Gaudas	Backward Class	
	Dangayat Gaudas	Backward Class	
	Dodukomoriya Gaudas	Backward Class	
	Dudukamoro Gaudas	Backward Class	
	Ladiya Goudas	Backward Class	
	Pullosoria Gaudas	Backward Class	
28	Magatha Gaudas—	Backward Class	
	Bennia Gaudas	Backward Class	
	Bodo Magatha Gaudas	Backward Class	
	Dangayat Gaudas	Backward Class	

(1)	(2)	(3)	(4)
	Ladya Gaudas	Backward Class	
	Poona Magatha	—	
	Gaudas	Backward Class	
	Sana Magatha Gaudas	Backward Class	
29	Secrithi Gaudas	Backward Class	
30	Holva	Scheduled Tribe	
31	Jadapus	Backward Class	
32	Jatapus	Scheduled Tribe	
33	Khatis—	Backward Class	
	Kati Komaro	Backward Class	
	Khati Labora	Backward Class	
34	Kodu	Backward Class	
35	Kommar	Backward Class	
36	Konda Dora	Scheduled Tribe	
37	Konda Kapus	Backward Class	
38	Kandhas—	Scheduled Tribe	
	Dasya Kondh	Scheduled Tribe	
	Dangaria Kondh	Scheduled Tribe	
	Kotia Kondh	Scheduled Tribe	
	Tikira Kondh	Scheduled Tribe	
	Yenity Kondh	Scheduled Tribe	
39	Kotia—	Scheduled Tribe	
	Baritika		
	Bentho Oriya		
	Dhulia or Dulia		
	Holva Paiko		
	Putiya		
	Sanrona		
	Sidho Paiko		
40	Koya	Scheduled Tribe	
41	Mala or Agency Malas	Scheduled Tribe	
	or Balmikis	Scheduled Tribe	
42	Malis—	Backward Class	
	Korchia Malis	Backward Class	
	Paiko Malis	Backward Class	
	Pedda Malis	Backward Class	

(1)	(2)	(3)	(4)
43	Manue	Backward Class	
44	Mannadora	Backward Class	
45	Mukha Dora or	Backward Class	
	Nokka Dora	— —	
46	Muli or Miulia	Backward Class	
47	Muria	Backward Class	
48	Ojulas or Metta Kansalis	Backward Class	
49	Omanaito	Backward Class	
50	Paigarapu	Backward Class	
51	Palasi	Backward Class	
52	Palli	Backward Class	
53	Pentias	Scheduled Tribe	
54	Bodo Parajas	Scheduled Tribe	
55	Daruva Parajas	Scheduled Tribe	
56	Didua Parajas	Scheduled Tribe	
57	Banda Parajas	Scheduled Tribe	
58	Jodia Parajas	Scheduled Tribe	
59	Mudili Parajas		
60	Pengu Parajas	Scheduled Tribe	
61	Saliya Parajas	Scheduled Tribe	
62	Pydi	Scheduled Tribe	
63	Reddi Doras		
64	Relli or Sarchandi	Scheduled Caste	
65	Ronas	Backward Class	
66	Savaras—	Scheduled Tribe	
	Kapu Savara	Scheduled Tribe	
	Khutu Savara		
	Maliya Savara	Scheduled Tribe	

Chapter III

(A) The Orissa Scheduled Areas Transfer of Immovable Property (By Scheduled Tribes) Regulations 1956 and Rules 1959 as amended from time to time

Orissa Regulation 2 of 1956

A Regulation to control and check transfer of immovable property in the Scheduled Areas of the State of Orissa by Scheduled Tribes.

Whereas, it is expedient to control and check transfer of immovable property by the Scheduled Tribes in the Scheduled Areas of the State of Orissa.

Now, therefore, in exercise of the powers conferred by Sub-paragraph (2) of Paragraph 5 of the Fifth Schedule to the Constitution, the Governor of Orissa, is pleased to promulgate the following Regulation made by him in the Seventh Year of the Republic of India.

1. Short title, extent and commencement.—(1) This Regulation may be called the Orissa Scheduled Areas Transfer of Immovable Property (By Scheduled Tribes) Regulations 1956.

(2) It extends to all the Scheduled Areas of the State of Orissa.

(3) It shall come into force at once.

2. Definition.—In this Regulation unless there is anything repugnant in the subject or context—

(a) "Agriculture" includes making land fit for cultivation, cultivation of land, improvement of land including development of sources of irrigation, raising and harvesting of crops, horticulture, farming seed farming, pisciculture, apiculture, sericulture, piggery, poultry farming and such other activities as are generally carried on by agriculturists, dairy farmer, cattle breeders, poultry farmers and other category of persons engaged in similar activities including marketing of agricultural products, their storage and transport, and the acquisition activity, and 'agricultural purpose' shall be construed accordingly.

(ab) "Competent authority" means the Collector and includes any other officer or officers appointed by the State Government by notification to perform all or any of the function of a competent authority under this regulation.

Orissa Regulation 2 of 1956

(b) "Gram Panchayat" and "Gram Sasan" shall respectively mean the Gram Panchayat and Gram Sasan as defined in the Orissa Gram Panchayats Act 1964

(c) "Immovable Property" does not include standing number, growing crops or grass.

(d-1) "Public financial institution" means:

(i) any bank to which the Orissa Co-operative Societies Act 1962 (Orissa Act 2 of 1963) applies;

(ii) a banking company within the meaning of the Banking Regulation Act 10 of 1989.

(iii) The State Bank of India constituted under the State Bank of India Act 23 of 1955.

(iv) A Subsidiary Bank with the meaning of the State Bank of India (Subsidiary Bank) Act 33 of 1959.

(v) a corresponding new bank within the meaning of the Banking Companies (Acquisition and Transfer of Undertakings Act 5 of 1970.

(vi) The Agricultural Refinance Corporation established under the Agricultural Refinance Corporation Act 1 of 1963.

(vii) The Agricultural-Finance Corporation Limited, a company incorporated under the Companies Act 1 of 1956.

(viii) the Agro-Industries Corporation.

(ix) any other financial institutions which may be notified by the State Government.

(e) "Scheduled Areas" and "Scheduled Tribes" shall respectively mean and Scheduled Areas specified in respect of the State of Orissa in the Schedule in respect of the State of Orissa in the Scheduled Areas (State of Bihar, Gujarat, Madhya Pradesh and Orissa) Order 1977 and the "Scheduled Tribes" specified respect of Orissa in the Constitution (Scheduled Tribes) Order 1950, as modified from time to time.

(f) "Transfer of immovable property" means mortgage with or without possession, lease, sale, gift, exchange or any other dealings with such property not being a testamentary disposition and includes a charge or contract relating to such property.

CASE LAW

Restoration of Possession.—Application for—Plea of Resjudicata Onus of proof—order passed by officer on special duty in earlier proceeding only quoted—Necessary documents not filed—Plea cannot be sustained: AIR 1992 Ori. 5.

Transfer by Scheduled Tribes without permission—Civil Court, Decree to such transfer in nullity: 40 (1974) CLT 134.

3. Transfer of Immovable Property by a Member of the Scheduled Tribe.—Notwithstanding anything contained in any law for the time being in force any transfer of immovable property by member of a Scheduled Tribe, except by way of mortgage excited in favour of any public financial institution for securing a loan granted by such institution for any agricultural purpose, shall be absolutely null and void and of no force or effect whatsoever unless such transfer is made in favour of another member of a Scheduled Tribe.

Provided that:

(i) nothing in this sub-section shall be construed as to permit any member of a Scheduled Tribe or his successor-in-interest to transfer any immovable property which was settled with such member of Scheduled Tribe by or under any authority of the State or the Central Government or under any law for the time being in force;

(ii) in execution of any decree for realisation of the mortgage, money no property mortgaged as above said, shall be sold in favour of any person not being a member of a Scheduled Tribe; and

(iii) a member of Scheduled Tribe shall not transfer any land if the total extent of his land remaining after the transfer will be reduced to less than two acres in case of irrigated land or five acres in case of unirrigated land.

Explanation 1.—For the purposes of this sub-section, a transfer of immovable property:

(a) in favour of a female member of a Scheduled Tribe, who is married to a person not belonging to any Scheduled Tribe, shall be deemed to be a transfer made in favour of a person not belonging to a Scheduled Tribe; and
(b) shall include a transfer of immovable property to a person belonging to a Scheduled Tribe for consideration paid or provided by another person not belonging to any such Tribe.

Explanation II.—For the purpose of Clause (iii) of the proviso, the expression "irrigated land" shall mean such land which is irrigated at least for one crop in a year, and the expression "unirrigated land" shall mean such land which is irrigated at least for one crop in a year and the expression "unirrigated land" shall be construed accordingly.

(2) Where a transfer of immovable property is made in contravention of Sub-section (1) the competent authority may, either on application by anyone interested therein or on information received from the Grama Panchayat or on his own motion and after giving the parties, an opportunity of being heard, order ejectment against any person in possession of or being heard, order, ejectment against any pension in possession of the property claiming under the transfer and shall cause restoration of possession of such property to the transferor or his heirs. In causing such restoration of possession the competent authority may take such steps as may be necessary for securing compliance with the said order or preventing any breach of peace;

Provided that if the competent authority is of the opinion that the restoration of possession of immovable property to the transfer or his heirs is not reasonably practicable, he shall record his reasons thereof and shall, subject to the control of the State Government settle the said property with another member of Scheduled Tribe or in the absence of any such member, with any other person in accordance with the provisions contained in the Orissa Government Land Settlement Act 33 of 1962:

Provided further that where it is decided by the competent authority to settle the said property with any person other than a person belonging to a Scheduled Tribe in accordance with the Orissa Government Land Settlement Act 33 to 1962, he shall obtain prior approval of the concerned Grama Panchayat, accorded with the concurrence of the Gram Sasan.

Explanation.—Restoration of Possession means actual delivery of possession by competent authority to the transferor or is heirs.

(3) Subject to such conditions as may be prescribed an appeal if preferred within thirty days of the order under Sub-section (2) shall, if made by the Collector lie to the (Revenue Divisional Commissioner) and if made by any other competent authority to the Collector, or any other officer specially empowered by the State Government in this behalf.

(3-a) (i) Any order passed by the competent authority under Sub-section (1) or under Sub-section (2) may within a period of five years from the date of such order, be revised, either on own motion or otherwise, by the Revenue Divisional Commissioner if the order was passed by the Collector and by the Collector if it was passed by any other competent authority, after giving the parties concerned a reasonable opportunity of being heard:
Provided that no order shall be revised under this sub-section if an appeal against such order has been entertained under Sub-section (3)

(ii) For the purpose of revising any order, the Revenue Divisional procedure as may be prescribed and shall have power to call for and examine the records of the proceedings wherein such order was passed and pass such order as he deems fit.

(4) Subject to any order passed under Sub-section (3) or Sub-section (3-a) the decision of the competent authority under Sub-section (2) shall be final and shall not be challenged in Court of Law.

CASE LAW

Expression 'transfer of immovable property'. Any transaction of dealing with immovable property which would have the effect of extinguishing title, possession or right to possess such property in a tribal and vesting the same in a non-tribal, would be included within the meaning of 'transfer of immovable property': 2004 (II) OLR (SC) 117.

Benami transaction—Prayer for eviction of opposite party No. 2 (Benamidar) and recovery of possession of the suit land, before the trial Court by O.P. No. 1—Trial Court rejected the application on the ground that allegation of Benami transaction and possession by O.P. No. 2 not proved—Reversing judgment of the appellate Court challenged in writ—Appreciation of evidence—Evidence laid by opposite party No. 1 does not prove the case of Benami transaction nor exclusive possession of the property by O.P. No. 2—Appellate Court passed orders on the assumption that O.P. No. 2 failed to prove that it was not a case of Benami transaction—Admittedly O.P. No. 2 did not contest the case—Burden on O.P. No. 1 prove the Benami transaction who has not discharged the same—Order of appellate Court set aside—Direction issued on action to be taken: 2004 (I) OLR 435: 97 (2004) CLT 528.

Transfer of immovable property by a member of scheduled tribe within the scheduled area is void if not supported by prior permission in writing of the competent authority—Sec. 3 of the Regulation does not authorise the competent authority to either entertain an application regarding a void transfer—In case of unauthorised occupation, Sec. 3A governs the field which was added in 1975—Authority entertaining an application regarding unauthorised occupation and not on the basis of any void transaction or transfer—Proceeding without jurisdiction—Order does not operate as resjudicata: 2004 (Supp.) OLR (NOC) 999.

Restoration of possession—Application for—Correct area in respect which restoration of possession was prayer for not given Order of offer on special duty directing delivery of possession of different areas than mentioned in application—Not liable to be set aside on that ground: AIR 1992 Ori. 5.

Duty of competent authority under, indicated: 73 (1992) CLT 357: AIR 1992 Ori. 293: 34 (1992) OJD 7 (Civil).

Requirements under-Transfer of land to non-Scheduled Tribe—Previous consent of competent authority—Necessity—According permission on the basis of application by transferee—Legality of: 73 (1992) CLT 356: AIR 1992 Ori. 294: 34 (1992) OJD 7 (Civil).

Question whether a person belongs to the Scheduled Tribe—the enquiry is to be made by the competent authority by observing the principles of natural justice—There is no scope for authorising another office to enquire and to act upon his report—In the instant case the competent authority transferred the enquiry to B.D.O. and acted on his report—Held, the order illegal: 1989 (I) OLR 473.

Constitution (Scheduled Castes) Order 1950—Part XIII—Constitution (Scheduled Tribes) Order, 1950—Part-XII-"CADE" or "Mudi"—Both are not the same as "ORANG" or "ORAON" as described in Constitution (Scheduled Tribes) Order 1950, Part XII, Entry 53—Even "ORANG" is not in any of the entries—Hence, the restriction in Sec. 3 of the Regulation of 1956 is not applicable: 1989 (II) OLR 157.

The explanation inserted by way of amendment in 1977 is apparently for the purpose of safeguarding against exploitation of tribals by person belonging to other communities by marriage to tribal woman which comes handy: 1989 (II) OLR 580.

Authority to see if the transferor and transferee belonged to Scheduled Tribes—Caste Certificate is not conclusive proof of Scheduled Tribe under any provision of law—The question has to be decided by authorities on the materials on record before them: 1987 (I) OLR 263.

Appeal filed 30 days after the period of limitation provided—Case heard at G. Udaygiri where the Adibasi Woman lives and engaged lawyer of local Bar—But order was passed at Balliguda without notice to party—Reasons stated in petition for condonation of delay—The beneficial purpose for the welfare Regulations enumerated-Held, appeal filed within time from the date of knowledge—Delay condoned: 1986 (II) OLR 641.

Transferee is a member of Scheduled Castes and transferor is a member of Scheduled Tribes—State Policy is to give protection on account of these classes being backward—Regulation makes an exception for a transferee belonging to Scheduled Castes: 1984 (I) OLR 633.

Even if sale is by Court contrary to permission sale is valid—AIR 1978 Supreme Court 1820.

3-A. Eviction of persons in unauthorised occupation of property.—(1) Where a person is found to be in unauthorised occupation of any immovable property of a member of the Scheduled Tribes by way of trespass or otherwise the competent authority may, either on application by the owner or any person interested therein or on information received parties concerned an opportunity of being heard, order of ejectment of the person so found to be in unauthorised occupation and shall cause restoration of possession of such property to the said member of the Scheduled Tribes or to his heirs.

(2) The provisions contained in Sub-sections (2), (3) and (4) of

Section 3 shall *mutatis mutandis*, apply to the proceedings instituted or initiated under Sub-section (1)

(3) In every case after finalisation of the proceedings under Sub-section (1) the competent authority shall make a report to the concerned Grama Panchayat about the order of ejection passed in respect of any person in unauthorised occupation of any immovable property of a member of a Scheduled Tribe and the restoration of possession of the property to such member or his heirs and in case of failure of such restoration, the reasons for such failure.

3-B. Reversion of land of members of Scheduled Tribes which was transferred by fraud.—(1) Every person who, on the date of commencement of the Orissa Scheduled Areas Transfer of Immovable Property (By Scheduled Tribes) Amendment Regulation 2000 (hereinafter referred to in this Section as the Amendment Regulation of 2000) is in possession of agricultural land which belonged to a member of a Scheduled Tribe at any time during the period commencing on the 4th October, 1956, and ending on the date of commencement of the Amendment Regulation of 2000 shall within two years of such commencement, notify to the Sub-Collector in such form and in such manner as may be prescribed, all the information as to how he has come in possession of such land.

(2) If any person fails to notify the information as required by Sub-section (1) within the period specified therein it shall be presumed that such person has been in possession of the agricultural land without any lawful authority and the agricultural land shall on the expiration of the period aforesaid, revert to the person whom it originally belonged and if that person be dead, to his heirs.

(3) On receipt of the information under Sub-section (1) the Sub-Collector shall make such enquiry as may be necessary about all such transactions of transfer, and if he finds that the member of Scheduled Tribe has been defrauded of his legitimate right, he shall declare the transaction null and void and,

(a) where no building or structure has been erected on the agricultural land prior to such finding, pass an order reverting the agricultural land to the transferor and if he be dead, to his heirs.

(b) Where any building or structure has been erected on the agricultural land prior to such finding, he shall fix the price of such land in accordance with the principles laid down for fixation of price of land in the Land Acquisition to pay to the transferor the difference, if any, between the price so fixed and the price actually paid to the transferor:

Provided that where the building or structure has been erected after the commencement of the Amendment Regulations of 2000, the provision of Clause (b) shall not apply:

Provided further that fixation of price under Clause (b) shall be with reference to the price on the date of registration of the case before the Sub-Collector.

CASE LAWS

Orissa Survey and Settlement Act, 1958—Sec. 15 (b)—Registered deed of sale of the year 1965 in favour of the petitioner and of the year 1987 in favour of the opposite party No. 1—Both parties laying claim of title and possession with respect to the disputed property claim of title and possession with respect to the disputed property on the basis of respective registered sale deeds—R.O.R supports the stand of the O.P. No. 1—Order of mutation and the Amin other supports the claim of the petitioner—Additional District Magistrate held that O.P. No. 1 is the purchaser of the case land—Petitioner's revision petition pending—Discussing the facts and contentions direction for deferring the orders by the Sub-Collector and action to be taken on Revision petition indicated: 2004 (I) OLR 251: 97 (2004) CLT 400.

Occupation of lands belonging to tribal persons by non-scheduled tribe persons—Sub-Collector and appellate authority held the possession to be unauthorised and illegal—Directed for eviction of petitioners—Plea of petitioners in occupation by adverse possession—Held, petitioners are in unauthorised possession of the lands—In view of Apex Court decision as reported in AIR 2004 SC 3782, the unauthorised occupants cannot claim adverse possession—No reason to interfere with the orders of eviction passed by the authorities below—Direction issued: 2004 (Supp.) OLR 947.

4. Inadmissibility of a dead for the purpose of registration.—Notwithstanding anything contained in the Indian Registration Act XVI of 1908 no deed of transfer of any immovable property executed in contravention of provision of this Regulation shall be accepted for registration.

5. Surrender or Relinquishment not valid unless Settled by Landlord.—(1) No surrender or relinquishment of any holding or a part of a holding by a tenant to a landlord under any law for the time being in force applicable to such tenancy, such tenant being a member of a Scheduled Tribe, shall be valid unless after such surrender of relinquishment the landlord thereof by whatever name called either settles the said holding or part of the holding, as the case may be with another member will any other person with the approval of the competent authority such member of a Scheduled Tribe is not available.

(2) Any surrender or relinquishment shall be deemed to be a transfer of immovable property within the meaning of this Regulation and except as otherwise provided in Sub-section (1) the other provisions of this Regulation shall, so far as may be, applied.

(3) Nothing in this section shall apply to any tenant holding immediately under the State Government.

6. Bar to Attachment of Immovable Property.—In execution of a money decree against a member of a Scheduled Tribe, no right, title or interest held by him in any immovable property within any Scheduled Area shall be liable to be attached and sold except as and if prescribed.

7. Punishment for Offences.—(1) If any person is found to be in possession of any immovable property in contravention of the provisions of this Regulation, then, without prejudice to his liability to ejectment under this Regulation, or where any person, having been evicted under any provision of this Regulation from immovable property belonging to a member of a Scheduled Tribe, continues to be in possession of the same, he shall be punishable with rigorous imprisonment for a term which may extend to two years, or with fine which may extent to rupees five thousand, or with both.

(2) Where any person, having been evicted under any provision of this Regulation from any immovable property belonging to a member of a Scheduled Tribe, reoccupies the same shall be punishable with rigorous imprisonment for a term which may extend to three years, or with fine which may extend to rupees ten thousand, or with both.

(3) When a Court imposes sentence of fine or a sentence of which fine forms a part, the Court may, when passing judgment, order the whole or any part, of the fine to be paid to the member of Scheduled Tribe to whom the immovable property belongs, or to his heirs.

7-A. Offences to be tried by Executive Magistrate and to be cognizable.—(1) The State Government may confer, on an Executive Magistrate, the powers of judicial Magistrate of the First Class or of the Second Class for the trial of the offence under this Regulation, and on such conferment of powers, the Executive Magistrate, on whom the powers are so conferred, shall be deemed, for the purposes of the Code of Criminal Procedure 1973, to be a judicial Magistrate of the First Class or of the Second Class, as the case may be.

(2) An offence under this Regulation may be tried summarily by a Magistrate.

(3) Every offence under this Regulation shall be cognizable.

CASE LAWS

Regulation 7-A—Survey and Settlement Act 1958, Sec. 15—Mayurbhanj Settlement Manual—Rule 563—Conclusions as to caste as described in sale-deed—R.O.R. entry not disputed—School admission Register shows the caste as "Bhuyan"—Conclusions arrived at by the forums below not accepting the caste as 'Khandual' as mentioned in sale-deed cannot be interested with: 1995 (I) OLR 412.

Scheduled Tribes—Santals—Sucession law is Hindu Law and not customary law: 77 (1994) CLT 219.

7-B. Consideration of Money Not Refundable in case of Invalid Transfer.—Notwithstanding anything contained in any law for the time being in force, where a transfer of immovable property is found to have been made in contravention of the provision of Sec. 3 and the transferee or any other person in possession of the property has been evicted or any other person in possession of the property has been evicted therefrom under the said section, the transferee shall not be entitled to the refund of any amount paid by him to the transfer by way of consideration for the transfer.

7-C. Burden of Proof and Power of Court to Ignore Admission.—Notwithstanding anything contained in any other law for the time being in force—

(a) If in any proceeding under this Regulations, the validity of the transfer or relinquishment of any immovable property is called in question or if such proceedings ar for the recovery of possession of immovable property, the burden of proving that the transfer of relinquishment was valid shall lie on the transferee (or any person claiming the right to the property through the transferee)

(b) The Court shall in any suit or proceeding relating to the transfer of immovable property a member of the Scheduled Tribes have power to require in face expressly or impliedly admitted by such member to be proved otherwise than by admission.

CASE LAW

Burden of proof lies on the transferee to prove his possession to be in accordance with laws—He should be given opportunity to discharge that burden: 1984 (I) OLR 633.

7-D. Amendment of the Limited Act 1963 in its Application to the Scheduled Areas.—In the limitation Act 1963 in its application to the scheduled areas in the Schedule, after the words "twelve years" occurring in the second column against Article 65, the words "twelve years" and "figure" but thirty years in relation to immovable property belonging to a member of a scheduled tribe specified in respect of the State Orissa in the Constitution (Scheduled Tribes) Order 1950 as modified from time to time shall be added.

CASE LAWS

Non-*Adivasi* cannot acquire or perfect title by adverse possession—on the land of Scheduled Tribe but Scheduled tribe can perfect title by adverse possession on the property of another Scheduled Tribe—State is custodian and trustee of the immovable property of tribals: 2004 (II) OLR 117: 2004 CLR (SC) 155.

Which came into force from 2nd October, 1973, Sec. 7-D. By the amended regulation 7-D, the period of limitation has been thirty years and not twelve years regarding adverse possession—The amendment has retrospective effect—But if title has already accrued after a period of twelve years by adverse possession prior to 2nd October, 1973—The period of thirty years would not apply—Adverse possession has to be proved it: 1994 (II) OLR 322.

Section 7-D (as amended in 1975)—Amendment is retrospective from 2nd October, 1973—Transfer by a member of the Scheduled Tribe to a member who is not a Scheduled Tribe is dated 26th June, 1954—Title of land stood extinguished by adverse possession of twelve years long prior to 2nd October, 1973. Transfer held, not affected—Proceeding for restoration of the disputed property is not maintainable: 1989 (II) 221.

7-E. Bar of Jurisdiction of Civil Courts.—No Civil Court shall have jurisdiction to try and decide any suit or proceeding so far as it relates to try and decide any suit or proceeding so far as it relates to any manner which any officer or other competent authority is empowered by or under this regulation to decide.

8. Rules.—(1) The State Government may from time to time make rules consistent, with the provisions of this regulations to carry out the purpose thereof.

(2) All rules made under the section shall be published in the Gazette and on such application shall have the effect as if enacted under this regulation.

9. Repeal.—(1) On and from the date of commencement of this regulation shall stand repealed, namely:

(a) The Agency Tracts interest and Land Transfer Act 1917 (Madras Act of 1917).

(b) The enactments mentioned in column 2 of the (Schedule to the extent specified in column 3 thereof insofar as they are in force (in the Scheduled Areas)

(2) Notwithstanding such repeal by this regulation the repeal shall not effect :

(a) The previous operation of such law or provisions so repealed or validity affect or consequence of anything done or suffered thereunder;

(b) any right title, privilege, obligation or liability acquired, occurred or incurred under the said law or provision;

or

(c) any investigation, legal proceeding or remedy in respect of such right, title, privilege, obligation or liability;

or

(d) any release or discharge from any debt, penalty, obligation, liability, claim or demand and any such investigation, legal proceedings or remedy may be instituted, continued or enforced and any such penalty, forfeiture of punishment may be imposed as if this Regulation had not been made.

SCHEDULE
(List of Enactment Repealed)
[*See Section 9*]

Sl. No.	*Number and Year*	*Short Title*	*Extent of Repeal*
1	Madras Act 1 of 1917	Agency Tracts interest and Land Transfer Act 1917	The Whole
2	Orissa Act IV of 1950	Orissa Merged State's Laws Act 1950	The words "Subjects to the restriction that no transfer of a holding from member of an aboriginal tribe to a member of a non-aboriginal tribe to a member of a non-aboriginal shall be valid unless such transfer is made with the previous permission of the Sub-divisional Magistrate concerned" in item 1 of Clause (d) of Section shall be omitted
3	Central Provinces Act XI of 1898.	Central Provinces Tenancy (b) Act 1989 Amendment by Orissa Act XIII of 1953	The provision to Clause Act (b) of Sub-Sec. (2) of Sec.46. shall be omitted.

THE ORISSA SCHEDULED AREAS TRANSFER OF IMMOVABLE PROPERTY (BY SCHEDULED TRIBES) RULES 1959
(As Amended by OSATIP Rules 2003)

The 17th August 1959

No. 34533: AG-60/59-R.—In exercise of the powers conferred by Section 8 of the Orissa Scheduled Areas Transfer of Immovable Property (By Scheduled Tribes) Regulations, 1956 (Orissa Regulation No. 2 of 1956) the State Government do hereby make the following Rules, namely:

1. Short Title and Commencement.—(1) These Rules may be called the Orissa Scheduled Areas Transfer of Immovable Property (By Scheduled Tribes) Rules 1959.

(2) Definitions.—In these rules unless there is anything repugnant in the subject or context:

(a) "Regulation" means the Orissa Scheduled Areas Transfer of Immovable Property (By Scheduled Tribes) Regulations. 1956.

(b) all words and expressions used in these rules and not defined herein shall have the same meaning as are respectively assigned to them in the Regulation.

3. Procedure for Transfer to Non-Scheduled Tribes.—(1) A member of a Scheduled Tribe who intends to transfer any of his immovable property situated within a Scheduled Area to a member of any non-Scheduled Tribe shall submit an application for the purpose and obtain the prior consent in writing of the competent authority under Section 3 (1) of the Regulation.

(2) On receipt of such application, the competent authority may cause necessary enquiries of summary nature to be made by an officer duly authorised by him for the purpose before passing orders the enquiring officer shall submit his report in formal appended to these rules.

4. Attachment of the Immovable Property.—(1) There shall be no attachment or sale of immovable property in execution of money decrees against a member of Scheduled Tribes within any Scheduled Areas without the written permission of the Competent authority.

The property at such sale shall be sold only to members of Scheduled Tribe unless otherwise specifically directed in writing by the competent authority.

5. General Control of Collector.—All orders except those against which an appeal lies, passed under these rules by any other competent authority shall be subject to general control of the respective Collector having jurisdiction.

6. Form and manner of filling information under Section 3-B(1).—(1) The information under Section 3-B(1) Regulation shall be filled in Form No. 2 accompanied by supporting documents mentioned therein.

(2) The Form No. 2 having been duly filled in shall be presented to the Sub-Collector personally by the person in possession of the agricultural land of Scheduled Tribe or by his authorised representative which shall be accompanied by a sworn affidavit to the effect that all the informations furnished in Form No. 2 are true to the best of the knowledge of the person submitting the information.

7. Manner of conducting Enquiry by the Sub-Collector.—(1) On receipt of information under Section 3-B(1) of the Regulation in the manner prescribed in Rule 6, the Sub-Collector shall cause the material particulars to be entered in a register, number the form, start a case record and fix a date of hearing not later than 30 days from the date of registration.

(2) The Sub-Collector then shall issue a notice to the person who submitted the information to appear on the date fixed for hearing with all his documents and material if any, in support of his claim.

(3) The Sub-Collector may also issue notice to any other person, whom he considers qualified to depose before him to arrive at a correct finding.

(4) The Sub-Collector may also serve a public notice on the village in which the land is situated, inviting their comments and views, if any, on the information within a period of 15 days from the date of service of notice. The notice shall be served in the manner prescribed in the Code of Civil Procedure.

(5) The Sub-Collector may, if considered necessary, call for any proper appreciation of evidence before him.

(6) The enquiry shall be summary in nature.

(7) The Sub-Collector may make such other enquiry as may be necessary about the transaction of transfer.

FORM I

Report of Officer Conducting an Enquiry on Application for Permission to Transfer Land by Scheduled Tribes to Non-Scheduled Tribes under Section (1) of Orissa Regulation No. 2 of 1956

[*See Rule 3*]

1. Name of the applicant ....
2. Tribe of the applicant..................................
3. Village, description of land, wet or dry areas, the rent payable of the land to be transferred (boundaries also to be furnished, the total area of land held by the applicant; the date of application; the number of his family members dependent on him; and his income from lands and other sources, if any)
4. Name and caste of persons to whom the land is to be alienated.
5. Kind of transfer proposed by the applicant (mortgage, sale, etc.) and his objection in asking for the transfer (the inquiring officer should satisfy himself that the object of transfer stated by the applicant is the true object. He should also mention whether the form of transfer which the applicant wants to make is in his best interest. If not, the officer should recommend some other form of transfer reasons).
6. If the Permission now applied for is only to satisfy any alienation already made, has the officer explained to the applicant that he can obtain possession of the land for mere asking of it ?
7. What is the present market value of the land proposed to be alienated (state reasons) for the valuation and what is the price at which the applicant propose to make the transfer ?
8. Has the officer advised the applicant to apply for a loan from Government ? If the object of alienation is for purpose enumerated under the L.I. Loans Act or A.L. Act ?
9. The officer should report whether the applicant agree to take a loan from Government and if so, whether transfer would still be necessary ? If he disagrees to take such loan reasons should be mentioned.
10. If the applicant induced by anybody to sell the land ?
11. Whether there is no other Scheduled Tribe man prepared to

have the land alienated in his favour for the market value of the land ?

12. Whether the officer has made fully and careful enquiries into the transaction and is personally, satisfied that it is genuine ? (Give reasons for holding that the transaction is genuine).
13. If the officer satisfied that the permission if granted would be in the best interest of the applicant ? (Reasons should be given for the opinion of the officer).
14. On how many former occasions has the applicant applied for any permission under Section 3 (1) of the Regulation granted?

Station..............

Date .... *Signature*..........

Designation of the inquiring officer

Order of the Competent Authority

Signature ....

Designation of the Competent Authority.

FORM II

1. Name of the person presenting the information.
2. His father's Name and Address
3. Name and address of the Scheduled Tribe, whose agricultural land, is presently in occupation.
4. Name of the village in which the land is situated, Khata, Plot number and area of the land, to be mentioned:
5. Source of occupation of the Scheduled Tribe land:
   (a) By purchase:
   (b) Through mortgage:
   (c) Through gift:
   (d) Through inheritance:
   (e) By order of a Competent Court:
   (f) Through trespass:
   (g) Through Exchange:
   (h) Any other—specify (Tick the item applicable in your case)
6. If in occupation of land through sale, gift or mortgage enclose a copy of the registration deed, if it was registered in any

Registration Office:

7. Was permission of the competent authority obtained before registration of the document ? If so, enclose a copy:
8. If the possession was obtained through Court's Order enclose a copy of the Court's Order:
9. If you are occupying the land through trespass, indicate whether with the knowledge of the Scheduled Tribe owner or any one of his legal heirs or without any one's knowledge:
10. Indicate the amount of consideration money:
    (a) Paid by towards the cost of the land at the time of purchase:
    (b) Did you pay the entire consideration money at the time of registration of the document or paid in full or a part of it before registration.
11. If you are in occupation through mortgage deed executed by the Scheduled Tribe, indicate the terms of mortgage and the amount, if any, paid by you to the Scheduled Tribe. If the mortgage is not registered, indicate the number of years you are in occupation and terms of mortgage.
12. If you are in possession through exchange of your land with the Scheduled Tribes, indicate the Khata No., Plot No., and area of your land, exchanged, with the name of the village in which the land is situated.

Chapter III (*Continued*)

AMENDMENT OF REGULATION II OF 1956
REGULATION 1975

With a view to safeguarding the interests of Tribals in Scheduled Areas more effectively and in proving their socio-economic conditions Regulation 11 of 1956 has been amended with effect from December 19, 1975. The amended Regulation has the following important provisions bearing on land alienation and land restoration in tribal areas.

1. The period of limitation for establishing title on the land transferred by a person belonging to a Scheduled Tribe has been increased from 12 to 30 years.
2. The restriction on the transfer of land by way of mortgage by a member of Scheduled Tribe in favour of different financing institutions has been relaxed in order to enable tribal to obtain a loan for agricultural purposes.
3. The right of alienation of land by tribals in favour of Co-operative societies, Co-operative banks and other financial institutions has been restricted only to enable tribal to obtain loans for agricultural purposes.
4. Power has been conferred on the courts to ignore admission by members of Scheduled Tribe to counteract collusive title suits.
5. Actual possession of the land to the transferor or his heirs in whose favour restoration of possession has been ordered by the competent authority has been ensured.
6. Eviction of unauthorised occupation of any immovable property of a member of a Scheduled Tribe by way of trespass or otherwise and restoration of such property to the said member of the Scheduled Tribe or his heirs has been ensured, and it has been provided that rigorous imprisonment for a term which may extend to two years or with fine which may

extend to Rs. 2,000 or both, may be imposed on those found guilty of such unauthorised occupation.

7. Summary eviction of a non-tribal transferee from the immovable property of a Scheduled Tribe person has been provided in addition to the higher penalty of Rs. 200 and payment of such person of the penalty as the competent authority may order to the transferer or his heir.
8. It has been further provided that the consideration money paid by the transferee to the transferer for such invalid transfer shall not be refunded. Steps are being taken to safeguard the interest of Scheduled Tribes in the Non-Scheduled areas of the State by making the necessary provision in the Orissa Land Reform Act of 1960 in the light of amendments to the Orissa Regulation II of 1956.

AMENDMENT OF 1989, BY T.A.C. TO THE ORISSA SCHEDULED AREAS TRANSFER OF IMMOVABLE PROPERTY (BY SCHEDULED TRIBES) REGULATION 1956

The following amendments to the Regulation II of 1956 are being implemented by the final recommendations of the T.A.C. held on 21st January, 1989

1. The Sivaraman Committee have recommended that the transfer of land between the Scheduled Tribe Community should be regulated and reduction of size of the holding below viability level should be prevented. The existing laws allow transfer of land by a tribal to any member of the Tribal community without any stipulations. But as a safeguard against indiscriminate and avoidable transfers, it is necessary to regulate such transfers whether within a tribal community itself or outside thereof.

It is, therefore, necessary to amend Section 3 of the Regulation to regulate and restrict transfers by Scheduled Tribe persons so that the person belonging to such tribe who transfers his land does not become landless as a result of such transfer. The viability level fixed is one standard acre. Thus, no tribal can transfer his land if by such transfer the transferer will have less than one standard acre of land.

2. As the minimum holding of a transfer will not be less than one standard acre, it is proposed to define the term 'standard acre' which will have the same meaning as in Orissa Land Reform Act 1961.

'Classes of land' will have the same meaning as defined in Orissa Land Reform Act 1980.

3. (i) At present there is no provision of appeal or review against the orders passed under Sub-section (vi) of Section 3 of the Regulation according to permission for alienation of Tribal land. If an order according such permission is passed on extraneous consideration or in an irregular manner, the mischief in curable. It is, therefore, necessary that the Collector should be vested with *suo motu* revisional powers so that he can devise any such order passed by any competent authority other than Item-I.

(ii) The Revenue Divisional Commissioner may be empowered similarly in respect of order passed by the Collector.

(iii) This power of revision may be exercised within a period of five years from the date of original order.

(iv) This amendment will, however, have prospective effect so that any order passed by a competent authority prior to the date of commencement of this amendment is not affected.]

4. Under Sub-section (3) of Section 3 of the Regulation, an appeal against an order of the Collector under Sub-section (2) of the Section lies to the Board of Revenue. But by virtue of Rule 7 of the Orissa Revenue Divisional Commissioners Rules 1959, the Revenue Divisional Commissioners exercise the appellate powers of the Board of Revenue. However it would be advantageous if Sub-section (3) of the said section if formally amended providing that the appeal against an order of the Collector under Sub-section (2) of the said section it formally amended providing that the appeal against an order of the Collector under Sub-section (2) of the said section shall to the Revenue Divisional Commissioner.

5. Section 7 provides for levy for penalty not exceeding Rs. 200 per acre per annum on a person who occupies the land of a Scheduled Tribe person in contravention of the provisions of the Regulation. In order to make the penal provision more stringent, it is proposed to amend the said section providing for the enhancement of the existing amount of penalty from 'an amount not exceeding Rs. 200 "to" an

amount not exceeding Rs. 2000 per acre for each year of unlawful possession.

6. In order to ensure that offences are tried expeditiously, it is proposed to confer on Executive Magistrate the power of Judicial Magistrate. Accordingly, it is proposed to amend Section 7A of the Regulation by a renumbering the said section of Sub-section (1) thereof and inserting a new Sub-Section thereunder in the following lines namely:

> "(2) For trial of offences under this Regulation the State Government may confer on an Executive Magistrate the powers of a Judicial Magistrate of the First Class or the Second Class, and on such conferment of power, the Executive Magistrate on whom the powers are so conferred, shall be deemed, for the purposes of the Code of Criminal Procedure 1973 to be a Judicial Magistrate of the first class or of the second class, as the case may be."

7. Clause (a) of Section 7-C of the Regulation provides that in case where validity of the transfer of relinquishment of any immovable property is called in question or where any proceedings are for the recovery of possession of immovable property, the burden of proof that the transfer or relinquishment was valid shall lie on the transferee. It is proposed to amend the section providing that the burden of proof lies on the person whosoever claim such right in the property. This will make the provision more broad based.

8. In order to prevent civil litigations, it is proposed to bar the jurisdiction of the civil court by inserting a new section in the following lines after section 7-D of the Regulation namely:

Bar of Jurisdiction of Civil Courts

"7-E. No Civil Court shall have jurisdiction to try and decide any suit or proceeding so far as it relates to any matter in which any officer or other competent authority is empowered by or under this Regulation to decide."

THE ORISSA GAZETTE
Extraordinary
Published by Authority

No. 391, Cuttack, Thursday, March 27, 1997/
Chaitra 6, 1919

LAW DEPARTMENT
NOTIFICATION
The 27th March, 1997

No. 7894-Legis.—The following Regulation made by the Governor of Orissa under sub-paragraph (2) of paragraph 5 of the fifth Schedule to the Constitution of India and assented to by the President on the 14th March, 1997 is hereby published for general information.

ORISSA REGULATION 1 OF 1997

THE ORISSA SCHEDULED AREAS TRANSFER OF IMMOVABLE PROPERTY (BY SCHEDULED TRIBES) AMENDMENT REGULATION, 1996

A

REGULATION

TO AMEND THE ORISSA SCHEDULED AREAS TRANSFER OF IMMOVABLE PROPERTY (BY SCHEDULED TRIBES) REGULATION 1996

WHEREAS it is expedient to amend the Orissa Scheduled Areas Transfer of Immovable Property (by Scheduled Tribes) Regulation 1956;

Now, therefore in exercise of the powers conferred by clause (a) of sub-paragraph (2) of paragraph 5 of the Fifth Schedule to the Constitution of India, the Governor of Orissa is pleased to make the following Regulation in the Forty-Seventh Year of the Republic of India:

1. This Regulation may be called the Orissa Scheduled Areas Transfer of Immovable Property (by Scheduled Tribes) Amendment Regulation 1996.

2. In the Orissa Scheduled Areas Transfer of Immovable Property (by Scheduled Tribes) Regulation 1956 (hereinafter referred to as the principal Regulation, in section 2—

(i) after clause (a) the following clause shall be inserted, namely: (b) "clauses of land" means—
Class I—Irrigated land in which two or more crops (i) were, in any years within a period of three years before the commencement of the Orissa Scheduled Areas Transfer of Immovable Property (by Scheduled Tribes) Amendment Regulation 1996, grown or (ii) can be grown in a year;
Class II—Irrigated land in which not more than one crop (i) was, in any year within a period of three years before the commencement of the Orissa Scheduled Areas Transfer of Immovable Property (by Scheduled Tribes) Amendment Regulation 1996, grown or (ii) can be grown in a year;
Class III—Land other than irrigated land, in which pady (i) was, in any year within a period of three years before the commencement of this Orissa Scheduled Areas Transfer of Immovable Property (by Scheduled Tribes) Amendment Regulation 1996, grown or (ii) can be grown in a year; and
Class IV—Any other land.

Explanation.—For the purpose of this clause—

(i) tanks, coconut gardens and orchards (except orchards growing banana) shall be deemed to be Class III land;
(ii) the existing clause (a-1) shall be renumbered as clause (ab); and
(iii) after clause (e), the following clause shall be inserted, namely—
(e-1) "standard acre" means the unit of measurement of land equivalent to one acre of Class I land, one and one-half acres of Class II land, three acres of Class III land or four and one-half acres of Class IV land.

Explanation.—For the purposes of conversion, one acre shall be equal to 0.4047 hectare'.

3. In Section 3 of the principal Regulation,—

(i) in sub-section (1), after the second provision, the following provision shall be inserted, namely—

"Provided also that a member of a Scheduled Tribe shall not transfer any land if the total extent of his land remaining after the transfer will be reduced to less than one standard acre";

(ii) in Sub-section (3) for the words "Boards of Revenue", the words "Revenue Divisional Commissioner" shall be substituted;

(iii) after Sub-section (3), the following sub-section shall be inserted, namely—

"(3-a) (i) Any order passed by the competent authority under Sub-section (1) or under sub-section (2) may, within a period of five years from the date of such order, be revised, either on own motion or otherwise, by the Revenue Divisional Commissioner if the order was passed by the Collector and if giving the parties concerned a reasonable opportunity of being heard:

Provided that no order shall be revised under this sub-section if an appeal against such order has been entertained under Sub-section (3).

(ii) For the purpose of revising any order, the Revenue Divisional Commissioner or, as the case may, the Collector shall follow such procedure as may be prescribed and shall have power to call for and examine the records of the proceedings wherein such order was passed and pass such order as he deems fit"; and

(iv) in sub-section (4) for the words brackets and figure "the provisions of sub-section (3)". the words, brackets and figures "any order passed under sub-section (3) or sub-section (3-a)" shall be substituted.

4. In section 7 of the principal Regulation, in sub-section (1), for the words "Rupees two hundred", the words "Rupees two thousand" shall be substituted.

5. In Section 7C of the principal Regulation, in clause (a), after the words "transferee"; the words" or any person claiming the right to the property through the transferee" shall be inserted.

6. After Section 7D of the principal Regulation, the following section shall be inserted, namely:

"7E. No Civil Court shall have jurisdiction to try and decide any suit or proceeding so far it relates to any manner which any officer or other competent authority is empowered by or under this Regulation to decide".

By Order of the Governor

P.K. Tripathy
Secretary to Government

THE ORISSA GAZETTE
Extraordinary
Published by Authority

No. 1429. Cuttack, Wednesday, September 4, 2002/ Bhadra 13, 1924

LAW DEPARTMENT
NOTIFICATION
The 4th September, 2002

NO.11714-Legis.—The following Regulation made by the Governor of Orissa under sub-paragraph (2) of Paragraph 5 of the Fifth Schedule to the Constitution of India and assented to by the President on the 20th August, 2002 is hereby published for general information.

ORISSA REGULATION 1 OF 2002

THE ORISSA SCHEDULED AREAS TRANSFER OF IMMOVABLE PROPERTY (BY SCHEDULED TRIBES) AMENDMENT REGULATION, 2000)

A
REGULATION

FURTHER TO AMEND THE ORISSA SCHEDULED AREAS TRANSFER OF IMMOVABLE PROPERTY (BY SCHEDULED TRIBES) REGULATION 1956

WHEREAS it is expedient to amend the Orissa Scheduled Areas Transfer of Immovable Property (By Scheduled Tribes) Regulation 1956;

NOW, THEREFORE, in exercise of the rowers conferred by sub-paragraph (2) of paragraph 5 of the Fifth Schedule to the Constitution of India, the Governor of Orissa is pleased to promulgate the following Regulation made by him in the Fifty-first year of the Republic of India:

1. This regulation may be called the Orissa Scheduled Areas transfer of Immovable Property (By Scheduled Tribes) Amendment Regulation 2000.
2. In Section 2 of the Orissa Scheduled Areas Transfer of Immovable Property (By Scheduled Tribes) Regulation 1956 (hereinafter referred to as the principal Regulation);
   (i) Clause (a) shall be omitted;
   (ii) for clause (b), the following clause shall be substituted, namely:
   (b) "Grama Panchayat" and "Gram Sasan" shall respectively mean the Gram Panchayat and Gram Sasan as defined in the Orissa Grama Panchayats Act 1964; and
   (iii) clause (e-1) shall be omitted.

3. In Section 3 of the principal Regulation,— (a) for Sub-section (1), the following Sub-section shall be substituted namely:

"(1) Notwithstanding anything contained in any law for the time being in force any transfer of immovable property by a member of a Scheduled Tribe, except by way of mortgage executed in favour of any public financial institution for securing a loan granted by such institution for any agricultural purpose, shall be absolutely null and void and of no force or effect whatsoever, unless such transfer is made in favour of another member of a Scheduled Tribe:

Provided that—

(i) nothing in this sub-section shall be construed as to permit any member of a Scheduled Tribe or his successor-in-interest to transfer any immovable property which was settled with such member of Scheduled Tribe by or under any authority of the State of the Central Government or under any law for the time being in force;

(ii) in execution of any decree for realisation of the mortgage money, no property mortgaged as aforesaid shall be sold in favour of any person not being a member of a Scheduled Tribe; and

(iii) a member of a Scheduled Tribe shall not transfer any land if the total extent of his land remaining after the transfer will be reduced to less than two acres in case of irrigated land or five acres in case of unirrigated land.

Explanation I—For the purposes of this sub-section, a transfer of immovable property:

(a) in favour of a female member of a Scheduled Tribe, who is married to a person not belonging to any Scheduled Tribe, shall be deemed to be a transfer made in favour of a person not belonging to a Scheduled Tribe; and

(b) shall include a transfer of immovable property to a person belonging to a Scheduled Tribe for consideration paid or provided by another person not belonging to any such Tribe.

Explanation II.—For the purposes of Clause (iii) of the proviso, the expression "irrigated land" shall mean such land which is irrigated at least for one crop in a year, and the expression "unirrigated land" shall be construed accordingly" and

(b) in Sub-section (2)—

(i) after the words "any one interested therein", the words "or on information received from the Grama Panchayat" shall be inserted; and

(ii) after the provision, the following provision shall be inserted, namely:

" Provided further that where it is decided by the competent authority to settle the said property with any person other than a person belonging to a Scheduled Tribe in accordance with the Orissa Government Land Settlement Act 1962, he shall obtain prior approval of the concerned Grama Panchayat, accorded with the concurrence of the Grama Sasan."

4. In Section 3-A of the principal Regulation—

(a) in Sub-section (1) after the words "any person interested therein" the words "or on information received from the Gram Panchayat" shall be inserted; and

(b) after Sub-section (2) the following Sub-section shall be inserted, namely:

"(3) In every case after finalisation of the proceedings under Sub-section (1), the competent authority shall make a report to the concerned Grama Panchayat about the order of ejection passed in respect of any person in unauthorised occupation of any immovable property to such member of his heirs and in case of failure of such restoration, the reasons for such failure."

5. After Section 3-A of the principal Regulation, the following Section shall be inserted, namely:

3-B. (1) Every person who, on the date of commencement of the Orissa Scheduled Areas Transfer of Immovable Property (By Scheduled Tribes) Amendment Regulation, 2000 (hereinafter referred to in this section as the Amendment Regulation of 2000), is in possession of agricultural land which belonged to a member of a Scheduled Tribe at any time during the period commencing on the 4th October, 1956 and ending on the date of commencement of the Amendment Regulation of 2000 shall, within two years of such commencement, notify to the Sub-Collector in such form and in such manner as may be prescribed, all the informations as to how he has come in possession of such land.

(2) If any person fails to notify the information as required by sub-section (1) within the period specified therein it shall be presumed that such person has been in possession of the agricultural land without any lawful authority and the agricultural land shall on the expiration of the period aforesaid, revert to the person to whom it originally belonged and if that person be dead, to his heirs.

(3) On receipt of the information under Sub-section (1) the Sub-Collector shall make such enquiry as may be necessary about all such transactions of transfer and if he finds that the member of Scheduled Tribe has been defrauded of his legitimate right he shall declare the transaction null and void and,—

(a) where no building or structure has been erected on the agricultural land prior to such finding, pass an order revesting the agricultural land in the transferor and if he be dead, in his heirs;

(b) Where any building or structure has been erected on the agricultural land prior to such finding, he shall fix the price of such land in accordance with the principles laid down for fixation of price of land in the Land Acquisition Act 1894; and order the person referred to in Sub-section (1) to pay to the transferor the difference, if any, between the price so fixed and the price actually paid to the transferor.

Provided that where the building or structure has been erected after the commencement of the Amendment Regulation of 2000, the provisions of clause (b) shall not apply;

6. For Section 7 and 7-A of the principal Regulation, the following sections shall be substituted, namely:

7. "(1) If any person is found to be in possession of any immovable property in contravention of the provisions of this Regulation, then, without prejudice to his liability to ejectment under this Regulation, or where any person, having been evicted under any provision of the Regulation from any immovable property belonging to a member of a Scheduled Tribe, continues to be in possession of the same, he shall be punishable with rigorous imprisonment for a term which may extend to two years, or with fine which may extend to rupees five thousand, or with both.

(2) Where any person, having been evicted under any provision of this Regulation from any immovable property belonging to a member of a Scheduled Tribe, reoccupies the same shall be punishable with rigorous imprisonment for a term which may extend to three years, or with fine which may extend to rupees ten thousand or with both.

(3) When a Court imposes sentence of fine or a sentence of which fine forms a part, the Court may, when passing judgement, order the whole or any part of the fine to be paid to the member of Scheduled Tribe to whom the immovable property belongs, or to his heirs.

7-A (1) The State Government may confer, on an Executive Magistrate, the powers of a Judicial Magistrate of the first class or and on such conferment of powers, the Executive Magistrate, on whom the powers are so conferred, shall be deemed, for the purposes of the Code of Criminal Procedure 1973, to be a Judicial Magistrate of the first class or of the second class, as the case may be.

(2) An offence under this Regulation may be tried summarily by a Magistrate.

(3) Every offence under this Regulation shall be cognizable."

By Order of the Governor
H. MOHAPATRA
Secretary to Government

(B) GOVERNMENT OF ORISSA
REVENUE DEPARTMENT

NOTIFICATION
No. 40955-R
Dated Bhubaneswar, the Ist September, 1962

In exercise of the powers conferred by Section 2 (a) of the Orissa Scheduled Areas Transfer of Immovable Property (by Scheduled Tribes) Regulation of the Government of Orissa in the Revenue Department No. 23071-Agency-14/57-R, dated the 13th December, 1959 and No. 39199-Agency 110/58-R dated the 8th November, 1958, the State Government do hereby appoint all Sub-divisional officers as the case may be, of the areas to which the said Regulation applicable to perform the functions of a competent authority under Section 3 of the said Regulation within their respective jurisdiction.

By Order of the Governor.

B.K. MISHRA
Secretary to Government

GOVERNMENT OF ORISSA
REVENUE AND EXCISE DEPARTMENT

NOTIFICATION
NO. AG 13/87—17800/R
Bhubaneswar, the 24th March, 1987

In exercise of the powers conferred by Clause (A-1) of Section 2 of the Orissa Scheduled Areas Transfer of Immovable Property (By Scheduled Tribes) Regulation 1956 (Orissa Regulation 2 of 1956 and in partial modification of the Notification of the State Government in

Revenue and Excise Department No. 32729 dated 19th May, 1986, the State Government do hereby appoint the Officers specified in the Schedule below to perform the function of a competent authority under section of the said Regulation within the Scheduled Areas of Koraput District as specified against each in column (4) and (5) respectively of the said schedule.

SCHEDULE

Sl. No.	*Name of the district*	*Designation of the officers on whom powers conferred*	*Section(s) of Reg. 2, 1956 for which power conferred*	*Jurisdiction of Scheduled area*
1	2	3	4	5
1	Koraput	Project Administrator I.T.D.A Koraput/Jeypore/ Malkangiri/ Nowrangpur	Section-3(1)	The Scheduled Areas under their respective jurisdiction
		Officer on Special Duty, Land Reform, Koraput.	All Sections except 3(1)	Koraput Sub-Division/Jeypore Sub-Division/ Malkangiri Sub-Division/ Nowrangpur Sub-Division.

By Order of the Governor
S. MISHRA
Secretary to Government

THE ORISSA GAZETTEER

Published by Authority

No. 5. Cuttack, Friday, January 29, 1988/Magha 1909

PART III

Statutory Rules, Orders, Notification, Rules etc., issued by the Government.

The 21st December, 1987

S.R.O. No. 938/87.—In exercise of the powers conferred by clause (a-1) of Section 2 of the Orissa Scheduled Areas Transfer of Immovable property (By Scheduled Tribes) Regulation 1956 (Orissa Regulation 2 of 1956) the State Government do hereby appoint the Officers specified in the Schedule below to perform the functions of a competent authority under Sections of the said regulation within the schedule areas located in different district as specified against each in column (4) and (5) respectively of the said schedule.

SCHEDULE

Sl. No.	*Name of District*	*Designation of the officers on whom power conferred*	*Section(s) of the Regulation 2 of 1956 for areas which powers conferred*	*Jurisdiction of Schedule*
1	2	3	4	5
1.	Koraput	Project Administrator ITDA (Koraput)	Section 3(1)	Koraput Sub-Division
		(P.A.) I.T.D.A	-do- Jeypore	Jeypore Sub-Division
		(P.A.) I.T.D.A Malkangiri	-do-	Malkangiri Sub-Division
		(P.A.) I.T.D.A Nawrangpur	-do-	Nawrangpur Sub-Division

(*Contd.*)

1	2	3	4	5
		(P.A.) I.T.D.A Rayagada	-do-	Rayagada Sub-Division
		(P.A.) I.T.D.A Gunupur	-do-	Gunupur Sub-Division
		Officer on Special Duty, Land Reforms, Koraput	All Sections except 3(1)	
		Officer on Special Duty, Land Reforms, Rayagada	-do-	
		Sub-Divisional	Section 3(2) Officer, Koraput	Koraput Sub-Division
		Sub-Divisional	-do- Officer, Jeypore	Koraput Sub-Division
		S.D.O. Malkangiri	-do-	Malkangiri Sub-Division
		S.D.O. Nawrangpur	-do-	Nawrangpur Sub-Division
		S.D.O. Rayagada	-do-	Rayagada Sub-Division
		S.D.O. Gunupur	-do-	Gunupur Sub-Division

This supersedes all notifications issued previously in this regard.

No.77064(L.R.C)-Ag-13/87-R

By Order of the Governor
B.C. PATNAIK
Secretary to Government

GOVERNMENT OF ORISSA
REVENUE AND EXCISE DEPARTMENT

NOTIFICATION
Dated the 21st September, 1992

No. 47153-R Ag. 84/92.—In exercise of the powers conferred by Sub-section 3 of Section (1) of the Orissa S.A.T.I.P (by ST) Regulation 1956 (Orissa Regulation 2 of 1956), the State Government, do hereby specially empower the Sub-Collector having jurisdiction over their respective Scheduled Areas to hear appeals under Sub-section (2) of the said section preferred against the orders passed by the competent authorities appointed under clause (A-1) of Section of the said Regulation.

By Order of the Governor
S.R. PAL
Principal Secretary to the Government

GOVERNMENT OF ORISSA
REVENUE AND EXCISE DEPARTMENT

NOTIFICATION
Bhubaneswar, the 21st September, 1992

No. Ag-84/92-51180/R.—In exercise of the powers conferred by clause (A-1) of Section 2 of the Orissa SATIP (By ST) Regulation 1956 (Orissa Reg. 2 of 1956) and in supersession of the Government of Orissa in the Revenue and Excise Department No. 72982-Ag 82/89, dated the 22nd December 1989, the State Government do hereby appoint the officers specified in column (3) of the Schedule areas hereto annexed to perform all the functions of a competent authority under the said Regulations with the Scheduled Areas located in different districts as specified against each in column (4) of the said schedule.

SCHEDULE

Sl. No.	*Name of the District*	*Designation of the officers on whom powers conferred*	*Jurisdiction of the Scheduled Areas*
1.	Koraput	Officers on Special Duty	Koraput Sub-Division (Land Reform) Koraput
2.	-do-	Officer on Special Duty (Land Reform) Rayagada	Rayagada Sub-Division
3.	-do-	Tahsildar Bisam Cuttack	Bisam Cuttack Tahsil
4.	-do-	Tahsildar, Gunpur Tahsil	Gunpur Tahsil
5.	-do-	Tahsildar, Jeypore	Jeypore Tahsil
6.	Koraput	Tahsildar, Boriguma	Boriguma Tahsil
7.	-do-	Tahsildar, Kotapad	Kotapad Tahsil
8.	-do-	Tahsildar, Malkaingiri	Malkinguri Tahsil
9.	-do-	Tahsildar, Motu	Motu Tahsil
10.	-do-	Tahsildar, Chitrakonda	Chitrakonda Tahsil
11.	-do-	Tahsildar, Nawrangpur	Nawrangpur Tahsil
12.	-do-	Tahsildar, Umarkote	Umarkote Tahsil
13.	-do-	Tahsildar, Kodigan	Kodigan Tahsil
14.	-do-	Tahsildar, Dabugan	Dabugan Tahsil

By Order of the Governor
S.R. PAL
Principal Secretary to Government

GOVERNMENT OF ORISSA
REVENUE AND EXCISE DEPARTMENT

NOTIFICATION
Bhubaneswar, the 19th April, 1993

No. ITTE-PT-S/93(PT)/R.—In exercise of the powers conferred by clause (A-1) of Section 2 of the Orissa Scheduled Areas Transfer of Immovable property (By Scheduled Tribes) Regulation 1956 (Orissa Regulation 2 of 1956) the State Government do hereby appoint the

Sub-Collector, Koraput to perform all the function of a competent authority under the said Regulation within the jurisdiction of Koraput Sub-Division in addition to his own duties as Sub-Collector, Koraput Regular O.S.D. (LR) Koraput.

By Order of the Governor
Sd/-
Under Secretary to Government

GOVERNMENT OF ORISSA
REVENUE AND EXCISE DEPARTMENT

Dated the 2nd September, 1993

No. 39883/R-Ag-49/93.—In exercise of the powers conferred by Sub-section (3) of Section 3 of the Orissa Scheduled Areas Transfer of Immovable Property (By Scheduled Tribes) Regulation 1956 and in supersession of all previous Notification issued on the subject, the State Government do hereby specially empowered the officers special duty in column (2) of the Scheduled hereto appended having jurisdiction over their respective Scheduled Areas to hear appeals under Sub-section (2) of the said section against the order passed by the competent authorities mentioned against each in column (3) thereof appointed under clause (A-1) of Section 2 of the said Regulation.

SCHEDULE

Sl. No.	*Appellate Authority*	*Competent Authority appointed under clause (A-1) of Section 2 of the Regulation of 1956*
1.	A.D.M.	Officer on Special Duty (L.R)
2.	Sub-Collector	Tahsildar/Revenue Officer

By Order of the Governor
S.R. PAL
Principal Secretary to Government

(B) Notifications issued under Regulation 2 of 1956

GOVERNMENT OF ORISSA
Revenue and Excise Department
NOTIFICATION
No. 39883/R, dated September 2, 1993

In exercise of the powers conferred by Sub-section (3) of Section 3 of the Orissa Scheduled Areas Transfer of Immovable Property (By Scheduled Tribes) Regulation, 1956 (Orissa Regulation 2 of 1956) and in supersession of all previous notifications issued on the subject, the State Government do hereby specially empowers the officers specified in column (2) of the Schedule hereto appended having jurisdiction over their respective Scheduled Areas to hear appeals under Sub-section (2) of the said section preferred against the orders passed by the competent authorities mentioned against each in column (3) thereof appointed under Clause (a-1) of Section 2 of the said Regulation.

SCHEDULE

Serial No.	*Appellate Authority*	*Competent authority appointed under Clause (a-1) of Section 2 of the Regulation*
1	2	3
1.	Additional District Magistrate	Officer-on-Special Duty (Land Reforms)
2.	Sub-Collector	Tahsildar

By Order of the Governor
S.R. PAL
Principal Secretary to Government

GOVERNMENT OF ORISSA

REVENUE DEPARTMENT

NOTIFICATION

Bhubaneswar, the 21st October, 2003

No. Ag-118/2003/49483/R.—In exercise of the powers conferred by Sub-Section (i) of Section 7-A of the Orissa Scheduled Areas Transfer of Immovable Property (By Scheduled Tribes) Regulation, 1956 (Orissa Regulation-2 of 1956), the State Government do hereby confer on the Executive Magistrate mentioned in column (3) of the Scheduled below belonging to the district mentioned against each in column (2) thereof, the powers of the Judicial Magistrate of the First Class for trial offences under the said Regulation within their respective jurisdiction appearing in column (4) of the said Schedule.

SCHEDULE

Sl. No.	*Name of the District*	*Designation of the officers on whom powers are conferred*	*Jurisdiction of the Scheduled Areas*
1	2	3	4
1.	Balasore	Sub-Collector, Nilgiri	Nilgiri Community
2.	Ganjam	Sub-Collector, Ghumsar (Headquarters at Bhanjanagar)	Development Block Suruda Tahsil excluding Gazalbadi and Gocha Gram Panchayats of Ghumsar Sub-Division 1. Rangada 2. Lokfisuni 3. Madhuaguma 4. Kanheisahi 5. Baduabada 6. Gaida 7. Jallara 8. Tuparda 9. Raikhula 10. Chandiapada 11. Karadabada

(Contd.)

1	2	3	4
			12. Mukaradoli
			13. Tubursingi
			14. Raghubalara
			15. Sanagam
			16. Dhobalingi
			17. Luhasingi
			18. Burudasingi
			19. Gambharikhol
			20. Gokhanasah
			21. Phulbani
			22. Aliara
			23. Titrisingi
			24. Achragada
			25. Dhanabada
			26. Gurusingi
			27. Tasaranga
			28. Mahulbada
			29. Masanibada
			30. Tadakasahi

(Contd.)

1	2	3	4
			31. Kalasahi
			32. Godango
3.	Kalahandi	Sub-Collector, Bhawanipatna	Thuamul-Rampur Block of Kalahandi Tahsil and Lugigar. Block in Bangarh and Kalahandi Tahsil of Bhavanipatnam Sub-Division
4.	Keonjhar	Sub-Collector, Keonjhar	Keonjhar Sub-Division
		Sub-Collector, Champua	Champut Sub-Division
5.	Koraput	Sub-Collector, Jeypore	Jeypore Sub-Division
		Sub-Collector, Koraput	Koraput Sub-Division
6.	Rayagada	Sub-Collector, Gunpur	Gunpur Sub-Division
		Sub-Collector, Raygada	Raygada Sub-Division
7.	Nawarangpur	Sub-Collector, Nawrangpur	Nawrangpur Sub-Division
8.	Malkangiri	Sub-Collector, Malkangiri	Malkangiri Sub-Division
9.	Mayurbhanj	Sub-Collector, Baripada	Baripada Sub-Division
		Sub-Collector, Bamanghati	Bamanghati Sub-Division
		Sub-Collector, Kaptipada	Kaptipada Sub-Division
		Sub-Collector, Panchapir	Panchapir (Karanjia) Sub-Division

(*Contd.*)

1	2	3	4
10.	Kandhamal (Phulbani)	Sub-Collector, Kandhamal Kandhamal (Phulbani)	Kandhamal Tahsil of Sub-Division
		Sub-Collector, Baliguda	Baliguda Sub-Division.
11.	Sambalpur	Sub-Collector, Kuchinda	Kuchinda Tahsil of Kuchinda Sub-Division
12.	Sundargarh	Sub-Collector, Sundargarh	Sundargarh Sub-Division
		Sub-Collector, Panposh	Panposh Sub-Division
		Sub-Collector, Bonai	Bonai Sub-Division
13.	Gajapati	Sub-Collector, Parlakhemundi	R. Udayagiri Tahsil, Guma Community Development Block of Paralakhemundi Tahsil of Paralakhemundi Sub-Division

Chapter III (*Continued*)

Notifications

GOVERNMENT OF ORISSA
REVENUE AND EXCISE DEPARTMENT
No. 6723 AG-7/66-R

From
Shri I.C. Dora. O.A.S
Under Secretary to Government

To
The Secretary
Board of Revenue, Orissa, Cuttack
Dated, Bhubaneswar, the 5th February, 1966

Subject: Tightening up control over transfer of land from *Adibasis* to non-*adibasis*.

Sir,

I am directed to say that it is noticed that there is a wrong impression in the minds of some of the field officers regarding the restrictions on transfer of lands by the *Adibasis* to the non-*Adibasis*. The correct position in the matter is explained below:

(1) Before merger of the ex-States occupancy tenants belonging to certain castes and tribes could transfer their lands only with the 12 (subsequently renumbered as paragraph 10) of the Administration of Orissa States Order 1948, which came into force in all the ex-States excluding Mayurbhanj on the 1st January, 1948, provided that an occupancy tenant would be entitled to freely transfer his holding subject to the restriction that no transfer of any holding by a member of an Aborginal Tribe in favour of one who is not a member of any of the aboriginal tribes shall be valid unless such transfer is made with the previous permission of the Administrator of the State concerned.

This power of the Administrator was subsequently given to the Sub-Divisional Magistrate by an amendment of the order. The term 'Aboriginal Tribe' was defined in the said order to mean any tribe that may from time to time notified as such by the Provincial Government for the purpose of this order. When the ex-State of Mayurbhanj was integrated with the State of Orissa a similar provision was also included in paragraph 11 of the Administration of Mayurbhanj State Order 1949. These provisions were repeated in Section 7 of the Orissa merged States (Laws) Act 1950. No notification was, however, issued by Government defining the term 'Aboriginal Tribe' until the 2nd May, 1962, when the term was defined in this Department notification No. 24507-Ten-15/62-R, dated the 22nd May, 1962.

(2) In 1956, the Orissa Scheduled Areas Transfer of Immovable Property (By Scheduled Tribes) Regulation 1956 (Regulation 2 of 1956) was passed and it put a restriction on the transfer of immovable property belonging to 'Scheduled Tribe' and not 'Aboriginal Tribes' The term 'Scheduled Tribe' has been defined in the regulation to have the same meaning as it has in the Constitution (Scheduled Tribes) Order 1950 as amended from time to time.

(i) Prior to merger i.e. before 1.1.1948	Ex-State laws of restriction in all ex-State except Mayurbhanj were applicable
(ii) Prior to merger. i.e. before 1.1.1949	Ex-State law was applicable in ex-State of Mayurbhanj
(iii) In ex-State of Sundargarh and Mayurbhanj	There was no restriction on transfer of land by an occupancy tenant whether or not he belonged to a Scheduled Tribe from merger till 3.10.56 (both days inclusive)
(iv) In the districts of Sundargarh and Mayurbhanj from 4.10.1956	Regulation 2 of 1956 is applicable.
(v) In other ex-States from merger till 21.5.1962.	There was no restriction on transfer of land by an occupancy tenant whether or not he belonged to a Scheduled Tribe.
(vi) In other ex-States from 22.5.1962.	The Merged States (Laws) Act is applicable.

Regulation 2 of 1956 applies to Mayurbhanj and Sundargarh districts only from 4.10.1956 and in respect of these two districts only the relevant provisions in the Merged States (Laws) Act stand repealed, from that date. So far restriction imposed by the Merged States (Laws) Act are still operative in other merged State from 22nd May, 1962.

(4) As regards agency area of ex-Madras area the position is as below:

(i)	Prior to the enforcement of the Regulation 2 of 1956, i.e. from the 4th October, 1956, in Koraput (excluding Kashipur) Agency portion of Ganjam district and Balli-guda Sub-division of Boudh Khondmals district.	The Agency Tracts Interest and Land Transfer Act 1917) was applicable.
(ii)	In Khondmals Sub-divisional of Boudh Khon-dmals	The Khondmals Laws Regulation 1936 districts from the enforcement of the Khondmals was applicable Laws Regulation 1936 till the enforcement of Regula-tion 2 of 1956.
(iii)	In Koraput (excluding Kashipur) Agency portion of Ganjam district, Balli-guda and Khondmals Sub-divisional of Boudh Khond-mals districts (excluding Pandakhol Mutha and Chakpad Khandam) from the 4th October, 1956.	Regulation 2 of 1956 is applicable
(iv)	In Pandakhol Mutha and Chakapad Khandm.	The Agency Tracts Interest and Land Transfer Act 1917 (Madras Act 1 of 1917)

(5) Proviso to Clause (b) of Sub-section (2) of Section 46 of the C.P. Tenancy Act 1898 as amended by the Orissa act XIII of 1953 which applies to Bargarh and Sambalpur Sub-divisions (excluding Mahadebpali Police Station area) and Raiyatwari villages of these Sub-divisions of Sambalpur district and provision to Clause (b) of Sub-section (1) of Section 12 of the C.P. Tenancy Act 1920 as amended by Orissa Act XV of 1953 which applies to Nawapara Sub-division of Kalahandi district and ex-Mahadebpali area of the Sambalpur Sub-Act 1891 as amended by Orissa act 27 of 1963 in respect of Raiyatwari villages of Sambalpur and Bargarh Sub-division, Section 61 of the Angul Laws Regulation 1936 also put certain restrictions regarding transfer of land. All these laws and regulations continued to be in force in the respective areas mentioned above till the 1st October 1965, when the Orissa Land Reforms Act 1960 was brought into force.

(6) In the remaining areas there were no such laws and hence there was no restriction on transfer of land by an *Adibasi* to a non-*Adibasi* till the date of enforcement of the Orissa Land Reforms Act 1960.

(7) According to Section 22 of the Orissa Land Reforms Act 1960, any transfer of a holding or part thereof by a raiyat belonging to a Scheduled Tribe is void unless made in favour of another member of a Scheduled Tribe. This restriction is now applicable throughout the State since the 1st October, 1965, except the Scheduled areas where Regulation 2 of 1956 is in force.

2. I am, therefore, to request that the above instructions may be explained to the field officers and they be asked to follow them strictly.
3. All Revenue Divisional Commissioners and all Collectors are being informed.
4. Receipt of the letter may please be acknowledged.

Yours faithfully
Sd/-
Under Secretary to Government

Chapter III (*Continued*)

(C) Instructions issued for dealing in with cases under Regulation 2 of 1956

GOVERNMENT OF ORISSA
REVENUE DEPARTMENT

No. 65704-Ag.-96/70-R

From

Shri Premananda Tripathy
Joint Secretary to Government

To

All Collectors

Dated Bhubaneswar, the 27th November, 1970

Subject: Enforcement of Legal Provisions against Illegal Transfer of *Adibasi* land to non-*Adibasis*.

Sir,

I am desired to say that it has been brought to the notice of Government that the problem relating to unauthorised occupation of lands belonging to members of Scheduled Tribes by non-*Adibasi* in increasing in various areas of the State. As a result of this there has been noticed a growing impatience amongst members of the Scheduled Tribe who, on account of their general ignorance, have found themselves in a pitiable conditions.

2. The Orissa Scheduled Areas Transfer of Immovable Property (by Scheduled Tribes) Regulation 1956) provides that any transfer of immovable property belonging to a member of the Scheduled Tribes to a person who does not belong to a Scheduled Tribe without the permission of competent authority can either *suo motu* or on receipt of application from the concerned member of the Scheduled Tribe, take steps to restore back the property to him, besides imposing such penalty as may be considered fit in accordance with Section 7 of that Regulation. This Regulation applies only to the Scheduled Areas of the State. Such protection to member of Scheduled Tribes in other areas of the State has been extended by the Orissa Land Reforms Act. Section 22 and 23 of the Orissa Land Reforms Act envisage that any transfer of a holding belonging to a member of the Scheduled Tribe except transfer where it is in favour of a person belonging to a Scheduled Tribe or in other cases, where the previous permission in writing of the Revenue Officer has been obtained, is illegal. Where transfer have taken place in violation of this provision the Revenue Officer may on his own information or on the application of the person interested make the required enquiry and cause restoration of the property to the transferer or his heirs under Section 23 of the Orissa Land Reforms Act. In view of these legal provisions. It should not be difficult to keep a strict watch on illegal transfer of land belonging to members of the Scheduled Tribes to persons not belonging to such Scheduled Tribes.

3. I am, therefore, to request that the present position regarding pendency of cases under Regulation 2 of 1956 and under Section 23 of the Orissa Land Reforms Act in respect of land belonging to members of the Scheduled Tribes may please be furnished in two separate Proforma enclosed herewith. A report by the 25th December, 1970, may please be sent.

Yours faithfully
PREMANANDA TRIPATHY
Joint Secretary to Government

Memo. No. 65705-R
Dated, the 27th November, 1970

Copy to all Revenue Divisional Commissioners/Secretary, Board of Revenue, Orissa Cuttack.

PROFORMA

Report on Cases under Regulation 2 of 1956 relating to Illegal Transfer of *Adibasi* Land

No. of Cases under Regulation 2 of 1956 Detected suo moto	*No. of cases under Regulation 2 of 1956 where Application has been filed by Members of Scheduled Tribes*	*Total No. of Cases (cols.1 &2)*	*No. of cases where Formal Proceedings have started*	*No. of cases disposed of*	*Balance pending for disposal*	*No. of cases out of col. 5 in which property has been restored to lawful owners belonging to scheduled tribes*	*Area restored under Col.7*	*Penalty collected since the beginning of the year*	*Remarks*

PREMANANDA TRIPATHY
Joint Secretary to Government

Memo. No. 65705-R
Dated, the 27th November, 1970

Copy to all Sub-divisional Offices.

PREMANANDA TRIPATHY

No. of Cases under Regulation 2 of 1956 detected suo moto	*No of cases under regulation 2 of 1956 where application has been filed by members of Scheduled Tribes*	*Total No of cases (cols.1 & 2)*	*No of cases where formal proceedings have started*	*No of cases disposed of*	*Balance pending for disposal*	*No of cases out of col. 5 in which property has been restored to lawful owners belonging to scheduled tribes*	*Area restored under Col. 7*	*Penalty collected since the beginning of the year*	*Remarks*

Joint Secretary to Government

Memo No. 4880-R
Dated the 29th January, 1971

Copy forwarded to the Secretary, Board of Revenue, Orissa, Cuttack/all Revenue Divisional Commissioners/Land Reforms Commissioner Orissa, Cuttack/Inspector-General of Registration, Orissa, Cuttack/Registrar, Co-operative Societies/Planning and Co-ordination Department/ Agriculture Department/Tribal and Rural Welfare Department/Community Development Department/ Finance Department for information and necessary action in continuation of this Department Memo. No. 55145R, dated the 23rd September, 1970.

2. Finance Department/ Secretary, Board of Revenue are requested to intimate the steps taken by them for timely indent-and supply of stamps to the Treasuries as decided in para 2 (5) of the proceedings. Para 2 to Finance Department and Board of Revenue only.

PREMANANDA TRIPATHY
Joint Secretary to Government

GOVERNMENT OF ORISSA
REVENUE DEPARTMENT
No. 9803-Act. 34/U-R

From: Sri Premananda Tripathy, Joint Secretary to Government

To

The Collectors Koraput, Mayurbhanj, Sundargarh, Ganjam and Khondmals.

Dated, the 22nd February, 1971

Subject.—Implementation of provision under Regulation II of 1956.

Sir,

I am directed to say that although the Orissa Scheduled Areas Transfer of immovable property (by Scheduled Tribes) Regulation, 1956 (Orissa Regulation II of 1956), has come into effect since the

1st October, 1956, the implementation of its provisions has not been paid adequate attention. Government have been noticing that the problems relating to unauthorised occupation of lands belonging to the members of Scheduled Tribes by non-*Adivasis* are gradually on the increase. As a result of this, there has been a growing discontent amongst members of the Scheduled Tribes who, on account of their general ignorance, have found themselves in a helpless condition. It is, therefore, felt necessary to bring to the notice of all field officers the importance of implementation of the said Regulations for their guidance.

2. The Orissa Scheduled Areas Transfer of Immovable Property (by Scheduled Tribes) Regulation 1956 (Regulation II of 1956) provides that any transfer of immovable property belonging to a member of the Scheduled Tribes to a person who does not belong to a Scheduled Tribes without the permission of competent authority (Sub-divisional Officers) under the above said regulation is completely null and void and where such illegal transfers have taken place, the competent authority can either *suo motu* or on receipt of application from concerned members of the Scheduled Tribes, take steps to restore back the property to him besides imposing such penalty as may be considered fit in accordance with Section 7 of the Regulation.

3. Normally the economic condition of the members of the Scheduled Tribes is quite poor and distress in this regard is on the increase on account of unbated transfer of their landed property to the non-*Adivasis*. Even though the law envisages booking of cases of illegal transfer of such land both on the application of the concerned member of the Scheduled Tribes as also on the own initiative of the competent authority, very few cases have been instituted in most of the Scheduled areas of the State. It has come to the notice of State Government that non-protection of the rights and interests of the Scheduled Tribes has, of late, led to serious law and order disturbances in some areas of the State. Government have, therefore, been pleased to decide that each Revenue Inspector, each Revenue Supervisor and each Tahsildar must ensure that he detects at least 3 such cases of illegal transfer and send reports to the Sub-divisional Officers concerned (Competent Authority) for taking action under the *suo motu* provision of law. It shall be the duty of the Sub-divisional Officers to register all cases and take up their disposal maintaining the usual court diary for the purpose. Disposal in Camp,

Courts may be given preference to disposal of the cases at headquarters.

4. It has further come to the notice of Government that competent authorities (Sub-divisional Officers) while passing order for restoration of the land to the members of the Scheduled Tribe under the Regulation are the tribal land owners. It is desirable that they invariably pass orders to give delivery of the land to the Scheduled Tribe owner, by means of delivery warrant in pursuance of provision of Rule 35 of Order XIX of Civil Procedure Code.

5. A number of complaints with regard to imposition of penalty under Section 7 of the Regulation particularly relating to Koraput district had been received by Government in the past. It had been alleged that factors like the extent of immovable property under unlawful possession, the period for which the property was unlawfully possessed circumstance of the case and the manner in which, i.e., whether by fraud, through mortgage, through purchase in another man's name or through a clean sale transaction the property had been occupied, the amount paid to the member of the Scheduled Tribe in the transaction and the amount of financial benefit that might have accrued to him as a result of the transaction and the peculiar condition of the person on whom the penalty is imposed amongst others, were not taken into consideration in a number of cases. While Government desire that the provisions of law should be implemented in all seriousness, these facts are brought to your notice for your guidance.

6. A quarterly review of the cases under Regulation 2 of 1956 may be made by you and sent to Revenue Divisional Commissioner, Board of Revenue and Government along with a return in the pro forma enclosed herewith. It may be ensured that the review and the return reach the above levels by 25th of the month following each quarter.

I am to request that the above instructions may please be kept in view. Suitable ancillary instruction may be issued to subordinate field staff where necessary.

Yours faithfully
P. TRIPATHY
Joint Secretary to Government

Memo. No. 9804-R
Dated the 20th February, 1971

Copy forwarded to all Revenue Divisional Commissioners/ Secretary, Board of Revenue, Orissa, Cuttack for information.

P. TRIPATHY
Joint Secretary to Government

Memo. No. 9805-R
Dated the 20th February, 1971

Copy forwarded to all Collectors (Expect Collector, Koraput, Mayurbhanj, Sundargarh, Boudh Khondmals and Ganjam) for information.

B.C. MOHANTY
Under Secretary to Government

Memo. No. 9806-R
Dated the 20th February, 1971

Copy forwarded to all Sub-divisional Officers for information.

B.C. MOHANTY
Under Secretary to Government

Memo. No. 9807-R
Dated the 20th February, 1971

Copy forwarded to all Tahsildars in Koraput, Mayurbhanj, Sundargarh, Boudh Khondmals and Ganjam district for information.

B.C. MOHANTY
Under Secretary to Government

No. of cases under Regulation 2 of 1956 detected suo motu	*No. of cases under regulation 2 of 1956 where application has been filed by members of Scheduled Tribes*	*Total No. of cases (cols.1 and 2)*	*No. of cases where formal proceedings have started*	*No. of cases disposed of*	*Balance pending for disposal*	*No. of cases out of col 5 in which property has been restored to lawfaul owners belonging to scheduled tribes*	*Area restored under Col.7*	*Penalty collected since the beginning of the year*	*Remarks*

2. For an adult with food Rs. 22.50 per month or Re. 0.75 per day.
3. For an adolescent (below 14 years) without food Rs. 30 per month or Re. 1.00 per day.
4. For an adolescent (below 14 years) with food Rs. 15 per month or Re. 0.50 per day.

By Order of the Governor
B.K. MISHRA
Secretary to Government

GOVERNMENT OF ORISSA
REVENUE DEPARTMENT
No. 44023-Ag-34/71-R

From

Shri B.C. Mohanty, O.A.S.,
Under Secretary to Government

To

All Collectors
Dated Bhubaneswar, the 10th August, 1971

Subject—Enforcement of legal provisions against illegal transfer of *Adivasi* land to non-*Adivasis*.

Sir,

In inviting the reference to this Department letter No. 65704-R, dated the 27th November, 1970, on the subject. I am directed to say that it has been brought to the notice of Government that delivery of lands to the members of Scheduled Tribes as provided under Regulation 2 of 56 and Section 23 of the Orissa Land Reforms Act 1960 is not being given on the file. Government desire that delivery of lands contemplated under the provisions of the aforesaid two legislations should be made at the spot without fail. The delivery of possession to the owners should be made by means of delivery warrant in pursuance of provisions of Rules 35 of Order Letter No. 9803-R, dated the 20th February, 1971, addressed to all Collectors of scheduled areas with copy to all other Collectors communicated in Memo No. 9805-R, dated the 20th February, 1971.

I am, therefore, to request that necessary instructions may be issued to Sub-ordinate field staff to ensure delivery of possession on the spot and Field Officers violating these instructions may be strongly dealt with.

Receipt of this letter may please be acknowledged.

Yours faithfully,
B.C. MOHANTY
Under Secretary to Government

TO BE SUBSTITUTED FOR THE LETTER BEARING THE SAME MEMBER AND DATE

GOVERNMENT OF ORISSA
REVENUE DEPARTMENT
No. 46816-CH-30/71-R

From

Shri B.C. Mohanty, O.A.S
Under Secretary to Government

To

All Collectors

Dated Bhubaneswar, the 25th August, 1971

Subject—Mutation of the beneficiaries in S.F.D.A./M.F.A.L. areas in priority

Sir,

I am directed to invite your attention to paragraph 5 of the proceedings of the Collectors' Conference held on the 8th May, 1971 on item sponsored by Department of Agriculture and Co-operation regarding Small Farmers Revenue Department Agency, etc., and to say that the Board of Revenue have moved Revenue Department for amending the existing settlement operations with a view to bring the record of rights up-to-date specially in respect of the beneficiaries in the S.F.D.A. and M.F.A.L. areas to enable them to avail the credit facilities from the institutional agencies. The Board's proposal is under examination.

2. Pending amendment to the settlement rules, Government desire that the Revenue Inspectors may be authorised to issue certificates to the extent of land the small farmers are in possession so that they could produce the same before the Banks and financing institutions in support of their loan applications. The certificates should be issued in the *pro forma* enclosed. A copy of the certificate issued should be kept in the office of the Revenue Inspector. During visit or inspection of to the Revenue Inspector Circle, the Tahasildar should make it a point to go through the office copies of the certificates issued by the Revenue Inspector and check about their correctness with reference to up-to date records. To facilitate keeping of copy of certificates granted by the Revenue Inspectors, the Revenue Inspectors may be supplied with adequate number of Certificate forms kept in bound books, the certificate in each case being prepared in duplicate and duplicate copy left with the Revenue Inspector. The books may be serially page numbered....

3. I am, therefore, to request that suitable instructions may be issued to all the Revenue Inspectors in this regard and a copy thereof sent to this Department for information of Government.

Yours faithfully
B.C. Mohanty
Under-Secretary to Government

GOVERNMENT OF ORISSA
REVENUE DEPARTMENT
No. 47416 AG-63/71R

From

Premananda Tripathy
Secretary to Government

To

All Collector,
Dated Bhubaneswar, the 27th August, 1971

Subject—Illegal Transfer of Lands belonging to the members of Scheduled Castes and Scheduled Tribes to non-Scheduled Castes and Tribes

Sir,

I am directed to say that Section 3 of the Orissa Scheduled Areas Transfer of Immovable Property (by Scheduled Tribes) Regulation 1956 (Regulation 2 of 1956) imposes restriction on transfer of immovable property by a member of Scheduled Tribe in the Scheduled Areas of the State. Similar restriction has also been imposed under Section 22 of the Orissa Land Reform Act 1960 in the non-Scheduled area of the State.

2. In spite of issue of repeated instruction to follow meticulously the spirit of Law in this regard, it has been brought to the notice of the Government that the problems relating to a unauthorised occupation of land belonging to the members of the Scheduled Tribe by non-Scheduled Tribe persons are on the increase. This has resulted in discontent amongst the members of Scheduled Tribes who, on account of their general ignorance, have found themselves in a helpless condition. Government, therefore, desire that the interests of the Tribals in the State should be fully protected and it may be ensured that they are not exploited on account of their ignorance of law.

3. The Sub-divisional Officers and Collectors who are in charge or General Administration have special responsibilities in this regard.

The transfer of land from an *Adivasi* to a non-*Adivasi* requires the sanctions of the Sub-divisional Officer in order that such transfer become legal and valid. In the past the Sub-Divisional Officers have treated requests for permission very liberally in complete disregard to the interests of the tribals. Government desire that you may issue necessary instructions to the Sub-divisional Officers to keep a strict watch on such illegal transfer of lands belonging to members of Scheduled Tribe to persons not belonging to Scheduled Tribe and to ensure that the interests of tribals in this regard are fully protected. While granting permission for transfer of lands in the above cases the application for transfer should be most carefully scrutinised and permission refused in all but the most genuine cases.

Yours faithfully,
P. TRIPATHY
Secretary to Government

Confidential

Copy of letter No. 72492/82, dated 11.11.86 of the Secretary, Revenue and Excise Department, Orissa, Bhubaneswar addressed to all Collectors and all P.A. (I.TD.A) in Memo No. 72493/82 of even date

Subject: Grant of permission for alienation of tribal land to non-tribals

Sir,

I am directed to say that Section 3(1) of the Orissa Scheduled Area Transfer of Immovable Property (By Scheduled Tribes) Regulation 1956 (Regulation 2 of 1956) provides that any transfer of Immovable Property situated within Scheduled Area, by a member of ST shall be null and void and no force or effect whatever unless made in favour of another member of ST of which previous consent in writing of the competent authority. Thus the competent authority under this regulation can grant permission for alienation of tribal land to a non-tribal. That a lot of mischief is committed while granting permission for alienation of tribal land to non-tribals has come to the notice of Government in a number of instances in the past. Since protection of interest of the tribals in their lands is utmost important the State Government has appointed all P.A.I.T.D. As located in Scheduled Areas. S.D.O. Nilgiri and A.D.M. (Revenue) Ganjam as competent authority for the Scheduled areas in their respective jurisdiction vide Notification No. 32729/R dated 19.8.1986.

2. In order to guard against or possible mischief and prevent indiscriminate transfer of tribal land, it has been decided by the Government that the competent authority before passing the final order for granting permission should invariably submit the case-record to the concerned Collector and obtain his approval so that *mala fide* sanction if any, on the part of competent authority is subject to prior scrutiny before such final order is passed.

Yours faithfully
Sd/- P.M. MOHAPATRA
Commissioner-cum-Secretary to Government

COLLECTOR OF KORAPUT
REVENUE SECTION
Dated the 4th December, 1986
No.4795/XXV-22/86-Rev

To

The P.A.I.T.D.A./S.D.Os in the District

Subject: Grant of Permission for Alienation of Tribal Land to Non-Tribals.

Sir,

In enclosing herewith a copy of letter of AG-89/86-72492/82 dated 11.11.1986 of Revenue Department, I am request you that the instructions issued in the above letter may strictly be adhered to and the case record in deserving cases be sent to Collector for scrutiny and approval, before, passing final order granting permission for sale of Tribal Land to non-Scheduled Tribe persons.

Yours faithfully,
Sd/-
A.D.M. Koraput

GOVERNMENT OF ORISSA
REVENUE AND EXCISE DEPARTMENT

No. 37431/R/Ag. 50/88
Dated the 7th June, 1988

From

B.C. PATNAIK
Secretary to Government

To

All Collectors,
All Project

Subject: Indiscriminate Alienation of tribal lands to the non-tribals.

Sir,

I am directed to say that Section 3 of the Regulation imposes restriction on transfers of immovable property by a member of ST and any Transfer made in violation in this provision in favour of a non-Scheduled person shall be null and void unless made with the previous permission of the competent authority. Similar restriction has also been imposed under Section 22 of the O.L.R. Act 1960 in the non-Scheduled areas of the State.

In spite of such provisions in the law, it has been brought to the notice of the Government that alienation of lands of Scheduled Tribes in favour of non-Scheduled Tribe person continue unabated. Officers vested with power to permit alienation of tribal lands are very often found exercising these powers rather liberally to the detriment of the interest of the Scheduled Tribe. In order to remove the shortcomings in implementation of the laws, government has been considering to bring certain amendment pending such amendment, it is imperative that the interest of Scheduled Tribes in their lands should be fully protected and officers at various levels empowered to accord permission for transfer of land under the law should observe the following guidelines meticulously while according permission for transfer of tribal lands in favour of non-tribals.

(I) Rules of O.S.A.T.I.P. (by ST) Rules 1959 provides that receipts of an application from a member of ST to transfer any immovable property to a member of non-ST, the competent authority may cause necessary enquiry before passing appropriate orders. The enquiry report is required to be submitted in Form I appended the rules. This report to form the basis for consideration the merit of the application. The competent authority may accord permission for the reasons to be recorded in writing only after he is satisfied that the transfer would be in the best interest of the applicant. It becomes incumbent on him to observe utmost caution and scrutinise the application and also the enquiry reports carefully before deciding to accord permission for such transfer. Permission for alienation of tribal lands in favour of non-tribals should be transferred only in extremely hard cases, as an exception rather than rules.

(II) Lands are being leased of the Scheduled Tribes in order to ameliorate their economic condition. It is, therefore, the duty of the Government to regulate and restrict such transfer of land belonging to a member of ST to another so that he does not become landless as a result of such transfer. At present a person whose total extent of land as a tenant or a raiyat held by all the members of family is less than one standard acre is considered landless. On this analogy, the maximum extent of land possession by a family should not be less than one standard acre.

While granting permission of transfer of tribal land, the competent authority should see that the extent of land left with the owner after such transfer does not come down one standard acre. This can, however, be relaxed only in exceptional cases where the applicant satisfies that he wants to sell the land to purchase some other suitable lands.

(III) It has been brought to the notice of the Government that in some cases where a transferer does not succeed in getting permission to alienate land in excess of what is actually require to meet his purpose he submits further applications for permission in various pre-text, real or imaginary. The competent authority should, therefore, be watchful to prevent such repeated transfer of land when a member of ST to a non ST person.

(IV) There are many instances of rich and influential person trying to purchase a tribal land at less than prevailing market price taking advantage of ignorance of the transferer. This happens when the competent authority fails to determine the proper market value of the land and treats the latter in a routine fashion. It is, therefore, necessary that a competent authority should scrutinise the enquiry report properly and ensure payment the prevailing market value to the seller.

(V) Instances have come to the notice of the Government that in a number of cases *benami* transaction takes place. Non-tribals purchase the land in the name of *Adivasis*. Before granting permission competent authority should satisfy himself that there is no '*benamidar*' behind the transactions.

The above instructions should be kept in view while according permission for transfer of lands in the above cases. Suitable instructions may also be given to the officers on special duty who have been vested with the power in this regard.

Yours faithfully,
Sd/-
Secretary to Government

NOTIFICATION

COLLECTORATE OF KORAPUT
No. 485/SS, Dated 8th August, 1986

To

The Sub-divisional Officers

The Special Officers under Regulation 2/56 in the district.

Sir,

It has been observed that permission is being granted under Regulation 2/56 in a very large number of cases. This defeats the purpose of the Regulation. You are hereby instructed that in future if the permission granted during a particular period exceeds more than of the cases died, prior clearance from the Collector must be obtained. Similarly in all the cases where the land is less than 5 acres, no permission should be granted without obtaining prior clearance of the Collector.

2. The above restriction will also apply to the provisions under the O.L.R. Act.

3. It is observed that virtually no cases are being detected and

disposed under Section 22 of the O.L.R Act and the corresponding provision under Regulation 2/55. Under the instructions of H and W. Department, every Welfare Extension Officer must detect at least 5 cases in a month. You are requested to review the performance of the Welfare Extension Officers. In all cases where the Welfare Extension Officer have not detected at least five cases, the same should be entered in the C.C.H. and will also be treated as negligence of duty.

4. The Rev. Inspectors so must be directed to detect at least five such cases in every month. Any failure of the R.I. should be reflected in the C.C of their C.C.R.s The performance in this regard should also be reflected in the C.C.R.s of the Asstt. Dist. Welfare Officers of your sub-division.

Yours faithfully
Sd/-
Collector, Koraput

COLLECTORATE, OF KORAPUT
No 4994/89 Revenue
Dated the 10th August, 1989

To

All P.A.I.T.D.A
All Sub-Collectors (in the district)

Subject: Effective implementation of the provision of OSATIP, Regulation 1956—Instruction issued.

Sir,

It is noticed that due to lack of proper enquiry and investigation as well as improper implementation of different provisions contained in OSATIP Regulation 2/56 illegal transfer of tribal land in the hands of the non-tribals continues unabated defaulting the very purpose of this protective legislation. Some of the problems which are generally confronted while disposing of cases under various sections of Reg. 2/56 are highlighted in the following para along with instructions to overcome these problems so as to safeguard the interest of the tribal and to check the illegal transfer of immovable property.

Instances have come to the notice that vested interest non-tribals are able to make application in the name of tribal persons to obtain permission under section 3(1) which fact the tribal concerned themselves even does not know. In such case attempts should be made to detect the fraudulent persons to book cases under criminal law. It is, therefore, necessary that the competent authority should simultaneously entrust the enquiry of such application both to the Tahsildar and ADWO concerned. Generally the non-tribals after accepting tribal land endeavour to regularise the transactions by obtaining the permission by hook or by crook.

Hence, it is imperative to enquire in the field as to who is in physical possession of the land in question. If the enquiry reveals that some non-tribals person is already in unauthorised occupation of tribal land it can well be inferred that the same non-tribal is a fake applicant. Basing on such finding, the enquiring A.D.W.O. will submit his report certifying this fact to the competent authority as well as to the Sub-Collector concerned for failing the cases under Cr.P.C. against the fake applicant similarly the enquiring Tahsildar will also send his report on the same line to the Sub-Collector concern to book the case under Section 3(A) of the Regulation 2/56. Not only this will deter the miscreants considerably but also create an awareness against such type of criminality.

2. It is found that sometimes the application are filled for permission under Section 3(1) without furnishing the correct particulars such as Khata No., Plot No., area and location, etc. These defective application may summarily rejected without any correspondence.

3. According to Rule 3(1) of OSATIP Rules, 1959, a summary enquiry is to be made by an officer authorised by the competent authority. Commonly the Tahsildars are entrusted with the enquiry who in turn assign this task to Revenue Inspectors. But the Rules are found conducting enquiry without proper application of mind and recommended almost all the cases for granting permission. It is, therefore, enjoined that A.D.W.O.s may also be entrusted with the work of enquiry to ensure proper investigation into the cases. While sending the enquiry reports of the Revenue Inspectors, the Tahsildar should certify regarding the correctness of the same.

Rule 3(1) of regulation 2 of 1956, requires that result of enquiry should be furnished in Form No. I. The Item No. 4 of this form requires the name and the caste of the proposed transferees. But in the majority of case of the enquiry reports, the names are not at all mentioned which means that the permission is granted to no specific individual. This will provide scope for *benami* transaction and to regularise the transaction already made. Therefore, failing which permission shall not be accorded. Similarly, in the order of permission the name, caste and address of the person to whom the immovable property is to be transferred should be written. This is very important.

4. The explanation to Section 3(1) envisages that transfer of immovable property in favour of female members of ST who is married to a non-tribal shall be deemed to be a transfer made in favour of a non-tribal person. Sincere effort should be made to find out the caste and social status of the husband of such tribal female member and action is to be taken accordingly. The Government servants who will submit either misleading or inaccurate enquiry report shall be taken to task under O.C.S. (C.C.A.) Rules.

5. For quick disposal, the cases may be organised Block-wise and data for hearing be fixed accordingly so that the Tahsildar and the A.D.W.O. can be able to complete the enquiry within the given time. The Project Administrator I.T.D.A. are advised to hold camp courts at different places for expedious disposal of the case and convenience of the tribal public.

6. Experience has shown that tribal person take consumption loans from private individuals when they fail to get it from government institutions. So while giving permission, Competent Authority should try to arrange for assistance from the I.T.D.A. income generating Scheme, if the tribal is eligible.

7. While granting permission under Section 3(1) a reasonable data line may be fixed within which time the sale has to be effected. If the sale is effected after a long lapse of time, the rate is fixed for the land in question loses its meaning due to change in market price.

8. Another prevailing mode of illegal transfer is that tribal having adequate land is used as middleman by non-tribal who acquire the tribal land. First, the rich tribal person purchases the land from the poor tribals at the instance of non-tribal person purchases the land from the poor tribals at the instance tribal person in which case the permission to sell the same to the non-tribal person in which case the permission is normally granted. Therefore, case should be taken at the enquiry stage to examine whether the same plot of land sold by the poor tribal in recent past is applied for transfer. In such cases permission should be refused.

9. Besides the permission is granted for sale of land for repaying the loan/certificate dues, copies of such permission order may be issued to the concerned certificate officer or Bank as far as practicable, to facilitate the collection of dues at the time of registration.

10. It is to be brone in mind that according to Section 3(A) even forcible occupation of the tribal land by another tribal person will attract the provisions of Regulation. In many cases non-tribals in occupation of tribal land employ tribals to cultivate the land to circumvent the provision of Regulation 2 of 1956. Similarly the tribal ceiling surplus land even after distribution of the same among the landless tribal beneficiaries. In such cases, eviction proceedings under Section 3-A of the Regulation 2 of 1956 could be initiated.

All concerned are requested to follow the above instructions meticulously while disposing of cases under Regulation 2 1956.

Yours faithfully,
Sd/-
Collector, Koraput

GOVERNMENT OF ORISSA

REVENUE AND EXCISE DEPARTMENT

No. 3546 /R, dated the 18th January, 1990

Ag. 82/89/(L.R.-A)

From

Shri Giridhari Nanda, I.A.S.,
Addl. Secretary to Government

To

All Collectors (Except Collector, Cuttack, Puri, Bolangir and Dhenkanal).

Subject: Vesting of powers of competent authority under Section 3(1) or Regulation 2 with Sub-Collector and Officers on Special Duty (Land Reforms)

Sir,

I am directed to invite a reference to this Department Notification

No. 77064/R, dated 21.12.1987 No. 79143/R, dated 19th December, 1988 wherein Officers on Special Duty (Land Reforms) and (Previously S.D.O.s) were declared as competent authorities to exercise powers under all Regulation 2 of 1956 except Section 3(1) and Project Administrators, I.T.D. as were vested with competent authority under Section 3(1) of the said Regulation.

2. In terms of this Department Notification No. 72982/R, dated 22.12.1989 copy of which communicated to you in Memo. No. 72984/R. 22.12.1989, powers of competent authority Regulation are no longer available to P.A. I.T.D.A.s Sub-Collectors and Officers on special competent authority in respect of the Regulation for specified areas. The Project Administrators may be requested to transfer the pending cases u/s 3(1) of the Regulation to the Sub-Officers on Special Duty (Land Reforms) as the case may be for disposal of the pending cases.

3. Occasions may arise where a post of an Officer on Special Duty may fall vacant due to his on long leave or the post not being filled up. In such contingencies, the cases in charge of an Officer Duty cannot be attended to by others without formal Notification by Government declaring them as authority in respect of that area. Powers of competent authority in the absence of the Officer can be conveniently transferred to the concerned Sub-Collectors.

4. I am to request that whenever the post of an Officer on Special Duty falls vacant or is vacant for a considerable period, proposals for exercise of powers by the concerned Sub-Collector furnished to this Department for issue of necessary notification, so that general public may not be inconvenienced due to absence of the Officer on Special Duty.

5. This Department G.P. No. 77474/R, Dt. 22.12.87 is hereby superseded.

Yours faithfully
Sd/-
Addl. Secretary to Government

Memo No. 3547/R, Dated 18.1.90

Copy forwarded to the H.&T.W Deptt. Board of Revenue, Orissa, Cuttack/L.R.C., Cuttack/All R.D.C.s / All Sub-Collectors/All Officers on Special Duty (L.R.)/Project Administrator of I.T.D. As Baripada/ Raingpur/Karanjia/Kaptipada/Keonjhar/Champua/Kuchinda/

Balliguda/Phulbani/Parlakhemundi/Thumul-Rampur/Koraput/Malkangiri/Nawarangpur/Raygada/Gunpur/Sundegarh/Panposh Boral for information and immediate necessary action.

Sd/-
Under Secretary to Government

GOVERNMENT OF ORISSA
REVENUE AND EXCISE DEPARTMENT

No. Ag.-69/.90/6860/R.
Bhubaneswar, the 13th February, 1991

From

Shri P.C. Rath, I.A.S.,
Joint Secretary to Government

To

The Secretary, Board of Revenue, Orissa, Cuttack
All Revenue Divisional Commissioners
All Collectors

Subject: Grant of permission for alienation of tribal land to non-tribals—Expeditious disposal of cases.

Sir,

I am directed to say that in order to restrict alienation of land belonging to Scheduled Tribes in the scheduled areas of the State. "The Orissa Scheduled Areas Transfer of Immovable Property (by Scheduled Tribes) Regulation prohibits alienation of tribal land to members not belonging to scheduled areas of the State. Section 3(2) and tribal land. The competent authority has also been empowered to initiate proceedings on his own motion or on an application filed by any party interested and restore the land to the transfer in case of illegally alienated or to the owner in case of the unauthorised occupation after giving the parties an opportunity of being heard. Penal provision has also been made in the Regulation to make the provision more effective.

2. Since protected of interest of the tribal community in their lands is of utmost importance, senior officers have been declared as 'Competent Authority' under the Regulation to excise powers within their respective jurisdictions. Instructions have from time to time been issued prescribing guidelines for grant of permission for alienation of tribal land and for expeditious disposal of the cases involving the interest of the tribals in their lands.

3. But it has come to the notice of the Government that in a number of cases permission for alienation is granted very liberally without going into the merit of the case to satisfy that the case of alienation is a genuine one. Besides, the case are dragging on for a considerable length of time in the court of the competent authority.

4. Economically, bulk of the scheduled tribe population of the State is backward and constitutes the weaker sections of the society. Necessity compounded by illiteracy and simplicity makes them as easy prey to the unscrupulous persons. It is, therefore, necessary that the cases relating to alienation of tribal land are properly and promptly enquired into and expeditiously disposed of. Besides, the cases of unauthorised occupation of tribal land also need to be disposed of with equal expediency.

5. I would, therefore, request you to please issue necessary instruction to the concerned competent authorities under your control to take immediate steps for speedy disposal of all the cases seeking permission transfer of land belonging to the tribals after following the procedure laid down in Rule 3 of the Regulation. Instruction also may please be issued to dispose of expeditiously the cases relating to unauthorised occupation the tribal land.

Yours faithfully,
Sd/-
Joint Secretary to Government

Memo No. 6861/R, Dated 13.2.1991

Copy forwarded to the Harijan and Tribal Welfare Deptt./All Officers on Special Duty (Land Reforms) all Sub-Collectors for information and necessary action.

Sd/-
Joint Secretary to Government

GOVERNMENT OF ORISSA
REVENUE AND EXCISE DEPARTMENT
No. Ag-84/92(p) 49919/R
Dated, Bhubaneswar, the 13th Oct., 92

From

Shri B.B Pattanaik, O.A.S
Deputy Secretary to Government

To

All Collectors (Except Collector, Cuttack, Puri, Bolangir and Dhenkanal)

Subject: Vesting of powers of competent authority under Sec. 3(1) of Regulation 2 of 1956 with Tahsildars and Officers on Special Duty (LR)

Sir,

I am directed to invite a reference to this Deptt. Notification No. 72982/R, dt 22.12.89 wherein Officer on Special Duty (L.R.) and Sub-Collectors were declared as competent authority to exercise powers under sections of the Regulation 2 of 1956.

In terms of this Deptt. Notification No. 47180/R, dt. 21.9.92 copy of which has been communicated you in this Deptt. Memo No.47182/R, dt. 21.9.92 powers of Competent Authority under different sections this Regulation are no longer with the Sub-Collectors, Tahsildars and O.S.D. (L.R.) have been appointed competent authority for specified areas. The Sub-Collectors in such a context may be requested to transfer the pending cases of Regulation 2 now with them to the respective Tahsildars immediately for disposal of the cases.

Yours faithfully,
Sd/-
Deputy Secretary to Government

Memo No. 49920/R, dated 13.10.92

Copy forwarded to the Secretary, Board of Revenue, Orissa, Cuttack/L.R.C. Orissa, Cuttack All R.D.C.s./ All Sub-Collectors/All O.S.D. (L.R.)/ Tahsildar, Nilgiri/Surda/Kalahandi/Thumul Rampur, Lanjigarh/Keonjhar/Telkoi/Ghatgaon/Champua/Barbil/Bissam, Cuttack/Gunupur/Jeypore/Boriguma/Kotpada/Malkangiri/Motu/ Chitrakonda/ Nawarangpur/Umerkote, Kodinga/Dabugaon/Baripada/ Betnoti/Rashgobindapur/ Rairangapur/Bahalda/Udala/Karnjia/Bonaj/ Kuchinda for information and necessary action.

Sd/-
Deputy Secretary to Government

Memo No. 49920/R, dated 13.10.92

Copy forwarded to the GOE (B).Br/L.R. (B) Br./L.R., (A) Br (20 copies) for information.

Sd/-
Deputy Secretary to Government

GOVERNMENT OF ORISSA
REVENUE AND EXCISE DEPARTMENT
No. A.G. 8/95/47875/R, the 30th October, 1995

From

Shri P.S. Guha, O.A.S., (i),
Joint Secretary to Government

To

The Collector, Balasore/Mayurbhanj/Keonjhar/Sundargarh/ Sambalpur/Kalahandi/Ganjam/Gajapati/Koraput/Raygada/ Nabrangapur/Malkangiri/Kondhamal.

Subject: Vesting of powers of competent authority under Regulation 2 of 1956 with Sub-Collectors.

Sir,

I am directed to say that Officers on Special Duty (Land Reforms) and Tahsildars/Revenue Officer were declared as competent authority under Regulation 2 of 1956 in Revenue and Excise Deptt. Notification No. Ag-84/92-47160-R; dt 21-10-1992. Due to administrative point of view, Government decided to withdraw the powers from Tahsildars and vest the same with Sub-Collectors besides Officers-on-Special Duty (Land Reforms) Accordingly, Government notification has since been issued vide this Department Notification No. 47173-R, dt. 26-10-95 and communicated to you in memo no 47175-R of even dated. As such powers of competent authority are no longer with the Tahsildars/Revenue Officer in scheduled areas of the State with effect from 26-10-1995.

In view of above, it is requested that (1) concerned Tahsildars/ Revenue Officer may be instructed to transfer the case records and other relevant papers/documents of the case instituted under Regulation 2 of 1956 now pending with them to the respective Sub-Collectors forthwith for disposal.

2. The Sub-Collectors may also be requested to furnish monthly progress reports under different sections of the Regulation taking into account of the achievement made in the court of Sub-Collectors prior to 21-10-1992 and the achievement made in the Court of the Tahsildars/Revenue officer under their jurisdiction (during 22.10.1992 to 25.10.1995). Such returns may be compiled at district level and submitted to Government in each month in time as usual.

In view of urgency, a copy of this letter is being sent to concerned Tahsildars/Revenue Officer/Sub-Collectors for immediate necessary action.

Receipt of this letter may please be acknowledged.

Yours faithfully
Sd/-
Joint Secretary to Government

GOVERNMENT OF ORISSA

REVENUE AND EXCISE DEPARTMENT

No L.R (A)-Ag 2/2003 177R, dated the 13th January, 2003

From

Sir R.L. Jamuda, IAS
Commissioner-cum-Secretary to Government

To

The Collector,
Koraput/Raygada/Malkangiri/Nabarangpur/Ganjam/Gajapati/Kalhandi/Kandhamal/Sambalpur/Sundargarh/Keonjhar/Mayurbhanj/Balasore

Subject: Implementation of Proviso (iii) of Section 3(1) of the Regulation 1 of 2002.

Sir,

With reference to the subject noted above, I am directed to say that as per proviso (iii) of Section 3(1) Regulation 1 of 2002 a member of a Scheduled Tribe shall not transfer any land of the total extent of his land remaining after the transfer will be reduced to less than two acres in case of irrigated land to five acres in case of the irrigated land has been explained [in Explanation II of Sub-section (i) of Section 3]. The ST land owners of scheduled areas might face difficulties to transfer their lands when the Registering Authorities demand evidence about extent of land held by the Tribal land owner. In fact it is necessary that the landowner produces evidence about the extent of his landholding to the Sub-Registrar/District Sub-Registrar so that the latter is satisfied that the transfer does not hit proviso (iii) of Section 3 (1) of Regulation 1 of 2002.

2. The matter was under consideration of the Government and after careful consideration, the Government have been pleased to decide that:

(a) The landowner belonging to S.T. in the scheduled areas shall wear an affidavit before First Class Magistrate/executive Magistrate as Annexure which discloses details of the land-held by the land owner.
(b) The landowner shall also furnish a certificate issued by the local Tahsildar as in Annexure-II. This certificate discloses details of land held by the landowner.
(c) The Sub-Registrar/District Sub-Registrar shall insist of production of these two documents before registration of documents purporting to transfer of land by 3 landowner belonging to ST in scheduled areas of the State.

(d) The Tahsildar should issue the certificate in Annexure-II to the landowner on plain paper application made to him in this regard. He may contact field enquiry, consult the ROR and hear the landowner to be satisfied about the landholding of the landowner.

(e) The Tahsildar shall issue the certificate within 30 days at the latest. While in no case issue of certificate should be delayed beyond 30 days. All possible steps be taken to issue the certificate quickly so that the landowner does not face difficulties to transfer his land.

3. It is, therefore, requested that suitable instruction may please be issued to all concerned for implementation of the decision.

Yours faithfully
Sd/-
Commissioner-cum-Secretary to Government

Memo No 1772/R Dt 13/1/03

Copy with copy of the enclosures forwarded to the I.G.R. Orissa, Cuttack for information and necessary action. She is requested to issue suitable instruction to all Registering Authorities of the Scheduled Areas for appropriate action by them.

Commissioner-cum-Secretary to Government

Memo No 1773/R, Dt 13/1/2003

Copy with copy of the enclosures forwarded to the Secretary. Board of Revenue Orissa Cuttack/L.R.C. Orissa, Cuttack / All R.D.C.s for information and necessary action.

Commissioner-cum-Secretary to Government

Memo No. 118/Rev-2003, Dated 14.1.2003

Copy forwarded to the Sub Collector, Koraput/Jeypore for information and necessary follow up action.

Copy to all Tahsildars is the district/All Sub-Registrars in the district for information and necessary follow up action.

Addl. Dist. Magistrate, Koraput

Forms of Affidavit

I .... Sri/Smt/Kumari/ Miss....................................Son/Daughter/Wife/Husband of...................... aged............ years, a permanent resident of village/ Town....................P.O......................P.S............Tahsil......................in the district of............................and.................. by profession do hereby solemnly affirm/make oath and state as follows.

That I am owner of/hold the land as in Schedule-A below free from all encumbrances, that I propose to transfer by way of sale/gift/ mortgage/lease acres..................land out of the same as per Schedule-B that I am aware of the provision of clause (iii) of proviso to Sub-Sec. (i) of Sec. 3 of the Orissa Scheduled Areas Transfer of Immovable Property (By Scheduled Tribes) Amendment Regulation 2000 (Regulation 1 of 2002) that after the proposed present transfer I shall remain holder of acres......................irrigated and or acres................unirrigated land which is permissible under clause (iii) of provision to Sub-section (i) of Section 3 of Orissa Scheduled Areas Transfer of immovable property (By Scheduled Tribes) Amendment Regulation 2000 (Regulation 1 of 2002) .

Schedule-A

Name of Mouza	*Khata No*	*Name of recorded land owners(s)*	*Plot No.*	*Areas*	*Classification*	*Irrigated/ Unirrigated*	*Remarks (if any)*
1	2	3	4	5	6	7	8

Schedule-B							
Name of Mouza	*Khata No*	*Name of recorded land owners(s)*	*Plot No.*	*Areas*	*Classification*	*Irrigated/ Unirrigated*	*Remarks (if any)*
1	2	3	4	5	6	7	8

Signature/Thumb impression of the deponent
Date......................

Son/Smt/Kumari/Miss .... Aged .... Years .... Son/Daughter/Wife/Husband of .... permanent resident of village .... at present .... by profession .... appears before me and states on oath ..... solemnly declaring that the contents of this affidavit are true to the best of his/her knowledge and belief.

Magistrate First Class
Executive Magistrate

Certificate of landholding of Sri/Smt/Miss/ Kumari............................ (This is to certify that Sri/Smt/Miss/ Kumari.............. Son/Daughter/Wife/Husband of.................. aged.....................years is a Town .... P.O. .... under ....C.A. of.....................................P.S. in..............................Tahsil of .... District we holds land as follows.)

Land Schedule

Name of Tahsil	*Name of Mouza*	*Khata No.*	*Recorded in the name of*	*Plot No.*	*Area*	*Kisssam*	*Irrigated/ Unirrigated*	*Remarks*

Tahsildar.......................................
Date ....
Seal ....

GOVERNMENT OF ORISSA
REVENUE DEPARTMENT

No. Ag. 5/05 18261/ R, dated the 2nd May, 2005

From

Sri S.N. Das
Joint Secretary to Government

To

All Collectors of Scheduled Areas.

Subject: Clarification on acceptance of return as required under Section-3-B (1) of amended Regulation 2000 by the Competent Authority.

Sir,

I am directed to say that the Section-3-B (1) of the Orissa Schedule the Transfer of Immovable Property (By Scheduled Tribes) Amended Regulation 2000 stipulation the period of limitation of two years for filling returns on landed properties in prescribed format to the concerned Sub-Collector with effect from 4.9.2002. But the OSATIP (By S.T.). Amendment Rules 2003 in corporating the prescribed format as required under the said Section was framed and published on 8.9.2003. A doubt arises as to whether the period of limitation as provided in the said Regulation will take effect from 4.9.2002 or 8.9.2003.

Keeping in view the above position, Government in consultation with Law Department have been pleased to clarify that the period of limitation for filling of return by a person having format as required under Section 3-B (1) of the amended Regulation 2000 will be effective with effect from 8.9.2003, i.e. from the date of notification of the Orissa Scheduled Areas Transfer of Immovable Property (By Scheduled Tribes) amendment Rules. 2003. As such the returns be accepted by the concerned Sub-Collectors till 7.9.2005.

This may be widely circulated among all the subordinate offices under your control as well as for information of general public.

This has been concurred in UOR-53/L dated 5.4.2005 by Law Department.

Yours faithfully
Sd/-
Joint Secretary to Government

Memo No. 18262/R, dated the 2.5.2005

Copy with 5 copies forwarded to the Law Department for kind information with reference to their UOR No. 53, dated 5.4.2005.

Sd/-
Joint Secretary to Government

Memo No. 18263/R, dated the 2.5.2009

Copy forwarded to Secretary, Board of Revenue/ L.R.C. Orissa, Cuttack/ All R.D.C.s for information and necessary action.

Joint Secretary to Government

Memo No.18264/R, dated the 2.5.2005

Copy forwarded to All Sub-Collectors of Scheduled areas/all OSDs of Scheduled Areas for information and necessary action.

Memo No. 18265/R, dated the 2.5.2005

Copy to L.R. (A) Section (10 spare copies).

Sd/-
Joint Secretary to Government

1. Name of the person presenting the Information:
2. His father's name and address:
3. Name and address of the Scheduled Tribe: whose Agricultural land, he is presently in occupation
4. Name of the village in which the land is situated, Khata, Plot number and area of the land, to be mentioned
5. Source of occupation of the Scheduled Tribe land:
   (a) by purchase

(b) through mortgage
(c) through gift
(d) by order of a competent court
(e) through inheritance
(f) through trespass
(g) through exchange
(h) Any other—specify

(Tick the item applicable in your case)

6. If in occupation of land through sale/gift or mortgage, enclose a copy of the registration deed, if it was registered in any registration office.
7. If a permission of the competent authority obtained before registration of the document ? If so, enclose a copy.
8. If the possession was obtained through Court's order enclose a copy of the Courts Order.
9. If you are occupying the land through trespass, indicate whether with the knowledge of the Scheduled Tribe owner ordinarily one of the legal heirs or without any one's knowledge.
10. Indicate the amount of consideration money:
    (a) Paid by you towards the cost of the land at the time of purchase
    (b) Did you pay the entire consideration money at the time of registration of the document or paid in full or a part of it before registration.
11. If you are in occupation through mortgage deed executed by the Scheduled Tribe. Indicate the terms of mortgage and the amount, if any, paid by you to the Scheduled Tribe. If the mortgage is not registered indicate the number of years you are in occupation and terms of mortgage.
12. If you are in possession through exchange of your land with the Scheduled Tribe's indicate the Khata No., Plot No. and area of the land exchanged with the name of village in which the land is situated.

Signature of the applicant
Dated: ....

GOVERNMENT OF ORISSA

REVENUE AND EXCISE DEPARTMENT

No. Ag. 5/2000-16324/R dt. 2.5.2006

From

Sri S.N. Das
Joint Secretary to Government

To

All Collectors of Scheduled Areas.

Subject: Clarification on procedure to be followed in case of the persons who failed to notify under Section 3-B of Regulation 2/56.

Sri,

I am directed to say that it has been clarified in this Department letter No. 10478/R, dt. 20.3.2006 that, if a non-Scheduled Tribe person is in possession of agricultural land of a S.T. person, fails to notify as required under Sub-section (2) of Section 3-B of Regulation 2/56 his occupation becomes unauthorised one and the competent authority can draw proceedings under sub-section (1) of Section 3-A of Regulation 2/56 for ejectment and restoration of unauthorised/ unlawful possession of agricultural land to whom it originally belonged and if that person is dead to his/her heirs.

You are, therefore, requested to intimate that action taken report on the aforesaid clarification to this department by return for review by Government.

Yours faithfully
Sd/-
Joint Secretary to Government

Memo No 16325/R, Dt. 2.5.2006

Copy forwarded to All R.D.C.s for information and necessary action with reference to this Deptt. Memo No. 10479/R, dt. 20.3.2006.

Sd/-
Joint Secretary to Government

Memo No.16325/R, Dt. 2.5.2006

Copy forwarded to the Secretary, Board of Revenue, Orissa, Cuttack/ Land Reforms Commissioner, Orissa, Cuttack for information and. necessary action with reference to this ex Deptt. Memo No. 10480/R. dt. 20.3.06.

Sd/ -
Joint Secretary to Government

COLLECTORATE OF KORAPUT
(REVENUE SECTION)

No. 3084 xvi 40/06, dated the 6th September, 2006

Copy forwarded to the Sub-Collector Koraput/Jeypore, O.S.D (L.R Koraput for information and necessary action taken on the matter may please be intimated to the Office).

Sd/-
Addl. District Magistrate, Koraput

GOVERNMENT OF ORISSA
REVENUE AND DISASTER MANAGEMENT DEPARTMENT

No. 5/2005/39328/RDM, dated the 5th October, 2006

From

Shri S.N. Das
Joint Secretary to Government

To

All Collectors

Subject: Submission of Reports on *suo motu* institution of cases under Section 3A of Regulation 2 of 1956.

Sir,

I am directed to say that in this Deptt. Circular No. 10478

dt. 20.3.2006 it has been clarified in Constitution with the Law Deptt. that a non-S.T person in possession of agricultural land of S.T. person if fails to notify as required under Section 3-B (2) of Regulation 2/56, his occupation becomes unauthorised and as such the competent authority can draw proceedings *suo motu* under Section 3A(1) of the said Regulation, for ejectment and restoration of unauthorised/unlawful possession.

In pursuance of the above clarification and subsequent reminder issued vide this Department letter No. 16324, dt. 2.5.2006 no report his yet been received from you as to action taken by the competent authorities in such cases.

You are, therefore, requested to send sub-division-wise progress of institution of *suo motu* cases u/s 3(A)(1) arising out of under Section 3(B)(2) of Regulation 2 of 1956 immediately by return fax for information of Government.

Further, you are requested to send a report if there is any such vacancy of the post of competent authority during which the above cases could not be initiated.

Yours faithfully
Sd/-
Joint Secretary to Government

Memo No. 38329/RDM, dt 5/10/2006

Copy forwarded to the Secretary, Board of Revenue, Orissa, Cuttack/Land Reforms Commissioner, Orissa, Cuttack/All Revenue Divisional Commissioner for information and necessary action in continuation to this Deptt. letter No. 16324 dt. 2.5.2006.

Sd/-
Joint Secretary to Government

The above provisions under Section 3B 3(b) and 3 (a) shall also apply to all cases which are pending adjudication after the amended provision came into force. Which may be disposed of immediately All Sub-Collectors and all Competent Authorities may be instructed accordingly.

Yours faithfully
Sd/-
Joint Secretary to Government

Memo No. 6901, dated 23.02.2007

Copy forwarded to Officer-on-Special Duty (LR) Panposh for information and necessary action with reference to his letter No.332, dated 03.06.2005.

Sd/-
Joint Secretary to Government

Memo No. 6902, dated 23.02.2007

Copy forwarded to the Secretary, Board of Revenue, Orissa, Cuttack/Land Reforms Commissioner, Orissa Cuttack. All Revenue Divisional Commissioner for information and necessary action.

Sd/-
Joint Secretary to Government

Memo No. 6903, dated 23.02.2007

Copy forwarded to all Sub-Collectors/all O.S.D (LR) for information and necessary action.

Sd/-
Joint Secretary to Government

GOVERNMENT OF ORISSA
REVENUE AND DISASTER MANAGEMENT DEPARTMENT

No. Ag. 20/2005 Dated 23rd February, 2007
Sri S.N. Das
Joint Secretary to Government

To

The Collector, Balasore/ Mayurbhanj / Keonjhar / Sundergarh / Sambalpur / Kalahandi / Kandhamal / Ganjam / Gajapati / Koraput / Rayagada / Malkangiri / Nabarangpur.

Subject: Clarification on application of provision of payment of compensation under section 3B in case if booked under Section 3(2) and 3-A of Regulation 2/1956.

Sir,

I am directed to say that subordinate offices on various occasions have raised the following issues in implementation of provisions of Regulation 2/1956 and sought for clarification of the Government.

1. Whether payment of compensation under section 3B, 3(b) will be applicable to cases under Section 3(2) and 3-A.
2. Whether O.S.D. (LR) action as Competent Authority can entertain cases under Section 3B like Sub-Collector.
3. Whether ST *raiyat* and Non-ST encroacher will enter into registration of any document on settlement of land and in case of payment of compensation, whether any modality and procedure for making award to be outlined.

After obtaining views of Law Department and views of Advocated General, Orissa, Cuttack, and after careful consideration, Government have been pleased to clarify that,

(a) In view of the decision of the Hon'ble Supreme Court of India, in case No. 11483 of 1996, *Amerendra Pratap Singh* Vs. *Tej Bahadur Prajapati and Others,* the payment of compensation under Section 3B, 3(b) to the S.T. owner of the encroached land is also applicable to the case under Section 3(2) and 3-A of Regulation 2/56 to determine the quantum of compensation and settlement of land in favour of Non-ST encroachers.

(b) The O.S.D. (LR) acting as Competent Authority can exercise power under Section 3(2) and 3(A) of Regulation 2/56 to entertain cases and to determine the quantum of compensation and settlement of land with non-ST persons in accordance with Orissa Government Land Settlement of Act 1962 at par with Section 3-B of said Regulation. Prior to settlement of land in favour of non-ST person, Sub-Collector or the Competent Authority shall obtain the prior approval of the concerned Gram Panchayat accorded with the concurrence of Gram Sasan. In case Gram Panchayat refuses approval for granting permission to record the land in favour of non-ST person it shall be referred to Government for taking decision as per the provision contained under Section 3(2) of Regulation 2 of 1956.

(c) The modality and procedure for making award for payment of compensation to the transferor (ST person) as provided under Section 3B 3(b) of Regulation 2/56 is *mutatis mutandis* applicable to the cases under Section 3(2) and 3(A) of said Regulation. On receipt of confirmation on quantum of compensation paid to ST person by non-ST encroacher the land may be settled in favour of non-ST encroacher and for which there is no need of execution of any document in the Registration Office. After settlement of land, the Competent Authority or the Sub-Collector shall send the land schedule along with copy of order to Tahsildar for correction of Records as per Rule 34 (c) of Orissa Survey and Settlement Rules 1962.

(d) The Sub-Collector or Competent Authority shall determine the extent of land over which construction were raised prior to the date of initiation of the proceeding, such determination shall be made by engaging a survey knowing commissioner who shall visit the sport and make measurement. The Sub-Collector or the Competent Authority shall examine such witness as may be necessary for determining the age of the constructions made on the disputed land.

(e) The Sub-Collector or Competent Authority shall, however, implement the order of eviction so far as the portions of the disputed land over which no constructions exists even before or after commencement of Amendment Regulation of 2000 published on 04-9-2002 and the disputed land over which the constructions have been raised after commencement of the Amendment Regulation of 2000. The land so evicted shall be restored to lawful Scheduled Tribe owner of the disputed land over which the constructions have been raised after commencement of the Amendment Regulation of 2000. The land so evicted shall be restored to the lawful Scheduled Tribe owner of the disputed land as per the provisions of Regulation 2 of 1956.

The above permissions under Sections 3B, 3(b), 3(2) and 3(a) shall also apply to all cases which are pending for adjudication after the amended provision came into force which may be disposed of immediately. All Sub-Collectors and all Competent Authority may be instructed accordingly.

Yours faithfully,
Sd/-
Joint Secretary to Government

GOVERNMENT OF ORISSA
REVENUE AND DISASTER MANAGEMENT DEPARTMENT
No. LR (A)-AG-40/2005/43529/ R&DM
Dated 13th October, 2008

From

G.V.V. Sharma
Commissioner and Secretary to Government

To

The Collector, Balasore/Mayurbhanj/ Keonjhar/ Sundergarh / Sambalpur/ Kalubandi/ Kandhamal / Gajapati/ Ganjam / Koraput/ Rayagada

Subject: Submission of information on institution and disposal of cases under Sections 3-B and 3-A of Orissa Scheduled Areas Transfer of Immovable Property (By Scheduled Tribes) Regulation 1956.

Ref: The Department L. No. (1) Ag.5/2005-18261/RDM dated 2.5.2005
12/C (2) L.No. 27798/R, Dt. 14.7.2005;
13/C (3) Memo No. 34197/R, Dt. 22.8.2005, and
(4) L.No. 10478/R, Dt. 20.3.2006 .

Sir,

I am directed to invite a reference on the subject noted above and to any that the Government has been asking you for furnishing information on institution and disposal of cases u/s 3-B of the Regulation 2 of 1956. But it has been seen that the progress requires systematization and improvement.

2. As you are aware, Section 3-B of the Regulation provides that all non-tribals in possession of agricultural land that belonged to a member of a Scheduled Tribe at any time from 4.10.1956 onwards, were required to furnish declaration in the prescribed format to the Sub-Collector by 7.9.2005. You are aware that the Sub-Collectors need to take up *suo mottu* cases under Section 3-A (1) read with 3(B) (2) by scrutiny of Record of Rights, i.e., wherever the non-tribal did not furnish the declaration prior to 7.9.2005 and if it revealed that the R.O.R. shows recorded tenant as a non-tribal in respect of any plot of agricultural land, which was tribal land as per Sabik record. You may note that detained comparative analysis of Sabik and Hal ROR will easily show up the cases requiring *suo mottu* examination by the Sub-Collector, Similarly, for cases in which the non-tribal give the required declaration before 7.9.2005 the Sub-Collector shall take up action as per Section 3-B (3).

3. Therefore, the Regulation requires the Sub-Collector to verify every single case of possession of any agricultural land, which was tribal land at any time after 4.10.1956 but which is now possessed by a non-tribal in Scheduled Areas. You may note that Section 3-B (2) has a presumption clause for non-tribals failing to notify within the stipulated date. The only choice is between Section 3-A (1) read with 3 (B) (2) or action competent authority. In case of the latter, the Sub-Collector will straight away take up the case. In cases where the non-tribal did not notify within 7.9.2005 the former course of action follows. You may please note that no third alternative has been provided in the law.

4. You are also aware that as required under Panchayats Extension to Scheduled Areas Act 1996, the Section 3-A (1) of the Regulation provides that Gram Panchayat can also intimate the competent authority the specific instances of persons in unauthorised possession of tribal lands. You are requested to launch a drive to educate the Gram Panchayat Sarpanches and ward members on this subject, so that they can bring the cases of violation, if any to the notice of the administration through a resolution of the Gram Panchayat.

You are, therefore, requested to take up a special review and report action taken by 30th November, 2008.

This must be treated as *Extremely Important*.

Yours faithfully,

Sd/-

Commissioner and Secretary to Government

Memo No. 43530 / R&DM, Date: 13.10.2008

Copy forwarded to all Sub-Collectors of Scheduled Areas/ All O.S.D. (LR) of Scheduled Areas for information and necessary action.

Sd/-
Joint Secretary to Government

Memo No. 43530 / R&DM, Date: 13.10.2008

Copy to Commissioner and Secretary, ST and SC Development Department / Commissioner and Secretary, Panchayati Raj Department for information.

Sd/-
Joint Secretary to Government

Chapter III (*Continued*)

(D) Judgements of Orissa High Court in 6 J.C. No. 723/68 and Supreme Court of India in C.A. No. 11483/66

202. *Himarika Ramudu and another* Vs. *Kondagori Buchanna and another* (O.J.C. No 723 of 1968) Decided on the 23rd September, 1969 (G.K. Misra C.J. and R.N Misra J.) Judgement delivered by G.K. Misra C.J

Orissa Scheduled Areas Transfer of Immovable Property (By Scheduled Tribes) Regulation 1961, Sections 2, 3 and 7 competent authority—it has power and jurisdiction to make an enquiry—If issue before a competent authority was tribal by Civil Court—Validity of transfer if petitioner disowns transaction and disclaimed the rights.

Legislature was well aware that the non-Scheduled Tribes were exploiting the member of the Scheduled Tribes and if the matter is left to be determined by the Civil Court only when a suit is filed, then in most of the cases justice cannot be meted out. Accordingly provision was made in Section 3(2) vesting power and jurisdiction in the competent authority to make an enquiry as to the real nature of the transaction. Where apparently a transfer is by a member of a Scheduled Tribe in favour of another member of the same Tribe belonging to the Scheduled area the transaction is valid and cannot be assailed. More important cases are where the apparent transaction conceals the real nature of the transaction and it is only in such cases that the competent authority would lift the veil and unveil the true character of the transaction. The power and jurisdiction have been conferred on the competent authority only in such cases. The exercise of this power is not dependent on the filing of an application by a party. The authority can make *suo motu* an enquiry on his own information. But as it involves determination of civil rights, the enquiry is to be made after giving full opportunities to the parties to be heard.

Law is well settled that under Section 9, Civil Procedure Code the Civil Court has got jurisdiction to decide all matters of civil disputes unless the same is barred either expressly or impliedly. Section 3(2) of the Regulation is an express provision vesting jurisdiction in the competent authority to determine questions of the aforesaid nature, namely whether the apparent transfer is a real one. Ordinarily such question are determinable by a Civil Court. But by express provision in Section 3(2) of the Regulation the Civil Court's jurisdiction must necessarily be outside and this is for obviously good reasons. The status was passed as a beneficial measures to prevent exploitation of a class of people belonging to the Scheduled Tribes.

Under the scheme of the Regulation a transfer by a member of the Scheduled Tribe in favour of a member of a non-Scheduled Tribe is wholly null and void. In no case a real transferee would admit that he claims any interest under an ostensible transfer. It is the duty of the competent authority to examine the real character of the transaction and even if the real transferee disclaims any title, it is open to the competent authority on evidence in the enquiry to come to the conclusion that he was the real transferee.

Writ application dismissed

2004(I) CLR (SC)-1

Civil Appeal No. 11483 of 1996
Decided on 21st November, 2003

R.C Lohoti and Ashok Bhan, JJ

Amrendra Pratap Singh—Appellant
Tej Bhadur Prajapati and Ors.—Respondent

A. Limitation Act 1963—Art. 65 and Sec. 27.—When Possession of wrong doer becomes adverse.

Every possession is not in law adverse possession. Under Art. 65 of the Limitation Act 1963, a suit for possession of immovable property or any interest therein based on title can be instituted within a period of 12 years calculated from the date when the possession of the defendant becomes adverse to the plaintiff. By virtue of Section 27 of the Limitation Act at the determination of the period limited by the Act any person for instituting a suit for possession of any property, his right to such property stands extinguished. The process of acquisition of title by adverse possession springs into action essentially by default or inaction of the owner. A person though having no right to enter into possession of the property of someone else, does so and continues in possession setting up title in himself and adversely to the title of the owner, commences prescribing title into himself and such prescription having continued for a period of 12 years, he acquires title not on his own but on account of the default or inaction on the part of the real owner, which stretched over 12 years results into extinguishing of the latter's title. It is that extinguished title of the real owner which comes to vest in the wrongdoer.

B. Doctrine of Adverse Possession: Conditions Necessary for Attracting the Applicability to the Doctrine

The nature of the property, the nature of the title vesting in the rightful owner, and the kind of possession which the adverse possessor is exercising are all relevant factors which enter into consideration for attracting applicability of the Doctrine of Adverse Possession. The right in the property ought to be one which is alienable and is capable of being acquired by the competitor. Adverse possession operates on an alienable right.

C. Orissa Merged States Laws Act 1950 Sec. 7 and Orissa Scheduled Areas Transfer of Immovable Property (By Scheduled Tribes) Regulation 1956—Regulations 3 and 3A Para 7-D inserted by way of amendment in the year 1975, Para 9—While the 1950 Act III imposed a restriction on the transfer of a holding by a member of an aboriginal tribe to a non-member except with the previous permission of the sub-divisional officer concerned, the 1956 Regulation enlarged the scope of the restriction by including, within the purview of prohibition, any transfer of any immovable property except with the previous consent of the competent authority.

HELD the definition 'transfer of immovable property' under the Regulation is very wide. Apart from the well-known modes of transfer such as mortgage, lease, sale, gift and exchange, what has been included therein "any dealing with such property" which is non-testamentary.

Regulation 7-D has amended the provisions of the third column of the Schedule to the limitation Act 1963. The effect of this amendment is that the period of limitation prescribed for suit for possession of immovable property or any interest therein in a suit based on title instead of being 12 years stands substituted by a period of 30 years in the limitation Act which period would begin to run from a point of time when the possession of the defendant becomes adverse to the plaintiff in its applicability to immovable property belonging to a member of a Scheduled Tribe.

D. Limitation Act 1963—Art. 65—Orissa Merged States Laws Act 1950–Sec. 7—Orissa Scheduled Areas Transfer of Immovable Property (By Scheduled Tribes) Regulation 1956 (as amended in 1975)—Sale of land by C and P who are persons belonging to an aboriginal tribe on 21.12.1962 to M who is a person belonging to Scheduled Tribe—M sold a portion of his purchased land to A non-tribal R on 7.4.1964—R sold a part of her purchased land to A non-tribal on 6.5.1975—Suit for declaration of title recovery of possession and permanent injunction by A in 1970—Defendants denied the title of A and pleaded their title by way of adverse possession over the suit land—Question is whether the suit is barred by limitation under Article 65 of the Limitation Act.

HELD, the period upto 6.4.1964 when the land belonged to the tribal has to be excluded from calculating the period of limitation. On 7.4.1964 the land having been sold by a tribal to non-tribal with the previous permission of the sub-divisional officer, the possession of the defendant-respondent No. 1 over the land on and from that shall be treated as hostile. In the suit filed by the plaintiff-appellant in the year 1970 the period of limitation shall have to be calculated by reference to Article 65 of the Limitation Act. By that time only a period of 6 years, i.e., between 1964 and 1970 had elapsed The suit was not barred by limitation.

E. Interpretation of Statutes—Words not defined in the status—Assignment of meaning to such words in the context and setting in which they have been used—Permissibility .

HELD the Court would place such construction on the meaning of the words as would enable the legislative intent being effectuated. Where the object of the legislation is to prevent any mischief and to confer protection on the weaker sections of the society the Court would not hesitate in placing an extended meaning, even a stretched one, in the word, if in doing so the status would succeed in attaining the object sought to be achieved.

Referred to:

(i) (1984) 3 SCR 502 1984(1) SCALE 632 *Manchegowda* Vs. *State*; 18
(ii) (1984) 2 SCR 244 *Lingappa* Vs. *State*; 18
(iii) (1965) 1 SCR 195 *Gamini* Vs. *Guraza;* 18
(iv) (1987) 1 Allear 20 (HL) *D* (a Minor) Vs. *Bershir;* 18
(v) AIR 1992 Orissa 5 *Laxmi* Vs. *Dandasi;* 28
(vi) 65 (1988) CLT 360: *Madhia* Vs. *Arjuna;* 28
(vii) (1986) 1 SCC 83 *Sanjay* Vs. *State;* 17
(viii) 1992 Sup (2) SCC 77 *Pendey* Vs. *Ram;* 18
(ix) (1977) 2 SCC 435 *State* Vs. *Babu;* 9
(x) AIR 1923 Privy Council 205 *Waman* Vs. *Rajhunath;* 24
(xi) AIR 1993 MP 132 *Jagdish* Vs. *State*; 21
(xii) 1992 Rev Nirmay 270 *Wajeram* Vs. *Kanram*; 21
(xiii) 1995 Reve Nimay 358 *Dimesh* Vs. *State*; 21
(xiv) AIR (36) 1949 Nagpur 265 *Kanmulkhan* Vs. *Bhanupratap.* 24

Result: Appeal allowed.

JUDGEMENT

R.C. Lahoti, J.—The suit property consists of piece of agricultural land situated in Sundergarh area of mouza Durgapur. Rourkela prior to the year 1962. The property belonged to Chard Oram and Pera Oram. Both of them belong to Oraon tribe, which is a Scheduled Tribe in the State of Orissa as notified *vide* the Constitution Scheduled Tribe Order 1950 issued in exercise of the powers conferred by clause (1) of Article 342 of the Constitution of India on 21.12.1962. Chand and Pera transferred their right and interest in 0.75 decimals of land in favour of one a Mangal Singh Manki. The said Mangal Singh Manki was also a person belonging to a Scheduled Tribe. Mangal Singh Manki, after obtaining the permission of the Sub-Divisional Officer, Panposh sold 0.40 decimals of land by a registered deed of sale dated 7.4.1964 executed in favour of one Ratnamani Mahapatra, and of the same day by another registered deed of land transferred of the remaining 0.35 decimals of land to one Harihar

Pradhan on 6.9.1975. Dr. Amarendra Pratap Singh, the plaintiff-appellant purchased 0.195 decimals of land out of 0.40 decimals from Ratnamani Mohapatra. It is this land purchased by the plaintiff has come to be numbered as plot No. 1147/1.

2. According to the plaintiff he raised construction in the year 1965 over 0.05 decimal area out of the land purchased by him. When he proposed to raise construction over the remaining area he was constructed in doing so by Harihar Pradhan, the owner of the adjoining land, whereupon the plaintiff got in touch with his predecessor in title Smt. Ratnamani Mahapatra. It was detected that in the map attached with the Sale Deed dated 6.9.1965 there was some error in description of the land forming the subject matter of sale. Smt. Ratnamani Mahapatra executed a deed of rectification dated 31.8.1968 in favour of the plaintiff appellant, after having the land demarcated by Amin.

3. During the course of demarcation proceedings it was found that the defendant-responded No. 1 had purchased some land under a registered deed of sale dated 25.4.1967 from Chand and Pera and constructed two buildings thereon. However, the defendant-respondent No. 1 who had purchased land plot thereon. However, the defendant-respondent No. 1 who had purchased land plot No. 1147 (new plot No. 956) belonging to the plaintiff-appellant.

4. The dispute between the parties led to the initiation of proceedings under Section 145 of the Code of Criminal Procedure in the year 1970, the plaintiff appellant filed a suit for declaration of title recovery 1970, the plaintiff appellant filed a suit for declaration of title, recovery of possession and issuance of permanent preventive injunction against the defendants. The defendant Nos. 1 to 3, who are the principal contesting defendants, denied the title of the plaintiff and pleaded their title by way of adverse possession on the suit land. The Trial Court decreed the suit and directed possession over the suit property to be restored to the plaintiff after demolition of the construction of the defendant No. 1 standing on the suit land. The defendant No. 1 preferred an appeal to the High Court. The High Court found the title of the plaintiff-respondent No. 1 to be the High Court. The High Court found the title of the plaintiff-respondent No. 1 to be proved but at the property for the prescribed statutory period of 12 years and, therefore, held the plaintiff-respondent No. 1 not entitled to a decree in the suit. The High Court reverse the judgement

and decree of the Trial Court and directed the suit to be dismissed feeling aggrieved, the plaintiff has filed this appeal by special leave.

5. On behalf of the plaintiff-appellant the correctness of the finding as to defendant No. 1 respondent being in adverse possession of the property and having perfected his title by being in continuous and uninterrupted possession of the property for a period exceeding 12 years time was seriously disputed, however, we are not inclined to enter into any revaluation of evidence and dislodge the finding of fact arrived at by the High Court. We would therefore proceed on an assumption that the defendant-respondent No. 1 has remainded in possession of the property for a period of more than 12 years before the date of the institution of the suit. The real question is—whether he can be said to have perfected his title by way of adverse possession? This question assumes significant because of the fact that the original owners of the land, namely, Chand and Pera, were persons belonging to a Scheduled Tribe and their successor-in-title Mangal Singh Manki was also a person belonging to the Scheduled Tribe.

6. The Orissa Merged States' Law Act 1950 was enacted by the Legislative Assembly of Orissa for the purpose of extending certain Acts and Regulation to certain area administered as part of the State of Orissa. It received the assent of the Governor on 26.2.1950, which was published in the Orissa Gazette on 3.3.1950 and on that date the Act came into force. Section 7 of the Act in so far as is relevant for our purpose provided as under Section 7 Modification of Tenancy Laws in force in the merged States—

Notwithstanding anything contained in the tenancy laws of the merged States as continued in force by virtue of Article 4 of the States Merged (Governor's Provinces) Order 1949—

× × × × ×

(b) An occupancy tenant shall be entitled.—(i) To freely transfer his holding subject to the restriction that no transfer of a holding for a member of an aboriginal tribe to a member of a non-aboriginal tribe shall be valid unless such transfer is made with the previous permission of the Sub-divisional Officer concerned.

(ii) To have full right over all kinds of trees standing on his holding.

(iii) To use the land comprised in the holding in any manner which does not materially impact the value of the land or renders it unfit for the purposes of the tenancy.

(iv) To the benefit of the presumption by any Court that the rent for time to time being payable by him is fair and equitable until the contrary is proved.

Explanation—(i) An occupancy tenant means tenant or a raiyat having occupancy right in his holding under the tenancy laws continued in force in the merged States.

(ii) An aboriginal tribe means any tribe that may from time to time be notified as such by the State Government.

7. Article 244 of the Constitution provides for the provisions of the Fifth Schedule being applicable to the administration and control of the scheduled area and Scheduled Tribe in any State other than the State of Assam, Meghalaya Tripura and Mizoram. Para 5 of the Fifth Scheduler provides *inter alia* for the Governor to make regulation which may prohibit or restrict the transfer of land by or among the members of the Scheduled Tribe in such area and/or to regulate the allotment of land to members of the Scheduled Tribe in such area.

8. In exercise of the powers conferred by sub-para 2 of paragraph 5 of the Fifth Schedule to the Constitution the Governor of Orissa Promulgated regulations known as the Orissa Scheduled Area Transfer of Immovable Property (By Scheduled Tribe) Regulation 1956 (hereinafter referred to as the Regulations in short) The assent of the President was received on 21.9.1956 and published in the Orissa Gazette Extraordinary on 4.10.1956 on which date the Regulations came into force. The preamble of the Regulation speaks that the same were promulgated as it was considered expedient to control and check transfer of immovable property by the Scheduled Tribe in the scheduled areas of the State of Orissa. Clause (f) of para 2 of the Regulation defines transfer of immovable property to mean mortgage with or without possession lease, sale, gift, exchange or *any other dealing with such property* not being testamentary disposition and includes a charge or contract relating to such property : emphasis supplied) Regulation 3 provides as under:

3. Transfer of Immovable Property by a member of the Scheduled Tribe.—(i) Notwithstanding anything contained in any law for the time being in force, any transfer of immovable property situated within a Scheduled Area by a member of a Scheduled Tribe shall be absolutely null and void and of no force or effect whatsoever unless made in favour of another member of a Scheduled Tribe or with the previous consent in writing of a competent authority.

Provided that nothing in this sub-section shall apply to any transfer by way of mortgage executed in favour of any public financial institution of securing a loan granted by such institution for any agricultural purpose.

Provided further that in execution of any decree for realization of the mortgage money no property mortgaged as aforesaid shall be sold in favour of any person not being a number of the Scheduled Tribe of the previous consent in writing of the competent authority.

Explanation—For the purposes of this sub-section, a transfer of immovable property in favour of a female member of a Scheduled Tribe, who is married to a person who does not being to any Scheduled Tribe, shall be deemed to be a transfer made in favour of a person not belonging to a Scheduled Tribe.

(2) Where a transfer of immovable property is made in contravention of Sub-section (1), the competent authority may either on application by any one interested therein or in his own motion and after giving the parties an opportunity of being heard order ejectment against any person in possession of the property to the transfer or his heirs in causing such restoration of possession the competent authority may take such steps as may be necessary for securing compliance with the said order or preventing any breach of peace.

Provided that the competent authority is of the opinion that the restoration of possession of immovable property to the transfer or his heirs is not reasonably practicable, he shall record his reasons thereof and shall subject to the control of the State Government settle the said property with any other person in accordance with the provisions contained in the Orissa Government Land Settlement Act 33 of 1962.

Explanation—Restoration of possession means actual delivery of possession by the competent authority to the Transfer or his heirs.

(3) Subject to such conditions as may be prescribed an appeal if preferred within thirty days of the order under Sub-section (2) shall, if made by the Collector, lie to the Board of Revenue; and if made by any other competent authority to the Collector or any other office specially empowered by the State Government in this behalf.

(4) Subject to the provisions of Sub-section (3) the decision of the competent authority under Sub-section (2) shall be final and shall not be challenged in Court of law.

(underlining by us)

9. Under Regulation 3A, where a person is found to be in unauthorised occupation of any immovable property of a member of the Scheduled Tribe by way of a trespass or otherwise the competent authority may either on application by the owner or any person interested therein, or on his own motion, and after giving the parties concerned an opportunity of being heard, order ejectment of the person so found to be in unauthorised occupation and shall cause restoration of possession of such property to the said member of the scheduled tribe or to his heirs.

10 In the year 1975 by Orissa Regulation No 1/1975 para 7-D was inserted by way of amendment along with a few other amendment Para 7-D read as under.

> 7-D. *Amendment of the Limitation Act, 1963 in its application the Scheduled Areas*—In the Limitation Act 1963 in its application to the Scheduled Areas in the Schedule *after the words* 'twelve years' occurring in the second column against Act 65, the word 'twelve years' and figure '30 years' in relation to immovable property belonging to a member a Scheduled Tribe specified in respect of the State of Orissa in the Constitution (Scheduled Tribe) Order 1950 as modified from time to time, *shall be added*)'

11 This amendment was given retrospective operation with effect from 2.10.1973

12. Para 9 of the Regulation partially repealed the Orissa Merged States (Laws) Act 1950. The relevant extracts is as under:

"**9. Repeal**—(1) On and from the date of commencement of this regulation shall stand repealed namely,

(a) xxx xxx xxx
(b) The enactments mentioned in column 2 of the Schedule to the extent specified in column 3 thereof in so far as they are in force in the Scheduled Areas.

SCHEDULE
List of Enactments Repealed

Number and Year	*Short Title*	*Extent of Repeal*
1	2	3
1. x x x	2. x x x	3. x x x
2. Orissa Act IV of 1950	Orissa Merged State Laws Act 1950	The Words Subject to the restrictions that no transfer of a holding from a member of an aboriginal tribe shall be valid unless such transfer is made with the previous permission of the Sub-divisional Magistrate concerned in item 1 of Clause (d) of the section shall be omitted.

13. The position emerging from the fact of the case found proved or undisputed and the relevant position of law, as emerging from the Act and the Regulation referred to herein above may be summed up. The original holders of the land, namely, Chand and Pera were persons belonging to an aboriginal 'tribe i.e. Oraon' Sundergarh the area where the land is situated is a tribal area. Chand and Pera Oram held the land as occupancy tenants. They could not have transferred their holding to a member of a non-original tribe though the transfer of holding by a member of one aboriginal tribe to a member of the same or another aboriginal tribe was permitted. This restriction contained to remain in force by virtue of Section 7-D of the Orissa Merged States' Laws Act 1950 from the year 1956. That restriction came to be deleted by a Para 9 read with Entry 2 to the Schedule to the 1956 Regulation. But then the same restriction came to be imposed independently by Para 3 of the Regulation. While the 1950 Act imposed a restriction of the transfer of holding by a member of an aboriginal tribe to non-member except with the previous permission of the sub-divisional officer concerned, the 1956 regulations enlarged the scope of the restriction by including, within the purview of prohibition any transfer of any immovable property except with the

previous consent in writing of the competent authority. The immovable property, referred to in para 3 of the Regulation. While the 1950 Act imposed a restriction on the transfer of a holding by a member of an aboriginal tribe to a non-member except with the previous permission of the sub-divisional officer concerned, the 1956 regulations enlarged the scope of the restriction by including, within the purview of prohibition any transfer of any immovable property except with the previous consent in writing of the competent authority. The immovable property, referred to in para 3 of Regulation, would obviously include a holding as well. The Regulations define transfer of immovable property. The definition is very wide. Apart from the well-known modes of transfer such as mortgage, lease, sale, gift and exchange what has been included therein is any dealing with such property" which is non-testamentary Regulation 7-D has amended the provisions of the third column of the Schedule to the Limitation Act 1963. The effect of this amendment is that the period of Limitation prescribed for suit for possession of immovable property or any interest therein in a suit based on title instead of being 12 years stands substituted by a period of 30 years in the Limitation Act which period would being to run from a point of time when the possession of the defendant becomes adverse to the plaintiff in its applicability to immovable property belonging to a member of a Scheduled Tribe such as 'Oraon' What is the scope of Regulation 7-D and to what immovable properties it would apply, shall be examined a little later.

14. It cannot be dispute that until 7.4.1964 the lands was owned by Chand and Pera and then by Mangal Singh, all the three being members of the aboriginal tribe and Scheduled Tribe. On 7.4.1964, the land came to be transferred to a person not belonging to any aboriginal tribe. Proceeding on the premise that in the year 1970 on the date of the filing of the suit (the exact date not being ascertainable) the defendant No. 1 had been in possession of the property for a period of more than 12 years. Can it be said that he had perfected his title by adverse possession or that the suit filed by the plaintiff had become barred by time on account of having been filed 12 years after the date when the possession of the defendant became adverse to the plaintiff or his predecessors-in-title? The period for which the defendant claims to be in possession had to be divided into period for which the defendant claims to be in possession had to be divided into two parts (i) the pre 7.4.1964 period when the ownership of the land vested in the person or persons who belonged to an aboriginal

tribe and (ii) post 7.4.1964 period when the ownership had come to vest in person belonging to a non-aboriginal tribe consequent upon a transfer made by the previous permission of Competent Authority. Two questions arise for consideration, firstly what is the meaning to be assigned to the expression 'transfer of immovable property' in relation to property owned by a member of a Scheduled Tribe to whom the Regulations apply; and secondly whether right by adverse possession can be acquired by a non-aboriginal on the property belonging to a member of an aboriginal tribe. The 1956 Regulations have chosen to assign an extended meaning to the expression 'transfer of immovable property' so as to include within its meaning not only such methods of testamentary disposition as are known to result in transferring an interest in immovable property but also and 'dealing' with such property as would have the effect of causing or resulting in the transfer of interest in immovable property is included therein. According to the Chambers Twentieth Century Dictionary (New Edition 1983) 'deal' as verb means [to divide to distribute], to throw about, to deliver and deal with means to have to do with, to treat of to take action in regard to: One of the meanings to the word 'deal' assigned in Black Law Dictionary (6th Edition) is to traffic. Dictionaries can be taken as safe guides for finding out meaning of such words as are not defined in the statute. However, dictionaries are not the final words on interpretation. The words take colour from the context and the setting in which they have been used. It is permissible to assign a meaning or a sense restricted or wider than the one given in dictionaries depending on the scheme of the legislation wherein the words has been used. The court would place such construction on the meaning of the words as would enable the legislative intent being effectuated. Where the object of the legislation is to prevent any mischief and to confer protection on the object of the legislation is to prevent any mischief and to confer protection on the weaker sections of the society, the court would not hesitate in placing an extended meaning, even a stretched one, on the word, if in doing so the statute would succeed in attaining the object sought to be achieved. We may refer to Principles of Statutory Interpretation by Justice G.P. Singh (Eighth Edition 2001) wherein at pp. 279-280 the learned author states—"in selecting one out of the various meaning of a word, regard must always be had to the context as it is a fundamental rule that "the meaning of words and expression used in an Act must take their colour from the context in which they appear".

Therefore "when the context makes colour from the context in which they appear". Therefore, "when the context makes the meaning of a word quite clear it becomes unnecessary to search for and select a particular meaning out of the diverse meanings a word is capable of according to lexicographers' Judge Learned Hand cautioned not to make a fortress out of the dictionary but to pay more attention to the sympathetic and fortress out of the dictionary but to pay more attention to the sympathetic and imaginative discovery of the purpose or object of the statute as a guide to its meaning".

15. Tribal areas have their own problems. Tribals are historically weaker sections of the society. They need the protection of the laws as they are gullible and fall pray to the tactics of unscrupulous people and are susceptible to exploitation on account of their innocence poverty and backwardness extending over centuries. The Constitution of India and the laws made thereunder treat tribal and tribal areas separately whether needed. The tribals need to be settled, need to be taken care of by the protective arm of the law, and be saved from falling prey to unscrupulous device so that they may prosper and by an evolutionary process join the mainstream of the society. The process would be slow. Yet it has to be initiated and kept moving. The object sought to be achieved by the 1950 Act and the 1956 Regulations is to see that member of an aboriginal tribe indefeatably continuous to own the property which he acquires and every process known to law by which title in immovable property is extinguished in one person indefeatably continues to own the property which he acquires and every process indefeatably continues to own the property which he acquires and every process known to law by which title in immovable property is extinguished in one person to vest in another person, should remain so confined in its operation in relation to tribal that the immovable property of one tribal may come to vest in another tribal but the title in immovable property vesting in any tribal must not come to vest in a non-tribal. This is to see and ensure that non-tribals do not succeed in making in-roads amongst the tribal by acquiring property and developing roots in the habit of tribals.

16. In support of the proposition that the expression 'transfer of immovable property' is capable of being assigned an extended meaning depending on the context and the setting in which it has been used so as to include in its meaning. We may refer to a few decided cases.

17. The Maharashtra Agricultural Lands (Ceiling on holdings)

Act 1961 imposed a ceiling on holding land and to effectuate the purpose sought to be achieved by the legislation, imposed restrictions on the transfer or partition of any land on or after the appointed date. Transfer was defined to mean transfer by and parties whether by sale, gift, mortgage with possession, exchange, lease or any other disposition (underlining by us) made inter vivos. This Court in *Sanjay Dinkar Asarkar* Vs. *State of Maharashtra and Anr.* (1986) SCC 83 placed an object-oriented interpretation on the term 'disposition' and held—"Though ordinarily the word 'disposition' in relation to property would mean disposition made by a deed or will but in the act it has to be given an extended meaning so as to include therein any disposition made by or under a decree or order of the Court".

18. In *Pandey Orson* Vs. *Ram Chander Sahu and Ors.* 1992 Supp.(2) SCC 77 the term 'transfer' as used in Section 71A of Chhotanagpur Tenancy Act 1980 came up for the consideration of the Court "Transfer" was not defined in the Act. It was held that considering the situation in which the exercise of jurisdiction is contemplated, it would not be proper to confine the meaning of 'transfer' to transfer under the Transfer of Property Act or a situation where 'transfer' has a statutory definition what exactly is contemplated by transfer in Section 71A is, where possession has passed from one to another and as a physical fact the member of Scheduled Tribe who is entitled to hold possession has lost it and a non-member has come into possession, would be covered by 'transfer' non-member has come into possession would be covered by 'transfer Their lordships observed "The provision is beneficial and the legislative intention is to extend protection to a class of citizens who are not in a position to keep their property to themselves in the absence of protection. Therefore, when the legislature is extending special protection to the named category, the Court had to give a liberal construction to the protective mechanism which would work out the protection and enable the sphere of protection to be effective than limit by its scope". Their Lordship referred to three earlier decisions of this court, namely. *Manchegowa* Vs. *State of Karnatake,* (1984) 3 SCR 502; *Lingappa Pochanna Appelwar* Vs. *State of Maharashtra,* (1984) 2 SCR 224; *Gamini Krishnayya* Vs. *Guraza Seshachalam* (1965) 1SCR 195 and a decision of House of Lords in *D* (a minor) *Vs. Bershire County Council,* (1987) 1 AIIER 20 (HL) laying down the proposition that a broad and liberal construction should be given to give full effect to the legislative purpose.

19. *State of Madhya Pradesh* Vs. *Babu Lal and Ors.,* 1997 (2) SCC 435 is an interesting case showing how this Court dealt with an artistic device employed by a non-tribal to deprive a tribal of his land. The MP Land Revenue Code 1959 imposed restrictions on the transfer of land by members of a Scheduled Tribe **Babu Lal** a non-tribal filed a suit for declaration against Baddiya, a Bhel, Notified Scheduled Tribe, for declaration that his name be recorded in the revenue record as Bhumiswami over the land of Baddiya. Baddiya did not contest the suit and the parties filed a compromise conceding to the claim of Babu Lal. The State Government intervened and filed a petition in the High Court seeking a writ of *certiorari*, submitting that the entire proceedings in the suit were in contravention of Sub-section (6) of Section 165 of the M.P. Land Revenue Code 1959. The judgement of the Civil Court based on compromise was sought to be quashed. The High Court dismissed the petition holding that the State could pursue the alternative remedy of filling a suit for declaration that the decree was null and void in appeal by special leave, this Court set aside the judgement of the High Court and issued a writ of *certiorari* to quash the judgement and decree passed in the civil suit it was held. One of the principles on which *certiorari* is issued, where the Court acts illegally and there is error on the face of record if the court usurps the jurisdiction, the record is corrected by *certiorari.* This case is a glaring instance of such violation of law. The High Court was in error in not issuing writ of *certiorari.* (underlining by us)

20. The law laid down by this Court is an authority for the proposition that the Court shall step in and annul any such transaction as would have the effect of violating a provision of law, more so when it is a beneficial piece of social legislation. A simple declaratory decree passed by a civil Court which had the effect of extinguishing the title of a member of a Scheduled Tribe and vesting the same in a non-member was construed as 'transfer' within the meaning of Section 165(6) of the M.P. Land Revenue Code 1959. Thus, we are very clear in our minds that the expression 'transfer of immovable property' as defined in clause (f) of para 2 of the 1956 regulations has to be assigned a very wide meaning. Any transaction or dealing with immovable property which would have the effect of extinguishing title possession or right to possess such property in a tribal and vesting the same in a non-tribal, would be included within the meaning of 'transfer of immovable property'.

21. In a series of decisions, the High Court of Madhya Pradesh has been consistently taking this view. The writ see *Jagdish* Vs. *State of Madhya Pradesh,* AIR 1993 MP 132; *Wajeram* Vs. *Kaniram*. 1992 Revenue Nirnaya 270; *Dinesh Kumar and Anr*. Vs. *State of Madhya Pradesh*, 1995 *Revenue Nirnya* 358.

22. What is adverse possession? Every possession is not, in law, adverse possession. Under Article 65 of the Limitation Act 1963, a suit for possession of immovable property or any interest therein based on title can be instituted within a period of 12 years calculated from the date when the possession of the defendant becomes adverse to the plaintiff. By virtue of Section 27 of the Limitation Act at the determination of the period limited by the Act to any person for instituting a suit for possession of any property, his right to such property stands extinguished. The process of acquisition of title by adverse possession springs into action essentially by default or inaction of the owner. A person, though having no right to enter into possession of the property of someone else, does so and continues in possession setting up title in himself and adversely to the title of the owner, commences prescribing title into himself and such prescription having continued for a period of 12 years, he acquires title not on his own but on account of the default of inaction on the part of the real owner, which stretched over a period of 12 years resulting into extinguishing of the latter's title. It is that extinguished title of the real owner which comes to vest in the Wrongdoer, the law does not intend to confer any premium on the wrong doing of a person in wrongful possession has defaulted and remained inactive for a period of 12 years, which the law considers reasonable for attracting the said penalty inaction for a period of 12 years is treated by the Doctrine of Adverse Possession as evidence of the loss of desire on the part of the rightful owner to assert his ownership and reclaim possession.

23. The nature of the property, the nature of title vesting in the rightful owner, the kind of possession which the adverse possessor is exercising, are all relevant factors which enter into consideration for attracting applicability of the Doctrine of Adverse Possession. The right in the property ought to be one which is alienable and is capable of being acquired by the competitor. Adverse possession operates on an alienable right. The right stands alienated by operation of law, for it was capable of being alienated voluntarily and is sought to be recognized by doctrine of adverse possession as having been alienated involuntarily, by default and inaction on the part of the rightful

claimant, who knows actually or constructively of the wrongful acts of the competitor and yet sits idle. Such inaction or default in taking care of one's own right over property is also capable of being called a manner of 'dealing' with one's property which results in extinguishing one's title in property and vesting the same in the wrong doer in possession of property and thus amounts of 'transfer of immovable property' in the wider sense assignable in the context of social welfare legislation enacted with the object of protecting a weaker section.

24. In *Madhavrao Waman Saundalegkar and Ors. Vs. Raghunath Venkatesh Deshpande and Ors.*, A.I.R. 1923 Privy Council 205, their Lordships of the Privy Council dealt with a case of Watan lands and observed that it is somewhat difficult to see how a stranger to a Watan can acquire a title by adverse possession for 12 years of lands, then alienation of which is, in the interests of the State, prohibited. The Privy Council's decision was notified in *Karimulakhan S/o Mohd. Ishaqkhan and Anr.* Vs. *Bhanupratap Singh,* A.I.R (36) 1948 Nagpur 265, and the High Court noted non-availability of any direct decision on the point and resorted to borrowing from analogy. It was held that title by adverse possession on Inam lands, Wata lands and Debutter, was incapable of acquisition.

25. Reverting back to the facts of the case at hand, we find that in the land, the ultimate ownership vests in the State on the principle of eminent domain Tribals are conferred with a right to hold land, which right is inalienable in favour of non-tribals. It is clear that the law does not permit a right in immovable property vesting in a tribal to be transferred in favour of a acquired by a non-tribals unless permitted by the previous sanction of a competent authority. The definition of 'transfer of immovable property' has been coined in the widest possible terms The definition makes a reference to all known modes of transferring right, title and interest in immovable property and to make the definition exhaustive, conspicuously employs the expression "any other dealing with such property" which would embrace within its sweep any other mode having an impact on right, title or interest of the holder, causing it to cease in one and vest or accrue in another. The use of the word 'dealing' is suggestive of the legislative intent that not only a transfer as such but any dealing with such property (though such dealing may not, in law, amount to transfer) is sought to be included within the meaning of the expression. Such 'dealing' because of the default or inaction of the tribal as a

result of his ignorance, property or backwardness, which shall be presumed to have existed when the property of the tribal is taken possession of or otherwise appropriated or sought to be appropriate by a non-tribal. In other words, a default or inaction on the part of a tribal which results in deprivation or deterioration of his rights over immovable property would amount to 'dealing' by him with such property, and hence a transfer of immovable property. It is so because a tribal is considered by the legislature not to be capable of protecting his own immovable property. A provision has been made by para 3A of the 1956 Regulations for evicting any unauthorized occupant, by way of trespass or otherwise, of any immovable property of the member of the Scheduled Tribe, the steps in regard to which may be taken by the tribal or by any person interested therein or even *suo motu* by the competent authority. The concept of *locus standi* loss its significance. The State is the custodian and trustee of the immovable property of tribals and is enjoined to see that the tribal remains in possession of such property. No period of limitations is prescribed by para 3A. The prescription of the period of 12 years in Articles 65 of the Limitation Act becomes irrelevant so far as the immovable property of a tribal is concerned. The tribal need not file a civil suit which will be governed by law of limitation, it is enough if he or anyone on his behalf moves the State or the State itself moves into action to protect him and restore his property to him. To such an action neither Article 65 of Limitation Act nor Section 27 thereof would be attracted.

26. In our opinion, the above said shall be the position of law under the 1956 Regulations where 'transfer of immovable property' has been defined and also under the 1950 Act where 'transfer of holding' has not been defined. Acquisition of title in favour of a non-tribal by invoking the Doctrine of Adverse Possession over the immovable property belonging to tribal is prohibited by law and cannot be countenanced by the Court.

27. The period upto 6.4.1964, during which the land belonged to the tribals, has to be excluded from calculating the period of limitation. Undoubtedly on 7.4.1964 the land having been sold by a tribal to a non-tribal with the previous permission of the sub-divisional officer, the possession of defendant-respondent No. 1 over the land on and from that date shall be treated as hostile. In the suit filed by the plaintiff-appellant in the year 1970 the period of limitation shall have to be calculated by reference to Article 65 of the Limitation Act. By

that time only a period of 6 years, i.e., between 1964 and 1970 had elapsed. The suit was not barred by limitation.

28. The learned counsel for the respondents relied heavily on Para 7-D of the 1956 Regulations and upon two decisions of the Orissa High Court rendered by reference thereto namely *Laxmi Gouda and Ors. Vs. Dandasi Goura (deceased by LR) and Ors.* AIR 1992 Orissa 5 and *Madhia Nayak Vs. Arjuna Pradhan and Ors.* 65 (1988) *Cuttack Law Times* 360. We have carefully perused both the decisions. The question which arose for decision therein was the effect of amendment made in Para 7-D of the Regulation and given a retrospective operation with effect from a back date. The High Court has held that if adverse possession extending over a period of 12 years had already stood perfected into acquisition of title before the date of the amendment, then the amended provision could not be read so as to extend the period of 12 years of acquisition of title by adverse possession substituted as 30 years even if such date fell after 2.10.1973, the date with which the amendment commenced operating. The question which is arising for decision before us namely whether a non-tribal can at all commence prescribing acquisition of title of adverse possession over the land belonging to a tribal and situated in a tribal area was neither raised before High Court nor decided by it. A judicial decision is an authority of what it actually decides and not for what can be read into it by implication or by assigning an assumed intention to the judges, and inferring from it a proposition of law which the judges have not specifically laid down in the pronouncement. Still we make it clear that the provision of Para 7-D of the Regulation are to be read in the light of the principle which we have laid down herein above. A tribal may acquire title by adverse possession over the immovable property of another tribal by reference to adverse possession over the immovable property of another tribal by reference to Para 7-D of the Regulations read with Article 65 and Section 27 of the Limitation Act 1963, but a non-tribal can neither prescribe nor acquire title by adverse possession over the property belonging to a tribal as the same is specifically prohibited by a special law promulgated by the State Legislature or the Governor in exercise of the powers conferred in that regard by the Constitution of India. A general law cannot defeat the provisions of a special law to the extent to which they are in conflict; else an effort has to be made at reconciling the two provisions by homogeneous reading.

29. Having held that the wrongful possession of the defendant-

respondent No. 1 over the land purchased by the plaintiff-appellant has not ripened into acquisition of title by adverse possession, the next question which arises for decision is in relation to the appropriate relief which should be allowed to the plaintiff-appellant. There was a controversy before the trial court as to the exact extent of land and of encroachment on the property belonging to the plaintiff appellant by the defendant-respondent, as the two properties are adjoining. The plaintiff-appellant relied on the report of Amin while the trial court had also got a survey conducted by a local commissioner who had filed his report. The High Court has not recorded any specific finding thereon because of the view taken by it on the plea of adverse possession resulting in dismissal of the suit.

30. The other question which arises is as to the construction made by defendant-respondent No 1 over the property of the plaintiff-appellant encroached upon by defendant-respondent No. 1 During the course of hearing, it was submitted by the learned counsel for defendant-respondent No. 1 that huge construction has come up over the property in suit, while according to the plaintiff-appellant some construction, rather a major portion thereof, has taken place during the pendency of the appeal in this Court as no interim relief was granted by the Court though it was prayed for by the plaintiff-appellant.

31. On these two aspects the case needs to be remanded to the trial Court for the ends of justice and determination of appropriate relief. We propose to made suitable direction in this regard in the operative part of the judgement.

32. *The appeal is allowed.* The judgement of the High Court is set aside. The case is remanded to the trial Court for decision in accordance with the following directions:

(1) The trial Court shall find if an undisputed or proved map of the land belonging to the plaintiff-appellant demarcating the area encroached upon by defendant-respondent No. 1 is available on record, and if so, the same shall be accepted and made a part of the decree; if not, the trial court shall appoint an Advocate Commissioner assisted by a person proficient in survey to draw up a map of the plaintiff-appellant's land and demarcate specifically therein the area encroached upon by defendant-respondent No. 1.

(2) The trial Court shall determine, after hearing the learned

counsel for the parties and if necessary by recording additional evidence whether a decree for demolition of the construction, made by defendant-respondent No. 1 and specific restoration of possession to plaintiff-appellant, is called for. In the alternative, the trial Court shall determine if, in spite of the encroachment having been proved, a decree for the award of suitable compensation in lieu of demolition and restoration of possession would be a more appropriate relief.

Chapter IV

(A) Extracts of Orissa Land Reforms Act and Rules

(A) Extracts of Sections 22, 22A. To 23-A, 23-B of Orissa Land Reforms Act and Rules as Amended from Time to Time

Section 22. Restriction on alienation of land by Scheduled Tribe.—(1) (Any transfer) of a holding or part thereof by a *raiyat*, belonging to a Scheduled Tribe shall be void except where it is in favour of—

(a) a person belonging to a Scheduled Tribe; or

(b) a person not belonging to a Scheduled Tribe when such transfer is made with the previous permission in writing of the Revenue Officers:

Provided that in case of a transfer by sale the Revenue Officer shall not grant such permission unless he is satisfied that a purchaser belonging to a Scheduled Tribe willing to pay the market price for the land is not available, and in case of gift unless he is satisfied about the *bona fides* thereof..

(2) The State Government may having regard to the law and custom applicable to any area prior to the date of commencement of this Act by notification direct that the restrictions provided in sub-section (1) shall not apply to land situated in such area or belonging to any particular tribe throughout the State or in any part of it.

(3) Except with the written permission of the Revenue Officer, no such holding shall be sold in execution of a decree to any person not belonging to a Scheduled Tribe.

---

1. Substituted by Act 13 of 1965.
2. Substituted by Act 9 of 1974.

(4) Notwithstanding anything contained in any other law for the time being in force, where any document required to be registered under the provisions of clause (a) to clause (e) of sub-section (1) of Section 17 of the Registration Act 1908 (16 of 1908) purports to effect transfer of a holding or part thereof by *a raiyat* belonging to a Scheduled Tribe, in favour of a person not belonging to a Scheduled Tribe, no registering officer appointed under that Act shall register any such documents, unless such documents is accompanied by the written permission of the Revenue Officer for such transfer.

(5) The provisions contained in Sub-section (1) to (4) shall apply *mutatis mutandis*, to the transfer of a holding or part thereof *a raiyat* belonging to the Scheduled Caste.

(6) Nothing in this Section shall apply—

(a) to any sale in execution of a money decree passed, or to any transfer by way of mortgage executed, in favour of any scheduled bank or in favour of any block to which the Orissa Co-operative Societies Act 1962 (2 of 1963) applies, and

(b) to any transfer by a member of a Scheduled Tribe within a Scheduled Area.

Case laws: Accordingly permission for sale of immovable property of person belonging to scheduled caste/scheduled tribe to a non-scheduled caste/tribe is necessary and as such even homestead lands would also come within the regions of the provisions. But only exception of such sale of homestead land is that the same should not be connected with incidental or ancillary to agriculture—85 (1998) CLT 411, (*Siba Behara* Vs. *Manguli*)

Land mortgaged long before the OLR Act came into force but sale deed was executed in the year 1973 without obtaining prior permission as contemplated. The transaction would be hit by Section 23 of the Act. But since possession was must prior to the coming of the Act in operation by virtue of mortgage, the transaction cannot be held to have made in contravention of Section 22 rather the same would be an unauthorised occupation and as such the R.O. has no authority to direct restoration of the disputed land—1998 (I) OLR 512. (*Kashinath* Vs. *Mohan*)

S.DP.'s order deciding the matter with respect to transfer of land by scheduled caste person to non-scheduled caste person not challenged in appeal and as such the same became final.

Such matter can not be agitated in the Supreme Court—1999 (II) OLR 182 (S.C) *Om Prakash Agarwal and other* Vs. *Batara Behara and Others.*

Sale of land by scheduled caste person to non-scheduled caste person without due permission of the competent authority held to be invalid. Land valued more than Rs. 100 must be transferred through a registered document. Further the object of the provision of Section 22 explained and it has been suggested by the Hon'ble Court that the law framers should consider the matter of fresh looking at the apathy of such genuine purchasers who have remained in long possession of the land and their names being duly mutated, 89(2000) CLT 316; *Laxmidhar Mahalik and other* Vs. *State of Orissa and Others.*

Provisions are not applicable to the lands not belonging to Scheduled Tribes, *Ramachandra Sahoo* Vs. *Collector, Mayurbhanj*, 82 (1996) CLT 155.

SYNOPSIS

1. Application of the provisions of this section.
2. Provisions are not unreasonable.
3. Benevolent and social piece of legislation.
4. Principles of *res judicata* would not apply.
5. Requisites for according permission and result of non-obtaining of permission.
6. The principles to be followed to decide caste of the child where one of the spouses belongs to Scheduled Caste.
7. Some cases where determination of Scheduled Caste/Tribe have been made.
8. The Constitution (Scheduled Castes) Order 1950 Extracts.
9. The Schedule, Part-IX Orissa Scheduled Caste, throughout the State.
10. The Constitution (ST) Order 1950 (Extracts)
11. List of Scheduled Tribes, Orissa.

1. Application of the Provisions of this Section

Unless the disputed land comes within the definition of 'homestead' of "land" as defined in clause (12) and (14) of Section 1, the provision of Section 22 would be attracted—71(1991) C.L.T. 390 (*Smt. Madarbait Laath* Vs. *S.D.O. Sadar, Sambalpur*).

2. Provision are not unreasonable

The Supreme Court while interpreting A.P. Schedule Areas Land Transfer Regulation (1959), observed that a legislation which in essence aims at restoration to the "tribal" and the "non-tribal" is not unreasonable. The community cannot shut its eyes to the competition between the "tribals" and the "non-tribals" partakes the character of a race between a handicapped, one legged person and able bodied, two legged person. (AIR 1988 S.C 1626 (*P. Rami Reddy and Other* Vs. *State of Andhra Pradesh*)

3. The Act is Benevolent and Social Piece of Legislation

This legislation is social legislation providing a protective umbrella to the weaker class of the society, namely, Scheduled Castes and Scheduled Tribes. By enacting the section, the legislature in its wisdom has demonstrated the intent and purpose of safeguarding the interest of the weaker sections of the society and improving their conditions by providing that any transfer except in terms of the provisions of Section 22 would be null and void—61 (1986) C.L.T. (1) O.L.R. (*Karunakar Goud* Vs. *Pitabas Sahu*).

4. Principal of *resjudicata* would not apply

Principal of the *resjudicata* will not be applicable as the same is the principal of procedure and is not to supersede the law. As such any sale even if in execution of a decree as well as confirmation having been prohibited by the provisions of Section 22(3) of the Act in absence of the written permission of the Revenue Officer, the party affected by the said decisions will not be percluded from challenging validity of the same—66 (1988) C.L.T 700 (*Satyabhamo Pandey* Vs. *Bhagirathi Jaipuria and Others*).

Sale is void if transferred without due permission as provided. Further the principles of constructive *res judicata* produce would not apply as much Section 2 to Section 22 of the Act was not there in statute book when notice was served on the judgement debtors under Order 21 Rule 22 of the Code of Civil Procedure even if no objection was filed in execution proceeding after receipt of the notice under aforesaid provision of the Code 72 (1991) C.L.T. 634. (*Jadumani Darji* Vs. *Kishanalal Bhagwan Firm and Others*).

5. Requisites for According Permission and Result of Non-Obtaining of Permission: Restriction on Transfer of Land

The opposite party No. 4 belonging to Scheduled Caste admits that the sales of different parcels of land in favour of the petitioner were fraudulent, so the sales cannot be declared void and petition as made by him u/s 22 of the Act would not be maintainable. But there being contrary contention taken by the parties and further there being no clear picture of the transaction as the relevant document, i.e., absence of registered deed of contract for sale, it was not possible to arrive of a conclusion and as such the matter was remitted back for thorough examination 69 (1990) C.L.T 375 (*Smt. Basanti Behera* Vs. *State of Orissa and Others*).

A person belonging to Scheduled Tribe cannot make a valid transfer of his lands in favour of a person, not belonging to Scheduled Tribe without obtaining the previous permission in writing of the Revenue Officer. Such provision of restriction also apply in case of Scheduled Caste. So the caste "Rajaka" being the literal synonymous for favour of a person belonging to Brahmin caste would be void—69 (1990) CLT 732 (SC) (*The Revenue Officers and Others* Vs. *Prafulla Kumar Pati and Others*.

Even though mere contract for sales on a future date would not be void. Where there is transfer of possession on the basis of such a contract it would require permission of the Revenue Officer. The purpose of such restriction as provided and explained —76(1993) CLT 367 (*Ramnaresh Singh* Vs. *Padma Lochan Jayapuria*). Further no Civil Court shall direct specific performance on contract of sale without prior permission of the Revenue Officer.

If the permission is invalid, the transfer would not be valid also. The permission was granted in excess of the interest of the transfer, so the same is bad, illegal and invalid to the extent of the excess of interest and as such possession of the transferee to such extent of land would be unauthorised. Further when an allegation is made that the transferee is an unauthorised occupant of the land, the Revenue Officer is obligated to make an inquiry into the matter in order to determine if the transferee has acquired a valid right, title as per the law. The revisional authority was in error by holding that if the permission is accorded then the transfer cannot be challenged—67 (1989) CLT (S.N.) 4.

While according to permission, the Sub-Divisional Officer (Revenue Officer) is to satisfy himself that a purchaser belonging to

Scheduled Tribe or Scheduled Caste willing to pay the market price for the land is not available. This is the prerequisite for according of permission to effect a sale to a non-Scheduled Caste and non-Scheduled Tribe person—61(1986) (I) OLR 14 (*Karunakar Goud* Vs. *Pitabas Sahu*).

Before according permission, the Revenue Officer is to satisfy himself that in the interest of the raiyat would not be affected adversely. But there is a distinction to be drawn when the proposed transfer is by way of sale and whether it is by way of mortgage, lease of gift. In case of a transfer by gift, the Revenue Officer has to satisfy himself about the *bona fides* thereof. In the case of a transfer by mortgage or lease he is to satisfy himself not only that the transfer is bonafides but that the terms are not usurious or detrimental to the interest of the raiyat. In the case of a transfer by a sale it is necessary for a Revenue Officer to satisfy himself that there is no person belonging to a Scheduled Caste willing to pay that market price and purchase the land. Thus, in the case transfer by sale any person belonging to a Scheduled Caste would be an interested person in proceedings under Section 23 of the Act provided the person is willing to purchase the land at the market price—44 (1977) CLT 332 (*Gangaram Singh* Vs. *Mayadhar*).

By virtue of Sections 22 and 23, the order where sale-deed held invalid and where permission was not granted and refused is accepted and appellate authority order not correct—Motive of transferees indicated rarely because the transferee have been in long possession is on the ground for right in their favour—*Laximadhar & Ors.* Vs. *State & Ors.* [89(2000) CLT 316; AIR 2000 Ori. 79]

6. Principle to be followed to decide caste of the child where one of the spouses belongs to Scheduled Caste

How the caste of a child is determined explained:– The crucial test to determine the caste of child where the father or mother is a member of Scheduled Caste community is whether the child has been accepted by the Scheduled Caste community as a member of their community or has been brought up in that surrounding and in that community. The nexus between the child and the community or class or caste is real test irrespective of the fact father the accommodating class or caste or community is Scheduled Caste community or a Hindu community. Even if the mother of the child is a member of the Scheduled Caste community, it is possible that the child is accepted by the community of his father and brought up in the surrounding of his father's relations. In the case, such a child cannot be treated as a member of the Scheduled Caste community. Similarly, when the mother belongs to a higher caste and the father is a Scheduled Caste, the father may remain away from the Scheduled Caste community and the child may be brought up in a different surrounding under the influence of his mother's relations and her community member of the Scheduled Caste community But where the child, irrespective of the fact father or the mother is a member of Scheduled Caste community, is brought up in the Scheduled Caste community as a member of such community, then he has to be treated as a member of the Scheduled Caste community and would be entitled to receive benefits as such available to be said caste: AIR 1959 S.C 1318 (1327); (AIR 1958 Assam 121; ILR 33 Madras 342) *V.V Giri* Vs. *D. Suri Dora*).

7. Some cases where determination of Scheduled Castes/Tribes has been made

The word "Rajaka" is literal synonym for the word "Dhoba" and as such a Scheduled Caste—69 (1990) CLT 732 (*Revenue Officer* Vs. *P.K. Pati* (SC).

"Niari" communities occupational activity is "Chudakuta" and "Mudhibhanj", but they are a class of "Keuta" or "Kaibarta" which caste is synonymous to that of "Dewar" and, therefore, such community comes within the Scheduled Caste list as per presidential order—73(1992) CLT 208 (*Sanantan Mangal* Vs. *State of Orissa*).

A question arose, whether "Jarasabar" can be construed to be the same class as "Sabar" appearing in Entry No. 59 of the Constitution (Scheduled Tribes) Order of 1950. After analysing a number of Supreme Court and as well as Orissa High Court decisions, the following points emerged in 54 (1982) CLT 475 (*K. Adikanta Patra* Vs. *G. Chaitanya*).

1. It would not be open generally to any person to lead evidence to establish that a particular caste, tribe is a part of caste/tribe notified in the Constitution (Scheduled Castes/Scheduled Tribes) Order.
2. Article 341 and 342 make it clear that in order to determine whether or not a particular caste/tribe is a Scheduled Caste/Scheduled Tribe within the meaning of Article 341/342 one

has to look at the public notification issued by the President in that behalf.

3. The name by which a tribe or sub-tribe/caste or sub-caste is known is not decisive. Even if the tribe/caste of a person is different from the name included in the Order issued by the President, it may be seen that the name included in the Order is a general name applicable to sub-tribe/caste.
4. Paragraph 2 of the Order is reported and aforesaid decision provided to the extent material that the tribes, or parts of or groups within the tribes specified in the Schedule to the Order shall also be deemed to be Scheduled Tribes.
5. An admission made by a party expressly or by implication that he is not a member of the Scheduled Tribe/Scheduled Caste is evidence against him, the same is not conclusive. Ultimately decided that "Jarasavars" a sub-tribe/groups within the tribe or tribal community of "Sabar" and are member of Scheduled Tribe.

Certain communities have been grouped together under a single entry in the light of Article 342 of the Constitution which requires parts of groups within a tribal community also to be specified in the order issued thereunder. It is, therefore, reasonable to hold that the communities mentioned against any specific entry are those which have mutual affinity amongst them AIR 1980 S.C 150 (*Dadaju* Vs. *Sakhadesbabu*)

The question arose whether "Kampa Saura" could be a member of the Scheduled Tribe within the State of Orissa. The High Court held that the public notification issued by the President is to be looked as to find out whether a particular tribe is a scheduled tribe or not. Even an admission by a party was not accepted as conclusive and President's Order is to be relied as final. In view of the position 'Kampa Saura' is held not a Scheduled Tribe within the State—1977 (2) C.W.R. 681 (*Prasanna* Vs. *Jain*)

The Presidential Notification stated only "Dewar". Dewar should be read as Dhewar. Whether it is Dewar or a Dhewar the real community to which reference is intended to have been made is Dhibar. Dhibara is not a community, and essentially refers to that section of people in the society, which take to the profession of catching of fish. Kaibarata and Keutas who are traditionally accepted to belong to Dhilbara profession should be taken to be a Scheduled

Caste as included in the term Dhibara—49 (1980) C.L.T 47 (*Narayan* Vs. *State of Orissa*)

On reconversion to Hinduism, a person can once again become the member of the caste in which he was born and to which he belonged before conversion to another religion if the members of the caste accept him as member—AIR 1976 S.C 939 (*C.M. Arumugam* Vs. *S. Rajgopal*)

The OLR Act does not define the terms 'Scheduled Tribe' and "Scheduled Caste" The Constitution (Scheduled Tribe) Order 1950 gives the following Tribes would be understood as those who are mentioned in the said Schedule. Similarly Scheduled Castes would mean the caste mentioned in the Constitution (Scheduled Caste) Order 1950.

Section 22.—A Surrender or Abandonment by Raiyat to Tenant—(1) No surrender to the landlord or abandonment of any holding or any part thereof a raiyat or a tenant shall be valid unless such surrender or abandonment has been previously approved by the Revenue Officer.

(2) Any raiyat or tenant desiring to surrender or abandon his holding or any part thereof may furnish information thereof in writing to the Revenue Officer.

(3) On receipt of information under sub-section (2) the Revenue Officer may, after making or causing to be made such inquiry and in such manner as may be prescribed, by order either approve or disapprove the proposed surrender or abandonment:

PROVIDED that no surrender or abandonment shall be disapproved unless the *raiyat* or tenant, as the case may be, has been given a reasonable opportunity of being heard in the matter.

(4) Where the surrender or abandonment of any holding or part thereof is approved by the Revenue Officer under this Section, the holding or part thereof so surrendered or abandoned shall be settled by the Government:

(i) Where such surrender or abandonment was made by a person belonging to a Scheduled Tribe, with another person belonging to the Scheduled Tribe; or

(ii) In case where no person belonging to a Scheduled Tribe is available or willing to take settlement under clause (i) or in any other case, with any other person in accordance with the priorities specified in sub-section (2) of Section 51.

(5) Where any *raiyat* or tenant surrenders, or abandons his holding or any part thereof without the previous approval of the Revenue Officer and holding or part thereof so surrendered or abandoned is taken possession of by the landlord, then, it shall be competent for the Revenue Officer (after giving to the landlord an opportunity of being heard) to impose on the landlord a penalty of an amount not exceeding rupees two hundred per area of the land so surrendered or abandoned for each year or any part thereof during which the possession is continued.

Note: Rule 22-F provides "surrender or abandonment by raiyat or tenant".

Form No. 18 provides that information is referred to in Sub-Section (2) of Section 22-A shall be furnished and such information shall be presented to the Revenue Officer personally by the applicant or his authorised agent.

SYNOPSIS

(i) Scope;
(ii) Object of the Section; and
(iii) Surrender of tenancy.

(i) Scope.—The provision of this Section provided that no surrender to the landlord or abandonment of any holding or any part thereof by a *raiyat* or a tenant shall be valid unless such surrender or abandonment is previously approved by the Revenue Officer. So the sale deed executed after the retrospective effective date of enforcement of the provisions, i.e., 2.10.1973 would be without consideration and deed of relinquishment would be invalid. Further necessary ingredients to constitute a sale also explained—74 (1992) CLT 843 (*Kachara Pradhan and Other* Vs. *Smt. Sushila Sundari Del*).

Section 22-A has no application to the surrenders prior to its insertion in the statute—(*Narayan Sahu* Vs. *Rama Ch. Sahu*) AIR 1985 Orissa 145.

(ii) Object of the Section.—The Orissa Tenants Relief Act 1955 and the Orissa Tenants Protection Act 1948 (Act prior to the Orissa Land Reforms Act) aimed to protect the tillers of the soil who had no interest in the land from discrimination and arbitrary eviction, until Permanent measures were taken by way of agrarian reforms. Thus came the Orissa Land Reforms Act 1960. It conferred better rights on such tenants and introduced agrarian reforms experienc of a decade and a half indicated that eviction of tenants was being effected through the dubious device of surrender of tenancy rights by tenants. Extensive surrender would be detrimental to the object and as such would frustrate aims of the Act. As such Section 22-A was introduced in the Status by Orissa Act 9 of 1974 which provided safeguards against frivolous and fraudulent surrenders. The object was to protect tenants from unscrupulous landlord who may resort to adopt the device of surrender for evicting tenants when a case of extinguishment of tenancy rights by surrender thereof is presented. The Courts should be circumspect and carefully scrutinise the plea of surrender advanced by the landlord—AIR 1985 Orissa 145 (*Narayan Sahu* Vs. *Rama Chandra Sahu*)

(iii) Surrender of Tenancy.—The landlord made claim for voluntary surrender of the land by the tenant against a petition of the tenant for relief under Section 32 (1-8) of the Bombay Tenancy and Agricultural Lands Act 1948. The Hon'ble Supreme Court held "We agree with the reasoning and conclusion of the Tribunal that surrender could have been made lawfully only under Section 15 read with Section 29(2) of the Bombay Tenancy and Agricultural Lands Act 1948 (BTAL Act) as it stood at the material time. There was no such order passed by any competent authority under the BTAL Act evidencing the surrender in accordance with the provisions of the Act. Under the circumstances the submission urged by the appellants that the tenant had surrendered his tenancy in favour of the appellants of February 21,1955 cannot be acceded to or sustained" and as such directed that the tenants be put in possession of the lands in question as early as possible—A.I.R 1987 S.C 1626 (*Abodul Ajij* Vs. *Dasharath*)

When Karnatak Act (1 of 1974) came into force tenant was in possession. Surrender by tenant not in accordance with Section 25 of the Act. It was held that tenant's possession must be presumed to have been continuing and tenant is entitled to temporary injunction in his suit restraining the landlord from interfering with tenant's possession—A.I.R 1975 Kant. 111 (*Thunga Bal* Vs. *Vishalakashi*).

Section 23. Effect of Transfer in Contravention of Section 22.—(1) in the case of any transfer in contravention of the provision of [sub-section (1) of Section 22] the Revenue Officer on his own information, or on the application of any person interested in the land may issue notice in the prescribed manner calling upon the transfer and transferee to show cause why the transfer should not be declared invalid.

(2) After holding such enquiry as the Revenue Officer deems fit and after hearing the persons interested may declare such transfer to be invalid and impose on the transferee a penalty of an amount not exceeding rupees two hundred per acre of the land so transferred for each year or any part thereof during which the possession is continued in pursuance of the transfer which has been declared to be invalid [and may also order such portion of the penalty as he deems fit, to be paid to the transferer or his heir].

(3) On a declaration being made under Sub-section (2) the Revenue Officer *suo motu* or on the application of any person interested cause restoration of the property to the transferor or his heirs and for the purpose may take such steps as may be necessary for compliance with the said order or preventing any breach of peace:

> [Provided that if the Revenue Officer is of opinion that the restoration of the property is not reasonably practicably, he shall record his reasons, therefore, and shall, subject to the control of the Government settle the said property with another member of a Scheduled Tribe or in the absence of any such member, with any other person in accordance with the provisions contained in the Orissa Government Land Settlement Act 1962 (33 of 1962).

Explanation—Restoration of the property means actual delivery of possession of the property to the transfer or his heirs.

(4) Where any transfer is declared under this Section to be invalid and the transfer or any other person in possession of the property has been evicted therefrom the transferor shall not be entitled to the refund of any amount paid by him to the transferor by way of consideration for the transfer.

Note: Form No. 16—It is prescribed under Rule 22-A for the issue of warrant by the Revenue Officer to give possession of land.

Corresponding Rules 22-A, 22-B, 22-C, 22-D, 22-E—Issue of writ and the procedure for delivery of possession.

Case Laws.—Burden to prove validity of transaction is on Transferee......... as by virtue of the Section the limitation period of 12 years as prescribed by Article 65 of Indian Limitation Act has been enhanced to 30 years—AIR 1995 Orissa 239 (F.B) 1995(1) OLR

75 (F.B.) *Trilochan Dandesena and Other* Vs. *State of Orissa and Others*).

Right acquired by way of adverse possession, prior to incorporation of Section 23-B enhancing the period of limitation is not affected—*Ghanashyam* Vs. *Bhima* (having died) *Lakhapait and Ors.*—2000 (II) OLR 275.

Revision application dismissed without any discussion on the point of limitation and further also without taking into consideration other points and decision of the Hon'ble High Court in the matter. The authority committed illegalities and as such order not sustainable. The matter was remanded—1996 (II) OLR 465 (*Bidya Mohananda* and after him his legal representative *Bahadur Mahanda and Others* Vs. *Gojendra Bhol and Others*).

Possession found based on report only, without any corroborating evidence. Matter remanded for hearing of the application made under the Section to be reheard after affording due opportunity of hearing to the parties-83 (1997) CLT 423 (*Dhruba Ch. Patra* Vs. *State of Orissa*).

SYNOPSIS

Corresponding rules and forms—

1. Scheme of the section.
2. Legislative intention.
3. Precondition of sale by Scheduled Tribe and Scheduled Caste.
4. Meaning of the words "may declare".
5. Penalty under Section 23 (2).

1. Scheme of the Section

Scheme of the Section explained, under sub-section (1) of this Section when the Revenue Officer on his own information or on an application of any person interested in the land comes to a conclusion that there has been a transfer in contravention of Sub-section 10 of Section 22, then he would hold an inquiry as he deems fit after hearing parties and would declare the transfer to be invalid and would impose penalty upon transferor as provided and further under provisions of Sub-section (3) he would either *suo motu* or on the application of any person interested could cause restoration of the property to the transferor or his heirs. So the contention of the petitioner that such an application can be filed under Sub-section (1) is unacceptable. Such an application can be filed independently by an interested person only after declaration under Sub-section (2) has been made—70 (1990) C.L.T 568 (*Jagannath Meher* Vs. *Anjana Dharuanl*).

Transfer affected prior to the Act came into force would not be affected, as such no application invoking the jurisdiction of the R.O. u/s 23(1) of the Act would be sustainable—70 (1990) CLT662 (*Nilambar Satpahty* Vs *Prema Ganda*). There being no finding in any of the orders that a disputed property was either used or capable of being used for agriculture purposes or was land ordinarily used as a house site ancillary or incidental to agriculture. The Revenue Officer does not get jurisdiction to proceed further in the matter as provided under the provisions of Section 23 and Revenue Officer is obligated to record such finding. The matter was remitted back for disposal of the proceeding afresh—71(1991) CLT 390 (*Smt. Modanbait Lath* Vs. *S.D.O Sadar, Sambalpur*) and further the purpose, interest and principles underlying both the provisions of Sections 23 and 23-A is to protect the properties belonging to the members of a Scheduled Caste/Scheduled Tribe who are usually subject to exploitation by other communities.

2. Legislative Intention

Legislative intention incorporation of these sections i.e., Section 22, 23-A and 23-B explained. The purpose is to provide a protective umbrella to the weaker sections of the society and improving and safeguarding their interest—76 (1993) CLT 367 (*Ram Naresh Singh* Vs. *Padmalochan Jaypuria*)

3. Pre-condition of Sale by Scheduled Tribe and Scheduled Caste

A Scheduled Caste person made an application for a permission of sale of the land, without indicating in the said application any particular provisions of law under which such permission was sought. The Sub-Divisional Officer (Revenue Officer) without enquiring under Section 22 of the O.L.R. Act took it to be an application under Regulation 2 of 1956 and after due enquiry granted permission under that regulation. When the permission was challenged, the High Court held "the learned Revenue Officer should have proceeded under Section 22 of the Act. However, there is no difference between the enquiry envisaged under Section 22 of the Act and that contemplate under Regulation 2 of 1956 because under both the provisions of law, the same type of enquiry is necessary for according permission for transfer of land by Scheduled Caste person or a Scheduled Tribe person and held" it would not vitiate the order granting permission 60 (1985) CLT 95 (*Shyam Sundar Khuntia* Vs. *Udayanath*)

On the date of registration of the sale deed, i.e., 29.12.1965 there was no permission as required u/s 22 of the Act and on the same day the vendor filed a petition for permission as required under Section 22 and obtained the same on 25.1.1996. It was also accepted that the possession of the land was not delivered immediately on sale but sometimes in January 1966. In a proceeding under Section 23 of the Act the Honourable High Court held that, on the date of registration of the sale deed there was no permission as required under Section 22 of the Act as such the sale deed itself is void and honest—61 (1986) CLT; 1986 (I) O.L.R. 14 (*Karunakar Gond* Vs. *Pitabas Sahu*).

Section 22 of the Act contains a restriction on alienation for land by a Scheduled Tribe. Under the said provision any transfer made by a raiyat belonging to a Scheduled Tribe in favour of non-Scheduled Tribe person without the previous permission in writing of the Revenue is void. The said restriction is also applicable in case of an alienation made by a Scheduled Caste person. Section 23 lays down the procedure to be followed by the Revenue Officer when a transfer is made in contravention of Section 22. For such a petition under Section 23 of the Act there was no period of limitation provided in the Act and, therefore, the twelve years period prescribed under Article 65 the Limitation Act 1963 applied. The Act was then added by the President Act 19 of 1973 and by the Scheduled provision. It was specifically provided that in the Limitation Act 1983 and its application to proceedings under Section 13 of the Act in Article 65, the period of limitation would be thirty years in the case of immovable property belonging to a member of Scheduled Tribe or a Scheduled Caste, specified in relation to the State of Orissa. This amended provision came into force with effect from 2.10.1973 and it was numbered as Section 23-A (2) of the Act. Though the Act provided a remedy in case of invalid transfers, but there was no remedy where a non-Scheduled tribe or non-Scheduled Caste person forcibly occupied the land of a Scheduled Tribe or a Scheduled Caste person without any document of title for the same. That mischief was remedied by the legislature by inserting another provision by Orissa Act 44 of 1976. Section 23-A of the principal Act was re-numbered as Section

2, 3-B and the new provision which was inserted by amendment in 1976 was numbered as Section 23-A-62 (1986) C.L.T 281 (*Sinai Nag* Vs. *Gobardhan*).

The land of the judgement debtor belonging to Scheduled Tribe was sold to a person not belonging to Scheduled Tribe in execution of money decree. Sale was confirmed, sale certificate was issued and possession was delivered to the purchase. Thereafter a proceeding was initiated challenging the sale and restoration of possession as permissible was not obtained under Orissa Scheduled Areas Transfer of Immovable Property (by Scheduled Tribe) Regulation No. 2 of 1956 for the sale. It was pleaded that the aggrieved person did not raise any objection during the execution proceeding before the civil court and as such the proceeding under Regulation No. 2 of 1956 is barred by the principle of constructive *resjudicata*. The High Court did not entertain such a contention, and directed restoration of possession in favour of Scheduled Tribe person—534 (1982) C.L.T. 475 (D.B) KJ. *Adikanda Patra* Vs. *Gandua*). Please also see *Satyabhama Pandey* Vs. *Bhagirathi Dalpurla*); 1988 (II) O.L.R. 420.

In an another similar matter a Scheduled Tribe person sold the land in an execution proceeding to a non-Scheduled Tribe man for satisfaction of the decretal amount. The sale was confirmed as no objection was raised against the sale. Subsequently in a suit filed by Scheduled Tribe person for declaration that the sale was void for non-compliance of Section 22(3) of the Act the Hon'ble High Court held that the suit would be barred by principles of constructive *resjudicata* as provision of Section 22 of the O.L.R. Act nowhere totally prohibit sale of such properties in favour of persons not belonging to a Scheduled Tribe—41 (1975) CLT 894 (*Pitambar Pujari* Vs. *Bhikari Mehera*).

As against the judgement of A.R.O. a petition filed and judgement was delivered which is reported in 1976 (1) C.W.R 509. Confirmed the view expressed by Hon'ble Justice Acharya in 41 (1975) C.L.T 894 following the Patna High Court reported in A.I.R 1962 Patna 72 wherein it was concluded "it is immaterial whether the sale of the lands in question is void or voidable because we have to consider at present the consequence of the judgment debtor not having the objection before the sale when he might and ought to have raised it. In accordance with the views which I have expressed, I hold that the judgement debtor is barred by the principle of constructive *resjudicata* from raising the objection on the ground of non-saleability of the *kasht* lands"

But in decision reported in 1988 (II) O.L.R. 420 the Hon'ble High Court took note of the amendment of Section 22 (33) by President's Act 17 of 1973 and came to a conclusion that a written permission of the Revenue Officer is a pre-condition for sale of a holding belonging to a scheduled tribe even in execution of a decree to a non-scheduled tribe person. Such a sale in contravention of the provision contained in Sub-section (3) of Section 22 must be held to be void. The party affected by such a sale would not be precluded from challenging the validity of the same subsequently under the rule of *resjudicata.*

Sub-section 8 of Section 23 has been inserted by Amendment Act 44 of 1976, without giving any retrospective effect. So barring refund of the consideration money would not be applicable to a pending suit—61 (1986) C.L.T. S.N. 55 (*Natabara Patra* Vs. *Debaki Naik*)

The transfer would be void in absence of previous permission and there is no talisman under any provision of the Orissa Land Reforms Act which can validate the transfer—44 (1977) CLT 332 (B.R) *Gangaram Singh* Vs. *Mayadhar Mund*).

A Scheduled Tribe person transferred the land in favour of a person belonging to a Scheduled Caste. The member, Board of Revenue held that the Scheduled Tribe and Scheduled Caste cannot be treated as one entity and the transfer of a holding raiyat belonging to a Scheduled Caste would be void in absence of the previous permission of the Revenue Officer.—43 (1977) CLT 162 (BR) *Prahallad Ghasi* Vs. *Smt. Vasani Kumari*).

"A" alleges mortgage in favour of *"B"* in application for possession. On the plea of *"B"* that *"C"* is in possession. *"C"* was added as a party who claimed to have purchased the land. The authorities came to the conclusion that though *"B"* is a member of Scheduled Tribe he was simply a name lender and real alience is *"C"* who is not a Scheduled Tribe man and directed restoration of possession. The Hon'ble High Court in the facts and circumstances of the matter rejected the plea of *Benami* and quashed the proceeding—1975 (1) C.W.R 198 (*Noro Kandilia* Vs. *Suti Digapuira*).

Transferor's brother made an application for registration. Even if the brother cannot be considered to be a person interested in the prohibition, yet it was open to the Collector to act *suo motu* when it was brought to his notice that a transfer was made in contravention of the provision of the Regulation. The order for registration passed by the Collector was not without jurisdiction. But the restoration cannot be made in favour of applicant having no interest. (*Smt. Suryomani Bhotta* Vs. *Doinu Naiku*) 40 (1974) C.L.T S.N.13. This decision though has been rendered under Orissa Scheduled Areas Transfer of Immovable Property (By Scheduled Tribes) Regulation 1956 would be equally applicable to Section 23 of the O.L.R. Act.

The son of the transferor (a man belonging to Scheduled Caste) made an application for declaring the transfer hold under Section 22 of the Act. No notice to the transferor under Section 23 (1) was given and the S.D.O. (Revenue Officer) held the transfer valid. The member Board of Revenue came to the conclusion that the failure the issue a notice under Section 23 (1) to the transferor and the consequent failure to give him the opportunity of being heard under Section 23 (2) vitiates the proceeding and renders the order of the Revenue Officer a nullity—42(1976) C.L.T 664 (BR) *Lamxan Saraj* Vs. *Artarana Bag*.)

4. Meaning of the Words "May Declare"

In absence of prior permission of the Revenue Officer the transfer would be void, under Section 22 (1) and the Revenue Officer has no option but to declare it invalid. "There is no talisman under any provision of the Orissa land Reforms Act which can validate the void transfer. The expression "may declare" there remains no element of discretion but merely connote the possibility that the Revenue Officer may well find, after holding such enquiry as he deems fit and after hearing the persons interested, that the ingredients of the transfer are not such as would render it void under Section 22 (1) 42 (1976) C.L.T. 664 (BR) *Laxman Saraf* Vs. *Artatrana Bag*).

5. Penalty under Section 23 (2)

By virtue of two sale deeds executed in the years 1968 and 1973 possession was delivered but the same were declared void under Section 23 and penalty as per the Amendment Act 17 of 1973 amounting to Rs. 200 per acre per each year for the period of possession was imposed by authorities. The Hon'ble High Court came to hold "Admittedly", the provisions is penal and, therefore, should not be given retrospective effect and would, therefore, have prospective effect particularly in the absence of anything to the contrary to the provision. At the time when the transfer took place, the unamended provisions was in force and all the maximum penalty eligible for the transaction was Rs. 200. We would accordingly allow the writ application to the extent of vacating the order of imposition of penalty and in lieu thereof direct that petitioner shall be subject to a total penalty of Rs. 200 as had been provided under Section 23(2) of the Orissa Land Reforms Act at the time the transaction took place"—A.I.R 1981 Orissa 196:52 (1981) CLT 218 (Parkhit Meher Singh). In view of this judgement the decision of Board of Revenue in case of *Shyama Sundar Bairk* Vs. *Jagannath Gond* reported in 42 (1976) CLT 450 is no longer good.

Revenue Officer's power to impose penalty explained.

If the transaction is made in contravention of Section 22 of the Act the same is void *ab initio* and the Revenue Officer is merely to declare it invalid after being satisfied upon enquiry, and given due notice to the parties concerned and hearing them. The jurisdiction and power to impose penalty arises only after declaration of invalidity is made. The transferee would be liable to be penalised for past possession, even though the transfer is declared subsequently to be invalid—44 (1977) CLT 217 (*Ramkrushna Panda* Vs. *The Sub-Divisional Officer*), A.I.R 1977 Orissa 219.

Even the sale and consequential delivery of possession of land belonging to a Scheduled Caste person by the Certificate Officer under the Orissa Public Demands Recovery Act for recovery of agricultural loan, without the permission under Section 22 of the Act is void—AIR 1985 Orissa 100 (*Somnath Sipka* Vs. *State of Orissa*) 1984 (I) O.L.R. 805.

Section 23-A.—Eviction of Person in Unauthorised Occupation of Property

[Where any person is found to be in unauthorised occupation of the whole or part of a holding of a raiyat belonging to a Scheduled Caste or of a raiyat belonging to a Scheduled Tribe within any part of the State other than a Scheduled Area, by way of trespass or otherwise, the Revenue Officer may, either on application by the owner or any person interested therein, or on his own motion, and after giving the parties concerned an opportunity of being heard, order eviction of the person so found to be in unauthorised occupation and shall cause restoration of the property to the said raiyat or to his heirs in accordance with the provision of Sub-section (3) of Section 23].

Case Law: Revision application dismissed without any discussion on the point of limitation and further also without taking into consideration the other points and decision of the Hon'ble High Court in the matter. The authority committed illegalities and as such order not sustainable. The matter was remanded—1996 (II) O.L.R. 465 (*Bidya Mahananda and legal representatives, Bahadur Mahananda and Other* Vs. *Gajendra Bhoi and Others*).

SYNOPSIS

(1) Scope of the Section explained.
(2) Distinction between Sections 23 and 23-A.
(3) Application of the Section.

1. Scope of the Section Explained

Scope of the section and circumstances in which the provisions can be invoked explained. Powers as provided under this Section are quite wise. But before exercising such powers it must be established that the person concerned is in unauthorised occupation by way of trèsspass or otherwise. But by the time the provisions of the Section came into force the person had perfected or acquired his title by way of adverse possession and as such the provisions cannot be exercised—70(1990) C.L.T. 662 (*Nilambar Satapathy* Vs. *Prema Ganda and Others*).

The Revenue Officer can pass order of eviction after extending due opportunity of hearing to parties when any person is found to be in authorised occupation of a holding belonging to a Scheduled Caste or a Scheduled Tribe by way of tresspass or otherwise and can cause restoration of the property to the said raiyat or to his heir. This provision is prospective in nature. In case of an unauthorised occupation coming within the ambit of Section 23-A of the Act the limitation of thirty years provided in Section 23-B (2) of the Act has no application. In this case the unauthorised occupant perfected title adversely being continuing in possession for more than twelve years before Section 23-A came to the Satute Book. (Section 23-A was inserted by amendment Act 44 of 1976 with effect from 25.10.1976). It was held that "Revenue Officer will have no jurisdiction to divest him of the said right in exercise of the powers under Section 23-A of the Act"—62 (1986) C.L.T 281(DB) *Siami Nag* Vs. *Gobardhan*)

Please also see (*Dama Maher* Vs. *Champeswar*) 64 (1987) C.L.T. 516; 1983 (I) O.L.R. 1.

An application under Section 23 of the Act was filed by the vendor previously by belonging to the Scheduled Caste but was dismissed on the ground that Section 23 is not applicable. After being unsuccessful another application was filed under Section 23-A with the same prayer for restoration of the land. It was held that the proceeding under Section 23-A of the Act would be hit by principle of *resjudicata* and as such not maintainable—64 (1987) C.L.T 12 (BR) (*Collector* Vs. *Mangalal Ganda*).

Once the land becomes the holding of a raiyat belonging to a Scheduled Tribe or Scheduled Caste, it is immaterial as to when the occupation took place and anyone sound to be in unauthorised occupation thereafter, such occupation by way of transfer in contravention of Section 22 or by way of trespass or otherwise, shall be evicted and the land would be restored to the raiyat or his heir.—[J.B.R. Vol. XIII (1977) Part 1 Page 13].

2. Distinction between Section 23 and 23-A

Distinction between the proceedings under Section 23 and 23-A explained. The period of thirty years of limitation as introduced in Art. 65 of the Limitation Act 1963 by amendment under Sub-Section 2 has no application to a proceeding u/s 23-A. In such case the period of limitation is twelve years as provided under Art. 65. The proceeding having been initiated in 1976, beyond 12 years from the date of transfer would not be maintainable being time barred—71 (1991) CLT 281 (*Butu Naik* Vs. *Annal Adhikari and Others*). Further the anomalous position with regard to limitation arising after going through the provision of Section 23, 23-A and 23-B also explained and it has been suggested to take suitable steps to amend Section 23-B (1) of the Act.

3. Application of the Section

Application of the provision of this Section would indicate that it is only when a person is found to be in unauthorised occupation of the holding of a raiyat belonging to a Scheduled Tribe within any part of the State after than the scheduled area, the provision will have no application, but so far as the holding of a raiyat belonging to a Scheduled Caste is concerned the fact that this land in a scheduled area will not make the provision inapplicable.

Further the contention that the petitioner had perfected his title by way of adverse possession would not stand as the land being *choukidari jagir* and had vested absolutely in the State Government free from all encumbrances by virtue of Orissa Officers of Villages Police (Abolition) Act. 76(1993) CLT 268 (*Goutam Kumar Mhapatra* Vs. *Karpatra*)

[Section 23 B—Burden of proof and amendment of Limitation Act 1963 in its application to proceedings under Section 23-(1)

If any proceedings under Section 23 [and Section 23-A] the validity of the transfer of any holding or any part thereof called in question, or if such proceedings are for the recovery of possession of such holding or part thereof the burden of proving that the transfer was valid shall, notwithstanding anything contained in any other law for the time being in force, lie on the transferee.

(2) In the Limitation Act 1963 in its application to proceedings under Section 23 in the Schedule, after the words "twelve Years" occurring in the second column against Article 65, the words, brackets and figure "but thirty years in case of immovable property belonging to a member of a Scheduled Tribe or a Scheduled Caste, specified in relation to the State of Orissa in the Constitution (Scheduled Tribes) Order 1950 or the Constitution Scheduled Caste) Order 1950, as the case may be" shall be inserted.

Case Laws: Burden to prove validity of transaction is on transferee as by virtue of the section, the Limitation period of 12 years as prescribed by Art. 65 of Limitation Act has been enhanced to 30 years—AIR 1995 Orissa 239. (F.B) 1995 (1) OLR 75 (F.B) *Trilochan Dandesena and Others* Vs. *State of Orissa and Others*.

SYNOPSIS

(1) Onus of the party
(2) Limitation.

1. Onus of the Party

The provisions of this Section provide that if the validity of transfer of a holding or part thereof is in question, the burden of proof that the transfer was valid shall notwithstanding anything contained in any other law for the time being in force lies on the transferee—69 (1990) C.L.T 732 (S.C) (*Revenue Officer and Others* Vs. *Prafulla Kumar Pati and Others*). Please also see 44 (1977) C.L.T 217.

2. Limitation

Limitation as contemplated under the provisions of Section 23-B(2) for prescription of title by adverse possession is 30 years—75 (1993) C.L.T. S.N 29 (*Ranjan Suna* Vs. *Nirabasan Bentakar and Others*).

In case of an unauthorised occupation coming within the ambit of Section 23-A of Act the limitation of thirty years provided in this Section has no application—(*Siani Nag* Vs. *Gobardhan*) 62 (1986) C.L.T. 281 (D.B.).

22-C. When the person directed to execute the warrant fails on the date fixed therein to put the transfer or his heir in possession, the Revenue Officer may issue another warrant to the same person or any other member of the staff.

22-D. The Revenue Officer may at any time recall or cancel any warrant issued under Rule 22-A or 22-B and may also order necessary police or other assistance to be rendered for the due execution of the warrant.

22-E. If on the dates specified in the warrant, for putting the transferor or his heirs in possession of lands, crops not ripe for immediate harvest are found on the land, the execution shall be postponed and a report of such fact shall be made to the Revenue Officer and on receipt of such report the Revenue Officer may postpone the execution till such time as the crops are harvested.]

22-F. Surrender or Abandonment by Raiyat or Tenant.—(1) The information referred to in Sub-section (2) of Section 22-A shall be furnished in Form No. 18.

(2) The information in Form No. 18 shall be presented to the Revenue Officer personally by the applicant or by his authorised agent.

(3) For every village there shall be a separate application in Form No. 18.

(4) The application shall, in each case, be made in triplicate.

(5) One copy of the application shall be published by the Revenue Officer in the village in which the land is situated and objections shall be invited to the proposed surrender or abandonment within a period of 30 days with effect from the date of the publication. Where the application is made by a tenant, a copy thereof shall be sent to his landlord by registered post with acknowledgement due.

(6) A date shall thereafter be fixed for hearing after issuing notices to the applicants and objections if any. Final orders in each case shall be passed after such hearing. While passing the final order,

the Revenue shall keep in view the circumstances of the proposed surrrender, as the case may be and determine whether the surrender or abandonment has been applied for due to natural reason, like inundation, sand casting, erosion, etc., or with a view to circumventing the provisions of any law for the time being in force or underlining the effect of any law, contract decree or order of a Court.

(7) Where the surrender or abandonment of any holding or part thereof is approved by the Revenue Officer under Sub-section (4) of Section 22-A, the holding or part thereof so surrendered or abandoned shall vest in the Government.

(8) A copy of the final order referred to in Sub-section (6) above shall be sent by the Revenue Officer to the Tahsildar entrusted with the maintenance of record-of-rights under Chapter IV of the Orissa Survey and Settlement Rules 1962]

(9) The Revenue Officer may make such enquiry as he deems necessary before passing orders allowing or disallowing the partition.

(10) Before passing orders, the Revenue Officers shall obtain the signature or the thumb impression of all co-sharer raiyats or their authorised agents on the body of the record signifying their consent to partition the holding on mutual agreement.

(11) When a portion is allowed, the order of the Revenue Officer shall clearly mention the plots of land allotted to the share of every co-share raiyat, the amount of rent, cess and other local dues payable by each co-sharer raiyat, after partition.

(12) In case of a dispute amongst the co-sharer raiyats, about the quantum of rent payable by each in respect of the new holding created after partition, prayer for partition shall be rejected.]

20. Notice under Sub-section (2) of Section 19.—(1) The notice envisaged under Sub-section (4) of Section 19 shall be in Form No. 4.

(2) The number of notices and copies thereof to be filled under Sub-rule (1) shall be the same as provided Sub-rules (2), (3) and (4) of Rule 14.

21. List under Sub-section (4) of Section 19.—(1) The list envisaged under Sub-section (4) of Section 19 shall in Form No. 5

(2) It shall be sent to the Revenue Officer by the Court either through a messenger or by registered post with acknowledgement due.

(3) The number of lists and copies thereof to be sent under Sub-rule (2) shall be provided in Sub-rules (2), (3) and (4) of Rule 14.

[21-A. The list envisaged under Sub-section (6) of Section 19 shall be in Form No. 5-A]

22. Manner of Application under Sub-section (1) of Section 20.—The application under Sub-section (1) of Section 20 shall be submitted in the same manner as provided in Sub-rules (3), (4), and (5) of Rule 10.

[22-A. On declaration being made under Sub-section (2) of Section 23, the Revenue Officer shall issue to any member of his staff or any other person a warrant in Form No. 16 to put the transferor or his heirs in possession of the land, if necessary, by removing any person bound by the order under Section 23 who refuses to vacate the land.]

22-B. The person to whom a warrant is issued under Rule 22-A shall after putting the transferor or his heirs in possession of the land, return the warrant and the Revenue Officer on being satisfied that the warrant has been duly executed, countersigning the same and keep it as a part of the records of the case.

FORM NO. 16

(See Rule 22.A)

Warrant to Officer to give Possession of Land

In the Court of Revenue Officer................Application No..................of Name(s) and address(es) of application(s).......................... Name(s) and address(es) of respondent(s).......................................

To

Whereas the land prescribed in the Schedule below has to be put into the possession of .... you are hereby directed to put the said person in possession of the same on the .... day of .... 20 .... and you are hereby authorised to remove any person bound by the order who may refuse to vacate the same. Should there be crops not ripe for immediate harvest on the land, the execution shall be given under my hand and seal this .... day of .... 20 ....

SCHEDULE

Date ....

Place ....

Revenue Officer

CERTIFICATE OF EXECUTION

I .... do hereby declare that the land schedule above has been put into possession of .... on the .... day of .... 20 .... in the presence of two witnesses described below:

Name and address and their signature of witness

1. 1. Address......................
2. 2. Address......................

Date...............................
Place ....

Signature of the Officer executing the warrant.

I/We declare that I/We have received today possession of the land in the schedule.

Name(s) and address(es) of the party receiving possession from the officer and the signature of such person.

Date...............................(Counstersigned)
Place............................. (Revenue Officer)

THE ORISSA GAZETTE
EXTRAORDINARY
Published by Authority

No. 1677 Cuttack, Tuesday, December 28 1993/Pausa 7,1915

LAW DEPARTMENT
NOTIFICATION
The 27th December, 1993

No.16431-Legis.—The following Act of the Orissa Legislative Assembly having been assented to by the present on the 30th November, 1993 is hereby published for general information.

ORISSA ACT 29 OF 1993
THE ORISSA LAND REFORMS (AMENDMENT) ACT 1992
An Act Further to Amend the Orissa Land Reforms Act 1960

BE IT ENACTED by the Legislature of the State of Orissa in the Forty-third year of the Republic of India as follows:

1. This Act may be called The Orissa Land Reforms (Amendment) Act 1960.

2. In the Orissa Land Reforms Act 1960 (hereinafter referred to as the Principal Orissa Act 16 in Section 59 for Sub-section (2) the following Sub-section shall be deemed always to have been substituted, namely:

> "(2) The Board of Revenue may, on being moved in that behalf by the Collector of a district or by the Land Reforms Commissioner, revise any order passed by any authority under this act within twenty-five years from the date of such order."

3. Notwithstanding anything to the contrary in any judgement, decree or order of any court or other authority, and order pass by the Board of Revenue in exercise of the powers of revision under Sub-section (2) of Section 59 of the principal Act as it stood prior to the date of publication of this Act shall, if such order has been passed within twenty-five years from the date of the order revised, be deemed, for all intents and purposes, to have been validly and effectively passed as if Sub-section (2) of Section 59 of the principal Act as amended by Section 2 of this Act was in force at all material times and, accordingly, no suit or other legal proceeding shall be instituted, maintained times and or continued in any court or before other authority on the ground that the Board of Revenue had exercised its power of revision under said Sub-section (2) of Section 59 without reasonableness and with undue delay.

By Order of the Governor
P.K. PANIGRAHI
Secretary to Government

Printed and Published by the Director, Printing, Stationery and Publication, Orissa, Cuttack-10 P/SB Ex.Gaz: 1179-216+s2,080

Chapter IV (*Continued*)

(B) Notifications issued under Orissa Land Reforms Act 1960

NOTIFICATION

The 25th September, 1965

No. 63382-Re60/65.—In exercise of the powers conferred by Sub-section (3) of Section 1 of the Orissa Land Reform Act 1960 (Orissa Act 16 of 1960), the State Government do hereby appoint the 1st day of October 1965 to be the date on which the said Act excepting Chapter III and IV thereof shall come into force.

By Order of the Governor
B.K. MISHRA
Secretary to Government

REVENUE AND EXCISE DEPARTMENT

NOTIFICATION

The 8th December, 1965

No. 786-Re78/65-R.—In exercise of the powers conferred by Sub-section (3) of Section 1 of the Orissa Land Reforms Act 1960 (Orissa Act 16 of 1960, the State Government do hereby appoint the 9th day of December 1965 to be the date on which the provisions contained in Chapter III of the said Act shall come into force.

By Order of the Governor
B.K. MISHRA
Secretary to Government

REVENUE AND EXCISE DEPARTMENT

NOTIFICATION

The 5th January, 1972

No. 916-Re88/72 R.—In exercise of the powers conferred by Sub-section (3) of Section 1 of the Orissa Land Reforms Act 1960 (Orissa Act 16 of 1960), the Government do hereby appoint the 7th day of January, 1972, to be the date on which the provisions contained in Chapter IV of the said Act shall come into force.

IMPORTANT NOTIFICATION DELEGATING POWER UNDER THE ACT

REVENUE AND EXCISE DEPARTMENT

NOTIFICATION

The 25th September, 1965

No. 63375-Re55/65-R.—In pursuance of Clause (28) of Section 2 of the Orissa Land Reforms Act 1960 (Orissa Act 16 of 1960) the State Government do hereby appoint all the Sub-Divisional Officers to discharge the function of a Revenue Officer under the provision of Section 22 and 23 of the said Act.

Superseded in Notification SRO 27/77-4.1.77

By Order of the Governor
M.P. NANDA
Deputy Secretary to Government

REVENUE AND EXCISE DEPARTMENT

NOTIFICATION

The 25th September, 1965

No. 63385-Re55/65-R.—In pursuance of Clause (28) of Section 2 of the Orissa Land Reforms Act 1960 (Orissa Act 16 of 1960) the State Government do hereby appoint all the Tahsildars and Additional Tahsildars to discharge all the function of a Revenue Officer under the provision of Section 22 and 23 of the said Act.

Superseded in Notification SRO 27/77-4.1.77

By Order of the Governor
M.P. NANDA
Deputy Secretary to Government

REVENUE AND EXCISE DEPARTMENT

NOTIFICATION

The 25th September, 1965

No. 63385-Re 59/65-R.—In pursuance of Clause (6) of Section 2 of the Orissa Land Reforms Act 1960 (Orissa Act 16 of 1960) the State Government do hereby appoint all Additional District Magistrates to discharge the function of Collector under Section 59 of the said Act within their respective jurisdictions.

By Order of the Governor
M.P. NANDA
Deputy Secretary to Government

REVENUE AND EXCISE DEPARTMENT

NOTIFICATION

The 25th October, 1965

No. 67971-Re54/65-R.—In pursuance of Clause (28) of Section 2 of the Orissa Land Reforms Act 1960 (Orissa Act 16 of 1960) and in supersession of the notification of Government of Orissa in the Revenue and Excise Department No. 63385-Re55/65-R, dated the 25th September, 1965, the State Government do hereby appoint all Tahsildars and Additional Tahsildars to discharge all the functions of a Revenue Officer under the provisions of the said Act excepting those specified in Section 22, 23 and Sub-section (2) of Section 55 within their respective jurisdiction.

By Order of the Governor
M.P. NANDA
Deputy Secretary to Government

Superseded in Notification SRO 28/77-4.1.77

REVENUE AND EXCISE DEPARTMENT

NOTIFICATION

The 10th June, 1969

No. 36607-Re18/69- R.—In pursuance of Clause (28) of Section 2 of the Orissa Land Reforms Act 1960, (Orissa Act 16 of 1960), the State Government do hereby appoint all Assistant Settlement Officer to be the Revenue Officers to exercise the powers and discharge the functions under the provisions of Clause (c) of Sub-section (I) of Section 19 of the said Act in areas where survey and settlement operation is in progress under the Orissa Survey and Settlement Act 1958 (Orissa Act 3 of 1959).

By Order of the Government
B.K. MOHANTI
Deputy Secretary to Government

REVENUE DEPARTMENT

NOTIFICATION

The 20th September, 1976

S.R.O. No. 961/76.—Whereas the State Government are satisfied that there are sufficient reasons for extending the period of limitation provided under the second proviso to Sub-section and the second provision to Sub-section (5) of Section 4 and under Section 36-A or Orissa Land Reforms Act 1960 (Orissa Act 16 of 1960)

Now, therefore, in exercise of the powers conferred by Sub-section (1) of Section 63 of the said Act the State Government do hereby extend the aforesaid period of limitation by a further period of one year with effect from the 2nd day of October, 1975.

No.75589-R.-357/76-R
By Order of the Governor
D.P. TRIPATHI
Secretary to Government

REVENUE DEPARTMENT

NOTIFICATION

The 20th February, 1976

S.R.O. No. 238/76.—In exercise of the powers conferred by the proviso to Clause (a) of Rule (4) of Rule 38-A of the Orissa Land Reforms (General) Rules 1965, the State Government do hereby exempt from payment of Court-fee in all cases of application from persons belonging to Scheduled Castes or Scheduled Tribes and other landless persons as defined in Clause (a) of Sub-Rule (2) of Rule 38-a for the settlement of ceiling surplus lands under Section 51 of the Orissa Land Reforms Act 1960 (Orissa Act 16 of 1960).

No. 12771-Re.-97/76-R
By Order of the Governor
S.M. PATNAIK
Secretary to Government

IMPORTANT NOTIFICATION DELEGATING POWERS UNDER THE ACT

REVENUE AND EXCISE DEPARTMENT

NOTIFICATION

The 25th September, 1965

No. 63375-Re55/65-R.—In pursuance of Clause (28) of Section 2 of the Orissa Land Reforms Act 1960 (Orissa Act 16 of 1960) the State Government do hereby appoint all the Sub-Divisional Officers to discharge the functions of a Revenue Officer under the provisions of Sections 22 and 23 of the said Act.

By Order of the Governor
M.P. NANDA
Deputy Secretary to Government

REVENUE AND EXCISE DEPARTMENT

NOTIFICATION

The 28th April, 1980

S.R.O. No 528/80.—In pursuance of the powers conferred by Section 69 of the Orissa Land Reforms Act 1960 (Orissa Act 16 of 1960), the State Government do hereby direct that the powers and functions exercisable by Government under the third proviso to Sub-section (1) of Section 51 of the said Act to accord prior approval on the proposal of the Collectors for setting apart of the surplus land for being utilised for any public purpose, other than the purpose of cultivation, shall also be exercisable by the Revenue Divisional Commissioner within their respective jurisdictions.

By Order of the Governor
S.N. MISHRA
Deputy Secretary to Government

REVENUE AND EXCISE DEPARTMENT

NOTIFICATION

The 29th October, 1986

S.R.O. No. 829/86.—In pursuance of Clause (28) of the Section 2 of the Orissa Land Reforms Act 1960 (Orissa Act 16 of 1960), the State Government do hereby appoint the Officer-in-Charge of Revenue Section of each headquarters office of Collectors to discharge the functions of a Revenue Officer under the provision of Sub-section (2) of Section 55 of the said Act.

By Order of the Governor
P.C. RATH
Deputy Secretary to Government

REVENUE AND EXCISE DEPARTMENT

NOTIFICATION

The 18th April, 1980

No. 287/96-Re-1-12/80—In exercise of the powers conferred by

Section 69 of the Orissa Land Reforms Act 1960 (Orissa Act 16 of 1960), the State Government do hereby direct that the powers under section (9) of Section 4, Section 8, Section 12 of the said Act shall also be exercisable by the Tahsildars and Additional Tahsildars, as the same may be within their respective jurisdiction in respect of the lands held directly under the State Government either by raiyat or a temporary lessor or a tenant.

By Order of the Governor
S.N. MISHRA
Deputy Secretary to Government

REVENUE AND EXCISE DEPARTMENT

NOTIFICATION

The 11th January, 1988

S.R.O. No. 52/88.—In pursuance of Clause (28) of Section 2 of the Orissa Land Reforms Act 1960 (Orissa Act 16 of 1960) and in supersession of the notification of the Government of Orissa in the Revenue and Excise Department No. 62652-Re-III-12/86-R.E dated the 26th September, 1986, the State Government do hereby appoint all the Additional District Magistrates in charge of land reforms in the district to discharge the functions of Revenue Officer under the provisions of Sub-Section (2) of Section 55 of the said Act.

No.1664-Re-160/87-R.E.
By Order of the Governor
P.S. RATH
Deputy Secretary to Government

REVENUE AND EXCISE DEPARTMENT

NOTIFICATION

The 23rd July, 1976

S.R.O. No 750/70.—In pursuance of Clause (6) of Section 2 of the Orissa Land Reforms Act 1960 (Orissa Act 16 of 1960), the State

Government do hereby cancel their notification No. 67842-Re-188/73-R, dated the 22nd October, 1973.

No. 58472-Re-272/76-R
By Order of the Governor
D.P. TRIPATHI
Secretary to Government

REVENUE AND EXCISE DEPARTMENT

NOTIFICATION

The 4th January, 1977

S.R.O. No. 28/77.—In pursuance of Clause (28) of Section 2 of the Orissa Land Reforms Act 1960 (Orissa Act 16 of 1960) and in supersession of the notification of Government of Orissa in the Revenue and Excise Departments No. 67971-Re-55/65-R, dated the 25th October, 1965, the State Government do hereby appoint all the Tahsildars and Additional Tahsildars to discharge the functions as Revenue Officer under the provisions of the said Act except those specified in Section 22, 23 and 23-A and Sub-section (20) of Section 55 within their respective jurisdiction.

No. 870-Re-181/76-R
By Order of the Governor
D.N. MOHANTY
Deputy Secretary to Government

REVENUE AND EXCISE DEPARTMENT

NOTIFICATION

The 4th March, 1977

No. 17365-Re-II-24/77-R.—In pursuance of Clause (28) of Section 2 of the Orissa Land Reforms Act 1960 (Orissa Act 16 of 1960) and in partial modification of the Notification of Government of Orissa in the Revenue Department No. 804-Re-181/76-R, dated the 4th January 1970 in S.R.O. No. 27/77 of even date published in the Orissa Gazette

No. 3, dated the 21st January 1977, the State government do hereby appoint all the Deputy Collector-in-Charge of Revenue Section of Sub-divisional Offices in the State to discharge the functions of a Revenue Officer under the provisions of Sections 22, 23, and 23-A of the said Act also.

2. The notification of the Revenue Department No. 90241-Re-389/76-R, dated the 22nd November, 1976, in S.R.O No 1170/76 of even dated published in the Orissa Gazette No. 52 dated the 24th December, 1976, is hereby cancelled.

By Order of the Governor
D.N. MOHANTY
Deputy Secretary to Government

REVENUE AND EXCISE DEPARTMENT

NOTIFICATION

The 31th March, 1980

S.R.O. No. 399/80.—In pursuance of Clause (6) of Section 2 of the Orissa Land Reforms Act 1960 (Orissa Act 16 of 1960) the State Government do hereby appoint all the Additional District Magistrates to discharge the functions of Collector under Section 38 of the said Act within their respective jurisdiction.

No. 24303-Re-148/80-R
By Order of the Governor
S.N. MISHRA
Deputy Secretary to Government

REVENUE AND EXCISE DEPARTMENT

NOTIFICATION

The 30th January, 1980

S.R.O. No. 161/80.—In pursuance of Clause (28) of Section 2 of the Orissa Land Reforms Act 1960 (Orissa Act 16 of 1960) and in partial modification of the notifications of the Government of Orissa in the Revenue Department No. 804-Re-181/76-R dated the 4th January 1976.

REVENUE AND EXCISE DEPARTMENT

NOTIFICATION

The 18th April, 1980

No. 287/96, Re. 1-12/80R.—In exercise of the powers conferred by Section 69 of the Orissa Land Reforms Act 1960 (Orissa Act 16 of 1960) the State Government do hereby direct that the powers and functions exercisable by Government as landlord under Sub-section (9) of Section 4, Section 8, Section 12 of the said Act shall also be exercisable by the Tahsildars and Additional Tahsildars, as the same may be within their respective jurisdictions in respect of the lands held directly under the State Government either by a raiyat or a temporary lessee or a tenant.

By Order of the Governor
S.N. MISHRA
Deputy Secretary to Government

REVENUE DEPARTMENT

NOTIFICATION

The 4th January, 1977

S.R.O. No. 27/77.—In pursuance of Clause (28) of Section 2 of the Orissa Land Reforms Act 1960 (Orissa Act 16 of 1960) and in supersession of the notification of Government in the Revenue and Excise Department No. 63375-Re-55/65-R dated the 25th September, 1965, the State Government do hereby appoint all the Sub-Divisional Officers to discharge the functions of a Revenue Officer under the Provisions of Sections 22, 23 and 23-A of the said Act.

No. 804-Re-181/76R
By Order of the Governor
D.P. MOHANTY
Deputy Secretary to Government

REVENUE AND EXCISE DEPARTMENT

NOTIFICATION

The 11th January, 1988

S.R.O. No. 52/88.—In pursuance of Clause (28) of Section 2 of the Orissa Land Reforms Act 1960 (Orissa Act 16 of 1960) and in supersession of the notification of the Government of Orissa in the Revenue and Excise Department No. 62652-Re-III-12/86-R.E. dated the 26th September, 1986, the State Government do hereby appoint all the Additional District Magistrate in-charge of land reforms in the districts to discharge the functions of Revenue Officer under the provisions of Sub-section (2) of Section 55 of the said Act.

No. 1664-Re-160/87-R.E
By Order of the Governor
P.C. RATH
Joint Secretary to Government

REVENUE AND EXCISE DEPARTMENT

NOTIFICATION

The 4th July, 1994

S.R.O. No. 669/94.—In pursuance of the explanation-I to Clause (9-b) of Section 2 of the Orissa Land Reforms Act 1960 (Orissa Act 16 of 1960), the State Government do hereby declare that for the purpose of the said clause the market value of 3,73,242 kilogram which is equivalent to one standard maund of paddy (common variety) through the State for the year 1994-95 shall be Rs. 116 (Rupees one hundred and sixteen only)

No. 29109-Re-1-49/94-R)
By Order of the Governor
P.K. CHOWDHURY
Joint Secretary to Government

REVENUE AND EXCISE DEPARTMENT

NOTIFICATION

The 25th October, 1995

S.R.O. No. 1175/95.—In pursuance of Clause (3-a) of Section 2 of the Orissa Land Reforms Act 1960 (Orissa Act 16 of 1960), the State Government do hereby appoint all Tahsildars as authorised Officers for the purpose of Section 8-A of the said Act in their respective jurisdiction.

No. 47759-Re-J-11/95-R)
By Order of the Governor
G.K. JENA
Deputy Secretary to Government

REVENUE AND EXCISE DEPARTMENT

NOTIFICATION

The 11th Marth, 1997

S.R.O. No. 117/97.—Government have been pleased to withdraw the Government of Orissa, Revenue and Excise Department Notification No. 17365-R, dated the 4th March, 1977, published in the Orissa Gazette the Deputy Collectors-in-charge of Revenue Section of Sub-Collectors Officers to discharge the functions of a Revenue Officer under Sections 22, 23 and 23-A of the said Act.

No. 11723-Re-1-114/96-R
By Order of the Governor
G.K. JENA
Deputy Secretary to Government.

REVENUE AND EXCISE DEPARTMENT

NOTIFICATION

The 8th December, 1997

No. 59535-Re-I-29/97-R.—In exercise of the powers conferred by Sub-sec. (3) of Section 8-A of the Orissa Land Reforms Act 1960 (Orissa Act 16 of 1960), the State Government do hereby specify the area as noted against each under Clauses (i), (iii), and (iv) of the said sub-section in the Schedule below:

SCHEDULE

1. Municipal area to come under Clause (i) of Sub-sec. (3) of Section 8-A	Area covered by Bhubaneswar Municipal Corporation, Cuttack Municipal Corporation, Sambalpur Municipality, Berhumpur Municipality, Rourkela Municipality.
2. Area to come under Clause (iii) of Sub-sec (3) of Section 8-A	Area covered by Municipalities and Notified Area councils other than the Municipal areas under Clause (i)
3. Area to come under Clause (iv) of Sub-Sec (3) of Section 8-A	Area covered by Development Plans/Master Plans but falling outside Municipalities/Notified Area Councils.

In all other areas premium shall be payable at the rate specified in Clause (v) of Sub-sec. (3) of Section 8-A of the said Act.

By Order of the Governor
J.K. MOHAPATRA
Commissioner-cum-Secretary to Government

CORRIGENDUM

The 27th December, 1997

No. 63137-Re-I-29/97-R.—The Clause (ii) appearing at the 3rd line of first paragraph of Revenue and Excise Notification No. 59539-Re.I/97-R, dated the 8th December,1997 published in the extraordinary issue of Orissa Gazette No. 1520, dated the 10th December 1997 bearing S.P.O. No 802/97 may be read as (iii).

By Order of the Governor
SRI HARI NAYAK
Additional Secretary to Government

Chapter IV (*Continued*)

(C) Instructions Issued for Disposal of Cases under O.L.R. Act 1960

GOVERNMENT OF ORISSA
REVENUE DEPARTMENT

No.-Re-I-6/01 763.R
Dated, Bhubaneswar the 7th January, 2003

From

Shri H. Behera,
Deputy Secretary to Government

To

The Collector, Cuttack

Subject: Clarification on implementation of Section 8-A of O.L.R. Act

Sir,

I am directed to invite a reference to Memo No. 5013 dated 2.9.2002 of Tahsildar, Salipur on the above noted subject and to say that the clarification sought for is made as follows:

(1) Section 34 of the OCH and PFL Act 1972 prohibits fragmentation of cultivable land forming a chack by way of partition and transfer. Partition and transfer in violation of provisions of Section 34 are void u/s 35 of the Act.

(2) An Authorised Officer may allow conversion of any agricultural land for non-agricultural purpose following

provisions of Sec. 8-A of O.L.R Act 1960 read with Rule 12-A of O.L.R. Rules 1965.

(3) It may, thus be seen that fragmentation of chack and conversion of agricultural land for non-agricultural purpose are quite different things and need be construed accordingly. In this connection, this Department letter No. 14726, dated 13.3.2002 especially paragraph 2 may also be referred to.

Yours faithfully,
Sd/-
Deputy Secretary to Government

GOVERNMENT OF ORISSA
REVENUE AND EXCISE DEPARTMENT

No. 9359/R., Bhubaneswar
Dated 15th February, 1999
Re-I-38/99

From

Shir D.K. Das OAS-i(SB)
Deputy Secretary to Government

To

The Secretary
Board of Revenue
Orissa, Cuttack

Subject: Clarification on exemption of Stamp Duty of effecting partition u/s 19(1) (c) and 19(6) of the O.L.R. Act 1960.

Sir,

I am directed to invite reference on the aforementioned subject and to say that the question whether partition of Joint holdings effected by the Revenue Officer upon mutual agreement in exercise of the powers conferred by Section 19(1) (c) of the Orissa Land Reforms Act 1960 is to be registered as usual by payment of stamp duty or it is exempted by virtue of the provision itself was enging the attention of the Government sometime past. Earlier this department, on the advice of the Law Department had clarified (vide letter No. 63670-R dated 16.8.1976 addressed to the Land Reforms Commissioner) that the order of the Revenue Authority under Section 19 (1) (c) of the Act is not exempt from stamp duty. This view was subsequently reiterated in Letter No. 48717/R dated 29.7.78 of Revenue Department.

2. This issue has been examined afresh in consultation with the Law Department. On that basis of our earlier view is hereby rescinded and the position is clarified as under.

3. Sub-section (1) of Section 19 of the Act sets out three distinct modes of partition of holdings namely, registered instruments, decree of a Civil Court and order of a Revenue Officer in the manner prescribed upon mutual agreement among the co-sharers. Quite clearly, therefore, partition of joint holding, upon mutual consent, through an order of the Revenue Officer has been conceived as a separated mode of partition distinct from a registered instrument.

4. Sub-section (6) of Section 19 of the Act envisages that an order of partition, upon mutual agreement, is required to be sent by the Revenue Officers the concerned Sub-Registrar for registration. The proviso to the sub-section provides that no 'charges' for such registration shall by payable. 'Charges' for registration does not mean or imply only registration fees. These charges include the stamp duty, additional stamp duty, and surcharge thereon payable for registration of documents/ orders. Therefore, even though orders of partition passed by the Revenue Officers in exercise of powers conferred by Section 19 (1) (c), upon mutual agreement, are required to be sent to the Sub-Registrar as provided under Section 6 for registration, neither of documents/orders. Therefore, even though orders of partition passed by the Revenue Officers in exercise of powers conferred by Section 19(1) (c) upon mutual agreement, are required to be sent to the Sub-Registrar as provided under Section 6 for registration, neither registration fees nor stamp duty, additional duty or any surcharge thereon is payable.

All concerned may be intimated accordingly.

This supersedes all previous instructions issued on the subject.

Yours faithfully,
Sd/-
Deputy Secretary to Government

BOARD OF REVENUE ORISSA, CUTTACK

No. XIV-2/99 340/L.R.
27th January, 2000

From

Shri G.C. Mandal, IAS
Land Reforms Commissioner

To

All Collectors

Subject: Instruction regarding filling of motion u/s 59(2) of O.L.R Act 1960 and u/s 38 (B) of O.E.A. Act 1951.

Ref: Board's letter No. 997 dt 20.2.99

Sir,

In inviting a reference to the Board of Revenue Circular No. 997 dt. 20.2.1999 on the above subject it was stipulated that all Revision cases u/s 59 (2) of O.L.R. Act 1960 and u/s 38 (b) O.E.A. Act 1951 are to be filled before the Hon'ble Member, Board of Revenue by the concerned Collectors through Land Reforms Commissioner for effective implementation of the provisions of O.L.R. and O.E.A. Act. It is now felt that the filling of the Revision cases through Land Reforms Commissioner is a time consuming affair. In order to avoid the unnecessary harassment to the parties concerned, it is worthwhile to file revisions under the above sections before the Hon'ble Member, Board of Revenue, directly instead of filling them through the Land Reforms Commissioner henceforth.

The above instructions should be followed strictly. This supersedes the earlier instructions issued from the Board under reference.

Yours faithfully,
Sd/-
Land Reforms Commissioner, Orissa

Board of Revenue, Orissa

LAND REFORMS BRANCH, CUTTACK

No. 9113-xv-63/71-L.R.

From

Shri V.K. Samantaray, O.A.S. (I)
Deputy Land Reforms Commissioner,
Board of Revenue, Orissa, Cuttack.

To

All Collectors

Cuttack, the 2nd December, 1971

Subject: Fixation of yardstick for disposal of O.L.R. Cases by the Sub-Divisional Officers, Tahsildars and Additional Tahsildars.

Sir,

I am directed to say that Board has been pleased to decide that the Additional Tahsildar specially posted for Land Reforms Act case should dispose of 60 cases per day. Where no Additional Tahsildars has been posted and one officer handle the cases under more than one Act the yardstick for disposal will be 20 cases per day.

The yardstick for the disposal of cases under Sections 22 and 23 of the O.L.R. Act by Submissional Officer has been fixed as 30 per day.

3. You are requested to please issue suitable instructions to all Sub-Divisional Officers /Tahsildars and Additional Tahsildars in your district to follow the yardstick without deviation. Their performance may also be reviewed periodically and review reports furnished for information of the Board.

4. A copy of this letter is being forwarded to all Sub-Divisional Officers, Tahsildars for their information.

Yours faithfully,
V.K. SAMANTARAY
Deputy Land Reforms Commissioner

Memo. No. 9114-L.R.
Dated the 2nd December, 1971

Copy forwarded to all Sub-Divisional Officers and Tahsildars for information and necessary action.

V.K. SAMANTARAY
Deputy Land Reforms Commissioner

File No. XV-71/70-No. 2017-L.R.

Dated the 25th May, 1971, from O.L.R.C., Orissa

Subject: Instruction in dealing with cases under Section 22 of O.L.R. Act.

In inviting reference to this office letter No. 14523 (13)-L.R. dated the 16th October, 1969 and No. 6466 (13)-L.R., dated the 2nd May, 1970, I am directed to say that in the aforesaid circular an elaborate procedure was prescribed indicating how the cases under sections 22 and 23 of the O.L.R Act should be dealt with. It has come to the notice of the Board that the said elaborate procedure has caused delay in the disposal of the cases. Issue of revised procedure was under the active consideration of Board. After careful consideration Board has been pleased to simplify the procedure and desire that the procedure outlined below should be followed while dealing with cases under section 2 of O.L.R. Act.

On receipt of an application for sale of land by a Member of Scheduled Tribe or Caste the Branch Clerk of the S.D.O. should scrutinise the application. If the application is defective in any details or Court fees are wanting, the applicant may be given a week's time to make good the omission. If the application is completed in all respects, the S.D.O. shall admit it and shall pass order of issue of proclamation inviting claims and objections within a month from the date of service of the notice. The applicant shall bear the proclamation fee. He shall file Court fee worth Rs. 1.50 for the purpose. One copy of the proclamation shall be served in the village, where the land situates and another copy at the village belonging to the seller, if the land situates in the different village, the proclamation shall be served either personally or by affixture, in which signature of 2 adult members of the community of the seller shall be obtained.

One copy of the proclamation shall be sent to the A.D.W.O. of the Sub-Divisional with direction to file objection, if any,

On the fixed date, if the proclamations have been duly served on all concerned, the S.D.O. shall hear the parties and if there are objections, shall hear the objections, their record their evidence in writing if necessary and pass order thereon. He shall grant permission for transfer, only when he is satisfied that no other member belonging to the community of the seller is willing to pay the market price for the land. The S.D.O. while considering the petition shall also consider the reasonableness of the price offered for the land. If the price does not appear to him reasonable, he shall refuse such permission.

If purchases, from the community of the seller are available who are willing to purchase the land on market price, their case should be given preference over the prospective purchase.

Immediately after passing order, the order should be communicated in the Form No. 'B' or 'C' prescribed under this Office letter No. 14523 (13), dated 16.10.1968 whichever is necessary.

A register of those cases in Form of (Revenue Misc. Case Regr). should be maintained in S.D.O.'s office. This supersedes the instruction issued in this office letter No. 14523 (12) L.R. dated 16th October, 1969, relating to disposal of cases under section 22 of O.L.R. Act.

Memo No. 2018
Dated the 25th March, 1971

Copy forwarded to all S.D.O. for information and necessary action.

Memo No. 2018
Dated the 25th March, 1971

Copy forwarded to the Joint Secretary to Government, Revenue Department, Bhubaneswar for information.

Memo No. 2018
Dated the 23rd March, 1969

Copy to Guard File of all Officers (L.R. Branch).

BOARD OF REVENUE, ORISSA
LAND REFORMS BRANCH, CUTTACK

No. 1423 (13)-XV-41/69
Dated the 16th October, 1969

From

Shri M.B.D.E O.A.S.
Deputy Commissioner, Land Reforms, Orissa

To

All Collectors

Subject: Instructions in dealing with cases under Sections 22 and 23 of the Orissa Land Reforms Act 1960.

Sir,

I am directed to say that section 22 of the Orissa Land Reforms Act 1960 imposes restriction on alienation of land by sale, gift or mortgage by a member of the Scheduled Tribes or Scheduled Castes to a person not belonging to such Scheduled Tribes or Castes. Section 23 of the Act provides for restriction of lands transferred in contravention of the provisions of the Section 22. It is noticed that adequate care and attention are not being given in the matter of grant of permission for transfer of land by Scheduled Tribes and Scheduled Castes or restoration of their land illegally transferred. In view of the importance of the matter it is considered necessary to issue the following instructions which should be strictly followed by the Sub-Divisional Officers and Tahsildars.

I. Cases under Section 22(i)(b) of Orissa Land Reforms Act:

1. Application should bear Court fee stamp of Rs. 1.10 P. (Section 62, Rule 46 and item I of the schedule to the Rules)
2. Proclamation of general notice fee of Rs. 1.50 P is leviable

in Court fee stamps in each case. (Item 6 of the schedule to the Rules).

3. If a portion of a Survey plea is sought to be transferred and permission accorded measurement fee of Rs. 2.00 per plot to be sub-divided should be paid in cash (item 7 of the Schedule to the Rules)
4. Application should be signed and verified by the Application. This is necessary as enquiries and proceedings under the Act are judicial proceedings (Section 64)
5. On filing of application the Bench Clerk of the Sub-divisional Officer should scrutinise and submit it with his note and an order sheet to the S.D.O. within 3 days. If the applications defective in any details or Court fees are wanting the applicant may be given a week's time to make good the commission. If the application is complete in all good the omission. If the application is complete in all respects, the Sub-Divisional Officer may admit it and send a copy thereof to the Tahsildar concerned alongwith the proclamation (duly signed by him) inviting claims and objection within a month. A copy of the proclamation should be sent to the D.W.O. and A.D.W.O. of the Sub-Division for filing objection, if any.
6. The Tahsildar should publish the proclamation in the village in which the land sought to be transferred is situated and return the served copy to the Sub-Divisional Officer. He should simultaneously get the details of the land verified by his Record Keeper with the R.O.R. (as in the case of a Mutation case) and if the details are found to be incorrect he may allow the applicant to rectify them within a week.

   If the area is unsurveyed, the Tahsildar should get the description, area and boundaries verified and recorded during the course of his enquiry.
7. The Tahsildar should, therefore, enquire into the application and submit a report in form A appended hereto. His enquiry should be searching so far as the genuineness of the necessity for transfer and voluntary nature of the application are concerned. If the need can be met by any other method (Institutional loans by Government or Co-operation) he should desist from recommending the case. As the Agent of the State Government, he should try to stick to the policy of the Government and discourage wanton or induced transfer

of land by Scheduled Tribes/Scheduled Castes. As in any scheme of welfare of weaker sections of the society, the Panchayati Raj Institutions should play a vital role, he should consult the concerned Gram Panchayat and obtain its views in the body of his report. If a transfer by sale is absolutely necessary, he should try to fix up a prospective purchase belonging to the concerned Scheduled Tribe/Scheduled Caste.

8. On receipt of the Tahsildar's report and claim and objections, if any, in response to the proclamation, the S.D.O. should consider them, hear the parties and pass orders giving his reasons therefor in the order sheet of the case record. His orders are appealable to the Collector under Section 58(1) read with Section 63 and Rule 44. The Sub-Divisional Officer is competent to review his orders under Section 60 for clerical mistakes.
9. Immediately after passing orders, the S.D.O. should communicate them in Form 'B' or 'C' appended hereto according permission on refusal as the case may be.
10. (a) A register of these cases in Form No. 8 (Revenue Misc case register prescribed in the Bihar and Orissa Register, and Return Manual 1932) should be maintained in the S.D.O's Office.
    (b) The papers in the case record should be classified into A.B.C. and D according to Para 238 and Appendix 'M' of the Orissa Records Manual, 1964 and case record consigned to the Record Room. The application. Tahsildar's report in form A and the S.D.O's order in form 'B' or 'C' should be treated as 'A' class papers.

II. Cases under Section 23 of the Orissa Land Reforms Act

1. The Sub-Divisional Officer can himself *suo motu* take up any case under this section. One of the important and reliable source of his information will be report from the concerned Tahsildar, who gets notices in Form No. 3 from the Registration Officer (Section 11 and Rule 14). If the Tahsildar finds that any transfer is not caused by the permission of the Sub-Divisional Officer, he should immediately send an intimation to the S.D.O. for action under Section 23. In such cases applicant and process fees should not be levied.

2. If an application ended under the section, it should bear court fee stamp of R 1 and process fee of Rs. 1.50 (items 1 and 6 of the Schedule to the Rules) and should be signed and verified.
3. The Orissa Land Reforms Act has only prospective effect. Section 23 does not cover illegal transfers made prior to the 1st October, 1965, in respect of illegal transfers made by Scheduled Tribes between the 22nd May, 1962, and the 30th September, 1965, the proviso of Section 7 (h) (i) of O.M.S.L. Act would apply).

   Secondly, notwithstanding the fact that a transfer without the prior permission of Sub-Divisional Officers is void or invalid under Section 22 (each) of the O.L.R. Act the law of prescription would prevaries, possession can be perfected after 12 years of adverse possession. Noted 21(k) under Act 65 of the Indian Limitation Act 1963 and para 12 of letter No. 2026-XXI /66-L.R.S. after the 25th February, 1966, from the Board of Revenue to the Settlement Officers.)

   The Sub-Divisional Officer's order of *suo motu* action or the application as the case may be should be the starting point of a case under section 23.
4. The Sub-Divisional Officer should himself take up enquiry in these cases. The enquiry, if made in the concerned village or at least at the revenue Circle headquarters, will be very useful. The requisite show cause notice should be issued to the persons interested.
5. A copy of the show cause notice should be sent to the D.W.O. and A.D.W.C. and the concerned Tahsildar. The D.W.O. may arrange financial aid to the applicant under the T.R.W. scheme. The Tahsildar may cause productions of relevant land records.
6. On completion on the enquiry, the Sub-Divisional Officer may pass order giving reasons therefor. His orders are subject to appeal to the Collector and revision against Collector's order lies to the Board of Revenue as in the case of application under section 22(1) (b) of the Act.
7. If the Sub-Divisional Officer's order as to restore the land to the transferer, he is to enforce his order by issuing a warrant of delivery of possession as under the Civil Procedure Code (Sec. 65 of the O.L.R. Act and Rule 47 thereunder)

8. On effective delivery of possession to the transferor to the Gram Panchayat in the circumstances stated on the proviso to Section an intimation should be sent to the Tahsildar concern for effecting correction of land records.
9. (a) A register of the case record should be maintained (in form No.8 of the Bihar and Orissa Register and Return Manual, 1932)
   (b) The paper in the case record should be classified and the record consigned to the Record Room as laid down in para 238 and Appendix 'M' of Orissa Records Manual 1964. The order of restoration, the evidence and the applications or the order of *suo motu* action by the Sub-Divisional Officer should be treated as 'A' Class papers.

Receipt of the latter may please be acknowledged.

Yours faithfully,
M.B.D.E.
Deputy Commissioner, Land Reforms Orissa

Memo No 14524 (11)-L.R.
Dated the 16th October, 1969

Copy forwarded to all Sub-Divisional Officers/all Tahsildars for information and necessary action.

M.B.D.E.
Deputy Commissioner, Land Reforms, Orissa

FORM-A

Report of the Tahsildar as applications for permission under action 22(i)/b/22(i) (b) and (4) of the Orissa Land Reforms Net, 1960 for transfer of land.

1. Same, father's name and address of the applicant.
2. Scheduled Tribe/Scheduled Caste of the applicant: (According to Scheduled Caste and Scheduled Tribes Lists (Modification) Order, 1956).
3. Particular of the total land held by the applicant: Village Khata No. Plot No. Area Kisam Rent (Note—The village in unsurveyed, five description, area, boundaries and rest of the land.)

4. Whether any portion on the land by the applicant was granted in Nayabadi basis; if so, the year of grant and extent of land—
5. (a) No. of his family members living in one mess.
   (i) His annual income from agricultural and other source separately.
6. Particulars of the portion of the land sought to be transferred. Village Khata No., Plot No., Area Kisam Rent.
   (*Note*—the village is unsurveyed, give description, area, boundaries and that of the land)
7. Object of the proposed transfer; whether this is genuine or induced or ill conceived.
8. Nature of the proposed transfer, whether the form of transfer is in his best interest, if not, recommend some other form of transfer which may be better (giving reasons).
9. Name, caste and address of the person to whom the land is proposed to be transferred.
10. If the permission applied for is only to satisfy and alienation already made, has the Tahsildar explained to the applicant that he can obtain possession of the land for the mere asking of it, subject to the law of prescription?
11. (a) Current market price of the land sought to be transferred by sale (give reasons);
    (b) What is the price at which the applicant proposes to transfer the land;
    (c) Whether any member of the Scheduled Tribe, Scheduled Caste is prepared to have the land alienated in his behaviour for the current market price of the land ? If so, give his name and address and tribe/caste.
12. If the proposed transfer is by way of gift (other than a gift to Government or a local authority for development projects) and whether it is genuine, voluntary and free from inducement.
13. What is the total indebtedness of the applicant from Government, Co-operative and private sources.
14. Whether the object of transfer is one that can be satisfied by a loan under the A.L. Act or L.I.L. Act or from a Co-operative society, If so, he may be advised to apply for such loan.
15. Whether he is the beneficiary of any financial aid from Government (T. and R.W. Deptt.) etc., if so, when and how much and for what purpose.

16. Whether the land proposed for transfer is a Bhoodan land and if so, whether the Orissa Bhoodan Samity granted any financial aid etc. to the applicant.

    Note—Guarantee of Bhoodan lands have no alienating rights in land except to offer them as security for loans from Government or Co-operative, Reft-Section 16 of the Bhoodan Yojana Act 1953.

17. Whether the land proposed for transfer is Bhoodan land and if so, whether the Orissa Bhoodan Samity granted any financial aid etc. to the applicant.
18. Whether permission was granted previously to the applicant. If so, when and for what extent of land. If permission was refused before, for what reasons.
19. If the applicant is a resident of the Juang pirhs, has the village community agreed to the transfer?

    Note— In the Juang prihs villagers pay rent to Government collectively. This ancient system will continue until the area is surveyed and settled.

20. Views of the concerned Gram Panchayat with the signature of the Sarpanch.
21. Views of the Tahsildar (with reasons).

Note—In these cases the State is also an objector in that it is the duty of its officers to ensure that the interest of the Scheduled Tribes/Castes are maintained due to the transfer and that they are not left in indignant circumstances after the sale of their lands—R.F. Board of Revenue letter No. 89 (b) Reve., dated 1st March, 1962.

Note—2 It would be other freely permit sale of lands by Scheduled Tribe, Caste with the possible effect of reducing them to landless condition, while on the other hand, the State has accorded high priority to them in the matter of lease of Government lands under the approved Lease Principal 1961.

Station

Dated .... Tahsildar

Memo No. .... Dated ....

Submitted to the Sub-Divisional Officer with reference to his letter No............ Dated...............

Tahsildar

FORM-B

Permission of the S.D.O. Under Section 22 (i) (a), 22(i) (b) and (4) of O.L.R Act 1960 Act 1960 for transfer of land.

1. Name, father's name and address of the applicant.
2. Name of the Scheduled Tribe/Scheduled Caste to which he belongs.
3. Details of the land permitted for transfer to other than a Scheduled Tribe/Scheduled Caste person.
   Village Khata No., Plot No., Area Kisam Rent)
4. (Nature of transfer)
5. Fair market price of the land if the transfer is by sale.
6. Purpose of transfer.
7. Reasons for the permission.

Station

Date (Sub-Divisional Officer

Memo No. ....   Dated ....

Forwarded to applicant (Through the Tahsildar...........) with reference to his application dated.............

Sub-Divisional Officer.

Copy to the Tahsildar................for information with reference to his report No.....................dated......................... . Necessary action should be taken on receipt of the notice in O.L.R. Form No. 3 from the Registration Office as required under Section II of the Orissa Land Reforms Act 1960 read with rules 14 of the general rules thereunder.

Sub-Divisional Officer

Memo No. ....   Dated ....

Copy to the Sub-Registrar for information.

Sub-Divisional Officer

Memo No. ....   Dated ....

Copy to the P.W.O., Keonjhar/A.D.W.O. of the Sub-Divisional/ B.D.O./ Sarpanch /G.P. for information.

They will please see that permit holder gets reasonable price and utilises the sale money for the purpose shown against items 6 of the above permission.

Sub-Divisional Officer.

FORM-C

Order of refusal to grant permission u/s 22 (i), (a) 22(i) (b) and (4) of the O.L.R. Act, 1960.

1. Name, father's name and address of the applicant.
2. Name of the Scheduled Tribe/Scheduled Caste to which he belongs.
3. Details of the land applied for transfer to other than a Scheduled Tribe/Scheduled Caste person:

   Village, Khata No., Plot No., Area, Kisam Rent

   (If unsurveyed, description, area, boundaries and rent)
4. (a) Purpose of proposed transfer, and

   (b) Nature of proposed transfer
5. Reasons for refusal of permission.
6. Name of the Scheduled Tribe/Scheduled Caste to which he belongs.
7. Details of the land applied for transfer to other than a Scheduled Tribe/Scheduled Caste person:

   Village, Khata No., Plot No., Area, Kisam Rent

   (If unsurveyed, description, area, boundaries and rent)
8. (a) Purpose of proposed transfer,

   (b) Nature of proposed transfer.

   Reasons for refusal of permission.

Station
Dated (Seal)
Sub-Divisional Officer

Memo No. .... Dated ....

Forwarded to the applicant (Through the Tahsildar...............with reference to his application dated ....)

Sub-Divisional Officer

Memo No. .... Dated ....

Copy to the Tahsildar .... for information with reference to his report No. .... dated

Sub-Divisional Officer

Memo No. .... Dated ....

Copy to the Tahsildar .... for information with reference to his report No. .... dated.

Sub-Divisional Officer

Memo No. .... Dated ....

Copy to Sarpanch..................................... G.P. for information.

Sub-Divisional Officer

BOARD OF REVENUE, ORISSA
Land Reforms Branch

CUTTACK
No. 4855-XV-7/72-L.R.
Cuttack, the 28th September, 1972

From

Shri G. Das, O.A.S.,
Asst. Land Reforms Commissioner, Orissa, Cuttack

To

All Collectors

Subject—Quick disposal of case u/s. 22 and 23 of the O.L.R. Act 1960.

Sir,

I am directed to say that in Board's letter No. 9113 L.R., dated 2nd December, 1971, target for disposal of O.L.R cases under section 22 and 23 of the Act was fixed at 30 per day.

It appears from the progress returns that the monthly target is not being adhered to. In the result, a large pendency of cases has accumulated for disposal. This spirit behind the protective provisions of the Act under Section 22 and 23 can be realised only if the case under the said sections are disposed of expeditiously and delay is avoided.

It is requested that necessary instruction may please be issued to all Sub-divisional Officers to keep in mind the instruction of the Board cited above in respect of the disposal of the pending cases.

The proforma prescribed for submission of monthly return under Sections 22 and 23 of the O.L.R. Act has been revised. A new column after col. 9 indicating the views of the Collectors on the progress of disposal of cases by each Court and the reasons for poor progress, if any, has been added to it.

The monthly return u/s 22 and 23 may please be furnished to the Board along with the other return in the revised proforma (enclosed) regularly and in time.

Yours faithfully
G. DAS
Assistant Land Reforms Commissioner

Memo. No. 4856-L.R.
Dated the 28th September, 1972

Copy forwarded to all Sub-Divisional Officers for information and necessary action.

G. DAS
Assistant Land Reforms Commissioner

Memo No. 4857-L.R.
Dated the 28th September, 1972
Copy to Guard file

G. DAS
Assistant Land Reforms Commissioner

Progress Report under Section 22 of the O.L.R. Act

Sl. No.	*Name of the Sub-Division*	*Total No of cases instituted till the end of the last month*	*No. of cases instituted during the month*	*Total Cols. (3+4)*	*Total No. of cases disposed of till the end of the last month*	*No. of cases disposed of during the month*	*Total Balance Cols. (6+7)*	*Views of the Collector on the performance of Sub-Divisional Officers and the reasons for poor performances, if any*	*Total No. of cases rejected out of the total disposal*	*No of cases in which permission granted for transfer of land.*
1	2	3	4	5	6	7	8	9	10	11

Progress Report under Section 23 of the O.L.R. Act

Sl. No.	*Name of the Sub-Division*	*Total No. of cases institu-ted till the end of the last month*	*No. of cases institu-ted during the month*	*Total Cols. (3+4)*	*Total No. of cases dispo-sed of till the end of the last month*	*No. of cases dispo-sed of during the month*	*Total Balan-ce Cols. (6+7)*	*Bal-ance*	*Views of the Collec-tor on the perfor-mance of Sub-Divisi-onal Officers and the reasons for poor perfor-mance if any*	*No of cases decal-red invalid*	*No of cases in which pro-perty resto-red.*	*No of Per-sons bene-fitted*	*Area invol-ved*
1	2	3	4	5	6	7	8	9	10	11	12	13	14

GOVERNMENT OF ORISSA
REVENUE DEPARTMENT

No.47416 AG-63/71-R

From

Premananda Tripathy
Secretary to Government

To

All Collector

Dated Bhubaneswar the 27th August, 1971

Subject: Illegal Transfer of Lands belonging to the member of Scheduled Castes and Scheduled Tribes to Non-Scheduled Castes and Tribes.

Sir,

I am directed to say that Section 3 of the Orissa Scheduled Areas Transfer of Immovable Property (by Scheduled Tribes) Regulation 1956 (Regulation 2 of 1956) imposes restriction on transfer of immovable property by a member of Scheduled Tribe in Scheduled Areas of the State. Similar restriction has also been imposed under Section 22 of the Orissa Land Reforms Act 1960 in the non-Scheduled area of the State.

2. In spite of issue of repeated instructions to follow meticulously the spirit of law in this regard, it has been brought to the notice of the Government that the problems relating to a unauthorised occupation of land belonging to the members of the Scheduled Tribe by non-Scheduled Tribe person are on the increase. This has resulted in discontent amongst the member of Scheduled Tribe who, on account of their general ignorance, have found themselves in a helpless condition. Government, therefore, desire that the interests of the Tribals in the State should be fully protected and it may be ensured that they are not exploited on account of their ignorance of law.

3. The Sub-divisional Officers and Collectors who are in-charge or General Administration have special responsibilities in this regard. The transfer of land from an *Adivasi* to a non-*Adivasi* requires the

sanctions of the sub-divisional officer in over that such transfer becomes legal and valid. If the past the sub-divisional officers have treated legal and valid. If the past the sub-divisional officers have treated requests for permission very liberally in complete disregard to the interests for the tribals. Government desire that you may issue necessary instructions to the sub-divisional officers to keep a strict watch on such illegal transfer of lands belonging to members of Scheduled Tribe to persons not belonging to Scheduled Tribe and to ensure that the interest of tribals in this regard are fully protected. While granting permission for transfer of lands in the above case the application for transfer should be most carefully scrutinised and permission refused in all but in most genuine cases.

BOARD OF REVENUE, ORISSA

Land Reforms Branch, Cuttack

No. 5339/L.R. Cuttack, dated the 7th August, 1979

From

S. Sundaranjan, I.A.S
Land Reforms Commissioner, Orissa

To

All Collectors,

Subject: Sale of land belonging to a Scheduled Tribe or Scheduled Caste in execution of a decree permission of Revenue Officer under Section 22 of the O.L.R. Act.

It has come to the notice of Board that some Tahsils while as Certificate Officer have sold away land belonging to a Scheduled Tribe or a Scheduled Castes in contravention of the mandatory provisions contained in Section 22 of the O.L.R. Act.

Section 22 of the O.L.R. Act restricts transfer of a holding or thereof by a raiyat belonging to a Scheduled Tribe or a Scheduled Castes to a person not belonging to such tribe or caste except with the permission of the Revenue Officer. Sub-Section (3) of Section

22, as good before the Amendment Act 17 of 1973 was brought into force, provided that even in the case of sale of land belonging to Scheduled Caste or Scheduled Tribe in execution of decree such permission shall be obtained. However, in such cases of sale in execution of a decree the permission of the Court executing the decree and not the Competent authority or Revenue Officer was necessary. Where the aforesaid conditions have not been fulfilled the sale would be *ab inito* void.

Sub-Section (3) of Section 22 was substituted through Act 1973. The new provisions which came into force on 2.10.1973 read except with the written permission of the Revenue Officer no such filing (belonging to a S.T) shall be sold in execution of a decree to any person not belonging to a Scheduled Tribe". This applies *mutatis mutandis* to scheduled land belonging to a Scheduled Tribe or a Schedule Caste in execution of decree to a person not belonging to the tribe or caste prior written permission of the Revenue Officer shall have to be obtained. Where such permission has not been obtained the sale becomes void *ab initio*. Therefore, in a case of a sale of land through execution certificate decree permission of the Revenue Officer will have to be obtained if the highest bidder in whose favour the sale is being confirmed does not belong to Scheduled Tribe or Scheduled Caste and where the recorded owner belongs to a Scheduled Tribe or Scheduled Caste. In all such cases before the sale in confirmed sale certificate issued by Certificate Officer should be obtained by the Revenue Officer of the area.

In the case of sale of land belonging to a Scheduled Tribe a person not belonging to a Scheduled Tribe in the scheduled area of State, prior permission of the competent authority shall have to be obtained as stipulated in the second proviso to Sec. 3 (1) of Regulation 2 of 1956.

It is requested that these instructions may be brought to the notice of all the Revenue Officers and Certificate Courts under your control for their guidance.

Yours faithfully,
Sd/-
Land Reforms Commissioner,
Orissa

Copy, with a copy of the letter No. 50772 dated 11.07.1979 of the Deputy Secretary to Govt. Revenue Department, Orissa

Bhubaneswar addressed to the B/R Orissa, Cuttack is forwarded to Collector, Koraput vide Memo No. 50774 of even date.

Subject: Enforcement of the provisions of Regulation 2 of 1956 in the newly defined scheduled areas of the State.

Sir,

I am directed to invite a reference to this Department latter No. 67253/R., dated 11.10.1978 and to say that with a view to bring the newly defined a scheduled Area Transfer of Immovable property (by Scheduled Tribe) Regulation 2 of the said Regulation 1956 Clause (3) of Section 2 of the said regulation has since been amended with effect from 12.6.1979. The Amendment regulation, viz., Orissa Scheduled Areas Transfer of Immovable Property (By Scheduled Tribe) Amendment Regulation, 1979 (Regulation 1 of 1979) has been published in the Extraordinary issue of Orissa Gazette No. 1244, dt. 12.6.1979. The present Scheduled areas of the State are as follows:

	District	*Sub-Division*	*Scheduled Areas*
1.	Mayurbhanj	All Sub-Divisions	Whole district.
2.	Sundargarh	-do-	-do-
3.	Koraput	-do-	-do-
4.	Sambalpur	Kuchinda	Kuchinda Tahsil
5.	Keonjhar	Keonjhar	Keonjhar and Telkoi Tahsil
6.	Boudha Kandhmals	Balliguada	Baliguda and G. Udayagiri
7.	Phulbani	Khandamals	Khandamals Tahsil
8.	Ganjam	Khandamals	Khandamals Tahsil R. Udaygiri Tahsil. Guma and Rayagada Blocks of Paralekhemundi Tahsil.
		Ghumsur	Suruda Tahsil (Excluding Gazalhadi and Gocha G.P.S.
9.	Kalahandi	Bhavanipatna	Thumal Rampur Block of Kalahandi Tahsil and Lanjigarh Block

10. Balasore	Nilagiri	Notified in Lanjigarh and Kalahandi Tahsils Nilagiri C.D. Block of Nilagiri Tahsil.

2. Transfer of immovable property belonging to the Scheduled Tribe of the above Scheduled Areas of the State Government notification conferring powers of competent authority on the Sub-divisional officers areas are being issued separately.

3. Suitable instruction may please be issued to all concerned to take adequate steps to tackle the land alienation problems belonging to tribals of the above Scheduled areas.

Yours faithfully
Sd/-
Deputy Secretary to Govt.

Copy of letter No. 72492/82, dated 11.11.86 of the Secretary, Revenue and Excise Department, Orissa, Bhubaneswar addressed to all Collectors and all P.A. (I.T.D.A.) in Memo No. 72493/82 of even date.

Subject: Grant of permission for alienation of tribal land to non-tribals.

Sir,

I am directed to say that Section 3(1) of the Orissa Scheduled Area Transfer of Immovable Property (By Scheduled Tribes) Regulation 1956, (Regulation 2 of 1956) provides that any transfer of immovable property situated within Scheduled Area by member of ST shall be null and void and no force or effect whatever unless made in favour of another member of ST or which previous consent in writing of the competent authority. Thus the competent authority under the regulation can grant permission for alienation of tribal land not a non-tribal. That a lot of mischief is committed while granting permission for alienation of tribal land to non-tribals has come to the notice of Government in a number of instances in the past. Since protection of interest of the tribals in their land is utmost important the State Government has appointed all P.A.I.T.D. As located in

Scheduled Areas. S.D.O. Nilagiri and A.D.M. (Revenue) Ganjam as competent authority for the Scheduled areas in their respective jurisdiction or vide Notification No. 32729/R dated 19.8.1986.

2. In order to guard against any possible mischief and prevent indiscriminate transfer of tribal land, it has been decided by the Government that the competent authority before passing the final order for granting permission should invariably submit the case-record to the concerned Collector and obtain his approval so that sanction if any, on the part of competent authority is subject to prior scrutiny before such final order is passed.

Yours faithfully
Sd/-
P.M. Mahapatra
Commission-cum-Secretary to Govt.

BOARD OF REVENUE, ORISSA
LAND REFORMS BRANCH

CUTTACK

No. V-122/86 3383/LR. Dated 16.4.1986

From

Shri Pratap Mukhopadhyay, I.A.S.,
Land Reforms Commissioner

To

All Collectors,

Subject: Extract from inspection note dt. 30.7.1982 of Member, Board of the Revenue, Orissa Cuttack on the Tahsil Officer, Bargarh regarding transfer of and belonging to Scheduled Caste persons to non-Scheduled Caste persons.

Sir,

I am directed to say that member, Board of Revenue during this inspection of Tahsil office, Bargarh, while reviewing O.L.R. case

No.18/79 had observed that the S.D.O. has allowed a non-Scheduled Caste person to purchase lands belonging to a Scheduled Caste person at the rate of Rs. 7,000 per acre in a village which is irrigated though the Tahsildar had reported the rate to be Rs. 10,000 to Rs. 15.000.

2. Member, Board of Revenue, is of the view that the S.D.O. is there to protect the interest of Scheduled Caste and Scheduled Tribe persons for getting adequate value for their lands.

3. Regulation 2 of 1956 deals with the transfer of land by Scheduled Tribe. The rules made thereunder prescribe a form of enquiry on the application seeking permission to alienate the land. But, under the O.L.R. Act no such provision is forthcoming.

4. In this context it may be stated that Section 22 of the O.L.R. Act provides that:

> "Any transfer of a holding, or part thereof, by a raiyat, belonging to Scheduled Tribe shall be void except where it is in favour of—
>
> (a) A person belonging to a Scheduled Tribe, or
>
> (b) A person not belonging to a Scheduled Tribe when such transfer is made with the previous permission in writing of the Revenue officer.

5. Provided that in case of a transfer by sale, the Revenue Officer, shall not grant such permission unless he is satisfied that a purchaser belonging to a Scheduled Tribe willing to pay the market price for the land is not available, and, in case of a gift, unless he is satisfied about the benefits thereof.

6. Similarly, Section 3 of the Orissa Scheduled Area Transfer of Immovable Property (by Scheduled Tribe) Regulation 1956, says that:

> "Notwithstanding anything contained in any law for the time being in force, any transfer of immovable property situated within a Scheduled Area, by a member of a Scheduled Tribe, shall be absolutely null and void and of no force or effect whatsoever unless made in favour of another member of Scheduled Tribe or with the previous consent, in writing, of the competent authority.

7. In the past, a number of instructions have been issued outlying the procedure to be followed by the Revenue permission of sale of land. In Board's circular No. XV-47/71-2017/LR, dated 25.3.1971, it was emphasised that the Revenue Officer shall grant permission for the transfer of land by Scheduled Tribe and Scheduled Caste only when he is satisfied that no other member belonging to the community of the seller is willing to pay market price for the land. S.D.O., while considering the petition, shall also consider the reasonableness of the price offered for the land and if the price does not appear to him reasonable, he shall refuse such permission, Further, it has also been specified that if purchasers from the community of the sellers are available, who are willing to purchase the land at market price, they should be given preference over the prospective purchaser/purchasers not belonging to the community of the seller.

8. Similarly, under Regulation 1 of 1956, a form has been prescribed for report of the Officer conducting enquiry on application of permission to transfer land by S.T. to non-Scheduled Tribe. Here, too, emphasis is on the market price of the land and, whether any other person of the community of the seller is available to purchase at market price of the land. A number of circulars have also been issued by the Government outlining the procedure for enquiry under the Regulation and grant of permission. Though the protective legislations do not provide for, in clear words, that permission shall not be granted unless the prospective buyer undertakes to purchase that land at the market rate, it is incumbent on the Revenue Officer/ competent authority to consider, before granting permission, that the purchaser is agreeable to pay market price and nobody from the community of the seller is available to purchase the land at the market price. These two are major factors to be taken, into consideration before granting permission. Board's circular dt. 25.3.71 referred to above, highlights the above points.

9. As the S.D.O. has committed either indiscretion or irregularity in granting permission to sell the land at Rs. 7,000 per acre when the price of the land is more than Rs. 10,000 even after issue of a number of instruction to that effect. I am, therefore, directed to reiterate the circulars issued earlier and make it clear that any laxity on the part of the Revenue Officer, the competent authority in such cases will be viewed seriously in future.

10. This may kindly be brought home to all concerned under your control.

Yours faithfully,
Sd/-
Land Reforms Commissioner,
Orissa

GOVERNMENT OF ORISSA

REVENUE AND EXCISE DEPARTMENT

No. 37431/R/Ag. 50/88, dated 7th June, 1988

From

B.C. Patnaik
Secretary to Government

To

All Collectors
All Project Officers T.D. Ps.

Subject: Indiscriminate alienation of tribal lands to non-tribals.

Sir,

I am directed to say that Section 3 of the Regulation imposes restriction on transfer of immovable property by a member of Scheduled Tribe and any transfer made in violation of this provision in favour of a non-Scheduled Tribe a person shall be null and void unless made with the previous permission of the competent authority, Similar restriction has also been imposed under Section 22 of the O.L.R. Act 1960 in the non-scheduled areas of the State.

2. In spite of such provisions in the law, it has been brought to the notice of the Government that alienation of lands of Scheduled Tribes in favour of non-Scheduled Tribe persons continue unabated. Very often found exercising these powers rather liberally to the detriment of the interest of the Scheduled Tribes. It has resulted in further alienation of tribal land in favour of non-Scheduled Tribes. In order to remove the shortcomings in implementation of the laws, Government have been considering to bring certain amendments.

Pending such amendment, it is imperative that the interest of the Scheduled Tribes in their lands should be fully protected and offices at various levels empowered to accord permission for transfer of lands under the law should observe the following guidelines meticulously while according permission for transfer of tribal lands in favour of non-tribals.

(i) Rule 3 of Orissa Scheduled areas transfer of Immovable property (By Scheduled Tribes) Rules 1959 provides that on receipt of an application from a member of Scheduled Tribe to transfer any immovable property to a member of non-Scheduled Tribes, the competent authority may cause necessary enquiry before passing appropriate orders. The enquiry report required to be submitted in the Form appended to the rules. This report is to form the basis for considering the merit of the application. The competent authority may accord permission for the reasons to be recorded in writing only after he is satisfied that the transfer would be in the best interest of the applicant. It becomes incumbent on him to observe utmost caution and scrutinise the applications and also the enquiry reports carefully before deciding to accord permission.

GOVERNMENT OF ORISSA

REVENUE AND EXCISE DEPARTMENT

No. Ag-90/94-13239/R.
Bhubaneswar, the 2nd March, 1994

From

Shir A.K. Tripathy, I.A.S.,
Commissioner-cum-Secretary to Government

To

The Collectors.

Subject: Enforcement of legal provisions against the illegal alienation/unauthorised occupation of land belonging to Scheduled Castes and Scheduled Tribes.

Sir,

I am directed to say that in order to safeguard the interest of the Scheduled Castes and Scheduled Tribes in their land protective provisions have been made in the Orissa Land Reforms Act 1960 and the Orissa Scheduled Area Transfer of Immovable Property (By Scheduled Tribes) Regulation 1956 Law empowers the Revenue Officer/Competent authority to initiate *suo motu* proceedings against the person(s) who have made illegal alienation or unauthorised occupation and restore such land with Scheduled Tribe/Scheduled Caste owners or with their legal heirs after evicting those unauthorised occupants. Since most of the persons belonging to Scheduled Castes and Scheduled Tribes are illiterate and are not well aware of these provisions, they are not coming forward to lodge their complaints, instructions were issued in the past to initiate *suo motu* proceedings by the Revenue field staff as well as by the welfare staff of Harijan Welfare Department and Tribal Welfare Department. Monthly targets were also fixed to detect and initiate such cases for such field staffs. As would be seen such instructions are not being carried out in the field. Many a times news items have appeared in the newspapers regarding unauthorised occupation. Of lands belonging to Scheduled Castes/Scheduled Tribes, which indicate that Revenue, Harijan and Tribal Welfare Department field staff have not discharged their duties satisfactorily.

2. The Parliamentary Committee on Welfare of Scheduled Tribes and Scheduled Castes during their visit to Koraput district noticed that tribal lands are being alienated on *benami* transactions as a result of those lands were being enjoyed by other freely. Three such cases were detected out of which lands were restored in two cases. Unless regular field survey is made by the field staff, it is very likely that such illegal transaction will not surface.

3. In view of the fact stated in foregoing paragraphs, it has been decided by Government to undertake a special drive in the following manner to know the magnitude of such illegal alienation/unauthorised occupation/*benami* transaction cases.

(a) The Tahsildar will prepare a firm programme for the Revenue Inspectors under his control to visit each village during the months of April-June 1994 to detect such cases. The programme of visit will have to be widely circulated in the locality to enable the villager to pass on the information to the Revenue Inspector and other visiting field staff. Clear 15 days notice to take up the survey should be given in the village as well as Harijan and *Adivasi Bustis* of the village(s) with copy to the local Ward Member and Sarpanch of the concerned Gram Panchayats. Notice should be issued both in Oriya and English and clearly indicate that those who want to file complaints about their illegal transfer/unauthorized occupation/lands restored but again taken back/land transferred without any document but possessed by any other person on verbal agreement/*benami* transactions if any made may submit a petition to the Revenue Inspector or visiting field staff on the stipulated date. Besides the protective provisions available for them in the law should be clearly spelt out in the notice.

(b) Soon after receiving those petitions, the Revenue Inspector should make enquiry into the facts mentioned on those complaint petitions, by making spot visit on the day of visit and then submit these papers along with his enquiry report to the concerned Revenue Supervisor within seven days.

(c) Revenue Supervisor on receipt of those petitions from the Revenue Inspectors should make twenty five percentum random check and then submit all those petitions alongwith his reports to the Revenue Officer/competent authority in next ten days.

(d) The Revenue Officer/competent authority on receipt of the complaint petitions and enquiry reports of Revenue Inspector/ Revenue Supervisor should initiate separate proceedings for each complaint under respective law and go ahead to dispose of the case as deemed proper.

4. To expedite this drive, the Collector of the district may utilize the service of Assistant Welfare Officers/Welfare Officers of Harijan and Tribal Welfare Department working in the district. The Additional District Magistrate (Revenue may be entrusted to look after this drive and the progress should be made to dispose of the cases instituted within four months for which the Revenue Officer/Competent authorities may be suitably instructed. As far as possible these cases should be decided in camp Courts so that advocates do not fleece the poor tribals and Scheduled Caste people and the landlords do not

pay the fare of the tribals who come to the Sub-divisional Headquarters. The issue of development of separate vehicles to O.S.D.S. will be examined after the drive is over and number of cases is known. For the present, on a day fixed for the camp Courts the vehicle of Sub-Collector should be spared for use by the O.S.D.S. under order to Collector and District Magistrates.

5. The receipt of this letter may please be acknowledged, Government in Revenue Department should be kept informed if the number of cases instituted/disposed of during a month by the 15th of the succeeding month. The Officer/Staff not achieving the interest fixed should be pulled up.

Yours faithfully,
Sd/-
Commissioner-cum-Secretary to Government

COPY OF REVENUE AND EXCISE DEPARTMENT

Letter No. AG-77/96-136259/R

All Collectors,

The 13th August, 1996

Alienation of land belonging to Scheduled Tribe/Scheduled Caste persons of Orissa in favour of Scheduled Tribe/Scheduled Caste persons of other States/Union Territories.

Section 3(1) of Regulation 2 of 1956 as well as Section 22 of O.L.R. Act 1960 prohibit the alienation of land belonging to Scheduled Tribes/Castes to persons of other communities. If any alienation is made without the prior permission in writing of the competent authority such transaction is null and void in law. It has come to the notice of the Government that some Scheduled Tribes/Scheduled Castes of this State on a large scale specially in the scheduled areas are in the belief that they will not attract the restrictive provisions of the above two laws as they belong themselves to Scheduled Tribes/ Scheduled Castes.

It may be made clear here that the aforesaid two laws have been enacted by State Government and the provisions incorporated therein are applicable to the Scheduled Tribes/Scheduled Castes of our State. The Minister of Home Affairs, Government of India have clarified in their letter No. BC-16014/1/82-S.C and BCD, dated the 22nd

February, 1985 (copy enclosed) that a Scheduled Tribe/Scheduled Caste person who has migrated from the State of origin to some other State will be deemed to be a Scheduled Tribe/Caste of the State of his origin only.

Since the Scheduled Tribe/Scheduled Caste persons of other States/ Union Territories will be deemed to be a Scheduled Tribe/Caste person of the State/Union Territories of the origin, any alienation made in their favour without valid permission will be null and void.

You are, therefore, requested to enquire if any land belonging to Scheduled Tribes/Scheduled Castes has been illegally alienated to persons of other States/Union Territories and if so, take prompt action for restoration of such lands to the Scheduled Tribe/Scheduled Caste transferor in terms of the provisions of Regulation No. 2 of 1956 and the Orissa Land Reforms Act 1960, as the case may be.

Yours faithfully,

Sd/-

Deputy Secretary to Government

CHAPTER V

Instructions issued regarding Restriction on Transfer of Lands in ex-State Areas by Aboriginal Tribe and recording of Caste in the Record of Rights

Copy of the letter No. 6165-XXI-172/64-L.R.S., dated the 5th June, 1956 from the P.A. to Director of Land Records and Surveys, Orissa, Cuttack, to all Settlement Officers/Charge Officers.

Subject: Restriction on transfer of lands belonging to occupancy tenants in the ex-State Areas.

I am directed to say that before the merger of the ex-State areas that is to say, before the 1st January, 1948 in respect of all ex-State excluding Mayurbhanj and before the 1st January, 1949, in case of Mayurbhanj occupancy tenants belonging to certain castes and tribes could transfer their lands only with the prior permission of the Durbar or some Revenue Authorities. Para 12 (subsequently numbered as para 10) of the Administration of Orissa States Order, 1948 which came into force in all the ex-States excluding Mayurbhanj on the 1st January, 1948, provided that an occupancy tenant would be entitled to freely transfer his holding subject to the restriction that no transfer of holding from a member of an "aboriginal tribe" to a member of a non-aboriginal tribal shall be valid unless such transfer is made with the previous permission of the Administrator was subsequently given to the Sub-Divisional Magistrate by an amendment of the order. The term aboriginal tribe was defined in the said order to mean any tribe that may from time to time be notified as such by the provincial Government for the purpose of this order. When the ex-State of Mayurbhanj was integrated with the State of Orissa on the 1st January,

1949, a similar provision in para. 11 of the Mayurbhanj State Order 1949 was also issued. These provisions were repeated in Section 7 (b) (i) of the Orissa Merged State (Laws) Act 1950. No notification tribe till the 22nd May, 1962 when notification No. 24507-Ten-15/62-R., dated the 22nd May, 1962 was issued explaining that aboriginal tribe shall mean any of the Scheduled Tribes specified in Part IX of Schedule III of the Scheduled Castes and Scheduled Tribes List (Modification) Order, 1956.

2. In 1956, the Scheduled Area Transfer of Immovable Properties (by Scheduled Tribes) Regulation (Regulation 2 of 1956) was passed and it put a restriction on the transfer of immovable property belonging to Scheduled Tribes and not Aboriginal Tribe. The term Scheduled Tribe has been defined in the regulation to have the same meaning as it has in the Constitution (Scheduled Tribes) Order, 1960, as amended from time to time.

3. It is thus clear that with effect from the date of merger any occupancy tenant in any ex-State could transfer his holding or part thereof without the prior sanction of any officer or authority in the absence of any restrictions. The caste or tribe of the tenant was irrelevant for this purpose. Only in 1956, a restriction to the effect that a person belonging to a Scheduled Tribe needs prior permission of a competent authority to transfer his immovable property was put by Regulation 2 of 1956. But this restriction was applicable to the Scheduled areas only, namely, Mayurbhanj and Sundargarh districts and it came into force. In respect of other ex-State areas the restriction came into force with effect from the 22nd May, 1962, when notification came into force No. 24507-Ten-15/62-R, dated the 22nd May, 1962, was issued defining the term Aboriginal Tribe. The conclusions therefore are:

Prior to Merger.—Transfer of land by castes and tribes prior to the merger of Princely State will be regulated by the laws then in force in those states.

On and from the Date of Merger

(i) In the ex-State of Sundargarh there was no restriction of transfer of land by any occupancy tenant irrespective of his caste or tribe from the 1st January, 1948 to 3rd October, 1956 (both days inclusive).

(ii) Similarly in Mayurbhanj district there was no restriction on transfer of land by an occupancy tenant whether he is a

Scheduled Tribe or not from the 1st January, 1949, to the 3rd October, 1956 (both days inclusive).

(iii) In other ex-States there was no such restriction from the 1st January, 1948 to the 21st May, 1962 (both days inclusive). The restriction was operative with effect from the 22nd May, 1962, when the notification defining aboriginal tribe was issued.

4. At some quarters there seems to be an impression that by the passing of the Regulation 2 of 1956, the restriction imposed by the Merged States (Laws) Act stands abrogated in all the Merged States. This is an erroneous impression. So far as the Merged States are concerned Regulation 2 of 1956 applies to the Mayurbhanj and Sundargarh districts only and in respect of these two districts therefore the relevant provision in the Merged States (Laws) Act stands repealed. The restriction imposed by the Merged States (Laws) Act is still operative in other Merged States though, as stated earlier, it came into force with effect from the 22nd May, 1962, only and not earlier.

5. Coming to the other areas, Regulation 2 applies to the Koraput district and some parts of the Ganjam and Baudh Khondmal district which are Scheduled areas. Even prior to the enforcement of the Regulation, there were certain laws in these agency areas regulating transfer of land by tribals to non-tribals. In the C.P. Tenancy Acts which are in force in Nawapara Sub-divisional of Kalahandi district and Bargarh and Sadar Sub-divisions of Sambalpur district, there are certain restrictions on the transfer of land by tribals to others. These laws are still in force. Angul and Kondhamal Laws Regulations which apply Angul and Kondhamals Sub-divisions respectively also put certain restrictions regarding transfer of land from tribal to non-tribals and these regulations continue to be in force. In the remaining areas, however, there are no such laws, and hence there is no restriction on transfer of land by tribal to a non-tribal and the tribal tenants in these areas have the same right to transfer land as any other tenants.

6. The above instructions may be kept in view during the preparation of record-of-rights.

Memo No. 6166

Dated, the 5th June, 1965

Copy forwarded to all Collectors for information and necessary action.

S.K. DAS

P.A to Director of Land Records and Surveys.

Extract of Letter No. 2026-101/66.2 R.S. 156, dated 25.2.1966 of Director of Lands Records and Survey, Orissa, Cuttack addressed to all Settlement Officers.

RESTRICTION OF ALIENATION OF LAND BY SCHEDULED CASTE AND SCHEDULED TRIBES

12. According to Section 22 of the Orissa Land Reforms Act any transfer of holding or part thereof by a riot belonging to Scheduled Tribe shall be void except where it is in favour of a person belonging to Scheduled Tribe when such transfer is made with the previous permission in writing of the S.D.O. This restriction shall also apply, *mutatis mutandis*, to a person who is a member of the Scheduled Caste. Similarly law already existed for transfer of lands by a member of the Scheduled Tribe in the scheduled areas, in the ex-State areas and in areas governed by the C.P. Tenancy Acts, 1898 and 1920. Under Regulation II of 1956, transfer made by a member of the Scheduled Tribe in favour of a person who is not a member of the Scheduled Tribe without the permission in writing of the S.D.O. has been prohibited with effect from the 4th October, 1956. This Regulation II of 1956 is applicable only to Scheduled Areas, namely, the district of Koraput, Sundergarh, Mayurbhanj and the Agency areas of Ganjam and the Sub-Divisions of Kondhamals and Baliguda in Phulbani district except Chokapad-Khandam and Pandakholmutha (Vide Letter No. XXXI-101/66-6770-LRS, dated the 3rd June, 1966). In other ex-States this restriction has been made with effect from the 22nd May, 1962, under the Orissa Merged State (Laws) Act. In Bargarh and Sambalpur Sadar Sub-Divisions (except Mahadevpali police-station), this restriction is applicable with effect from the 9th July 1953, under the amendment to C.P. Tenancy Act 1920. Now this restriction regarding transfer of land made by Adibasis in favour of persons who are not Adivasis, has been made applicable to all

other areas of the State under the Land Reforms Act with effect from the 1st October, 1965. Besides, similar restriction regarding transfer of land by a member of Scheduled Caste has also been made applicable under the Land Reforms Act throughout the State of Orissa, with effect from the 1st October, 1965. Transfer made prior to the date mentioned above in different areas of the State should not be considered as illegal. Moreover, lands in occupation of persons by way of such illegal transfer for a continuous period of 12 years should be recorded in favour of the transfer as they have perfected their title by adverse possession.

BOARD OF REVENUE, ORISSA

No. 15104-XXXI-496/66-L.R.S.

From

Shri Susil Kumar Das, O.A.S
P.A to D.L.R. & S. and Ex-Officio Under Secretary,
Board of Revenue Cuttack

To

All Settlement Officers/Charge Officers

Subject: Recording of caste in the record-of-rights in respect of persons belonging to Scheduled Castes and Scheduled Tribes.

Sir,

I am directed to say that Book Circular No. 20 issued by Government on the 27th April, 1949, which prohibited the recording of caste in settlement papers was subsequently revised in Book Circular No. 26 dated the 6th September, 1952. In the latter circular it was stated that the forms used for the preparation of record-of-rights stands on a different footing and in view of the varied utility of settlement papers, recording of caste in the settlement records was reintroduced.

2. In the context of the above, the question has come up as to the manner in which the caste of persons belonging to Scheduled Castes and Scheduled Tribes should be recorded, in case it is found that any such person has adopted Christianity as his religion. The proprietary transactions, that the Field Officers are most concerned with during the preparation of record-of-rights, relate to transfer and succession. It is patent from the existing personal law, applicable to different communities, that after conversion of a Hindu to Christianity, the provision of the Mitakshari Law or those of the Hindu Succession Act 1956, are no longer applicable to him. Notwithstanding this, the mention of the pre-conversion case of a Scheduled Caste or Scheduled Tribe member becomes indispensable in order to give him necessary protection in respect of the transfer of his immovably property. In Scheduled areas, to which the provisions of Regulation of 1956 are applicable, a person, belonging to Scheduled Tribe, cannot freely transfer his land to another, not belonging to such tribe. In the areas which have not been declared as Scheduled areas, such restrictions have been imposed by the provisions of the Orissa Land Reforms Act 1960. Similarly, both in Scheduled as well as non-Scheduled areas restriction on the transfer of occupancy holdings, belonging to the member of Scheduled Castes, have also been imposed by the provisions of the Orissa Land Reforms Act.

3. In view of the above restriction, it is but necessary that the caste of persons, belonging to Scheduled Castes and Scheduled Tribes, is also mentioned in the record-of-rights, so that the provisions of Regulation 2 of 1956 and those of the Land Reforms Act 1960 may be given effect to expediently. In case of the persons of Scheduled Caste who have been converted to Christianity, the caste of the person may, therefore, be mentioned as "Pan Christian", "Damba Christian", etc. Similarly, the caste of the persons of Scheduled Tribes, who have adopted Christianity", etc. Similarly, the caste of the persons, as "Kondha Christian", Munda Christian", etc.

4. This disposes of letter No. 4487-XX-19/66-STs, dated the 17th October, 1966, from the Settlement Officer, Sambalpur.

Yours faithfully,
S.K. DAS
P.A. to Director of Land Records
and Surveys, Orissa

Index